THE LAYMAN'S BIBLE COMMENTARY

THE LAYMAN'S BIBLE COMMENTARY
IN TWENTY-FIVE VOLUMES

THE LAYMAN'S
BIBLE COMMENTARY

Balmer H. Kelly, *Editor*

Donald G. Miller   *Associate Editors*   Arnold B. Rhodes

Dwight M. Chalmers, *Editor, John Knox Press*

VOLUME 9

THE BOOK OF
PSALMS

Arnold B. Rhodes

JOHN KNOX PRESS

ATLANTA

10 9 8 7 6 5 4 3

Complete set: ISBN: 0-8042-3086-2
This volume: 0-8042-3069-2
Library of Congress Card Number: 59-10454
First paperback edition 1982
Printed in the United States of America
John Knox Press
Atlanta, Georgia 30365

PREFACE

The LAYMAN'S BIBLE COMMENTARY is based on the conviction that the Bible has the Word of good news for the whole world. The Bible is not the property of a special group. It is not even the property and concern of the Church alone. It is given to the Church for its own life but also to bring God's offer of life to all mankind —wherever there are ears to hear and hearts to respond.

It is this point of view which binds the separate parts of the LAYMAN'S BIBLE COMMENTARY into a unity. There are many volumes and many writers, coming from varied backgrounds, as is the case with the Bible itself. But also as with the Bible there is a unity of purpose and of faith. The purpose is to clarify the situations and language of the Bible that it may be more and more fully understood. The faith is that in the Bible there is essentially one Word, one message of salvation, one gospel.

The LAYMAN'S BIBLE COMMENTARY is designed to be a concise non-technical guide for the layman in personal study of his own Bible. Therefore, no biblical text is printed along with the comment upon it. This commentary will have done its work precisely to the degree in which it moves its readers to take up the Bible for themselves.

The writers have used the Revised Standard Version of the Bible as their basic text. Occasionally they have differed from this translation. Where this is the case they have given their reasons. In the main, no attempt has been made either to justify the wording of the Revised Standard Version or to compare it with other translations.

The objective in this commentary is to provide the most helpful explanation of fundamental matters in simple, up-to-date terms. Exhaustive treatment of subjects has not been undertaken.

In our age knowledge of the Bible is perilously low. At the same time there are signs that many people are longing for help in getting such knowledge. Knowledge of and about the Bible is, of course, not enough. The grace of God and the work of the Holy Spirit are essential to the renewal of life through the Scriptures. It is in the happy confidence that the great hunger for the Word is a sign of God's grace already operating within men, and that the Spirit works most wonderfully where the Word is familiarly known, that this commentary has been written and published.

THE EDITORS AND
THE PUBLISHERS

THE

PSALMS

INTRODUCTION

The Appeal of the Psalms

Our love for and frequent use of the Psalms today is nothing new. We follow in the train of our fathers in the faith through the centuries. These lyric poems spring from encounter with God and lead men in every age to an encounter with him. Some of them were used by the ancient Israelites at various sanctuaries. Psalms were vehicles of worship in Solomon's Temple (957-587 B.C.), in the Second Temple (537-19 B.C.), and in Herod's Temple (19 B.C.—A.D. 70). They were used in Jewish synagogues and homes. On the basis of manuscript discoveries we know that the Book of Psalms was one of the most popular biblical writings in the Dead Sea Scrolls community. To the present day the Psalms have been loved and recited by the Jewish people.

According to the flesh Jesus was a Jew, and his life was nourished on the Psalms of his people. At his baptism his vocation as the Messiah and Servant of the Lord was confirmed by quotations from Psalm 2:7 and Isaiah 42:1 (Matt. 3:17; Mark 9:7; Luke 3:22). The hymn which Jesus sang with his Apostles at the Last Supper (Mark 14:26 and parallels) was probably the Egyptian Hallel (Pss. 113-118; see comment) or a part of it (Pss. 115-118). In the agony of the Cross, Jesus meditated upon Psalm 22:1, "My God, my God, why hast thou forsaken me?" (Matt. 27:46; Mark 15:34). And according to Luke 23:46 it was with words from another Psalm (31:5) upon his lips that he died. Millions of Jesus' disciples, in their hour of deep need, have also found help in the Psalms.

The hymns which Paul and Silas were singing in the Philippian jail (Acts 16:25) were probably some of the Psalms. Paul recommended the singing of Psalms to the congregations addressed in Ephesians (5:19) and Colossians (3:16). Isaiah and Psalms are the Old Testament books most often quoted by the writers of the

New Testament. From the earliest days to the present the Psalms have played a vital part in the life of the Christian community, whether this community be thought of in relation to public worship, private devotion, monastery, convent, Eastern Orthodoxy, Roman Catholicism, Protestantism, or sectarianism. They have been used by slaves, martyrs, emperors, Puritans, poets, reformers, men of letters, and just plain people.

There is manifold justification for this strong and persistent appeal of the Psalms. Their language is so simple that it is meaningful to a child, yet their thought goes so deep that the philosopher cannot exhaust its treasures. They are beautiful in thought and content both in Hebrew and in translation. All the moods of the human heart are expressed in them—complaint and praise, penitence and innocence, pessimism and optimism, imprecation and intercession, hate and love, sorrow and joy—yet all the psalmists moved within the realm of faith in God. In the Psalms men wrestle with the universal problems of suffering, sin, and death. The Psalms are, in fact, the faith of the Old Testament set to music.

The Psalms in Their Larger Setting

The Psalms are a part of Near Eastern literature and yet they are genuinely distinctive. There were forerunners of the Israelite Psalms in the literatures of the Sumerians, Babylonians, Canaanites, and Egyptians. This should not surprise us, because Israel did not live in a vacuum and her contacts with her neighbors were positive as well as negative. The closest parallels are found in Canaanite poetry. Such Psalms as 29, 68, 74, and 82 can be more easily understood in the light of evidence from Canaanite literary materials found at Ras Shamra, which is located in what is now known as Syria. Even in literary form the Hebrew Psalms reached heights never attained in any of the other Near Eastern cultures, but the chief distinctiveness of the biblical Psalms lies in their theology. The Psalms bear witness to the historical revelation of the one true God, whereas the poems of these other peoples are for the most part polytheistic and mythological. One point at which the distinctiveness of the Israelite Psalms is most apparent is in their deep penetration of the nature of sin and its forgiveness.

The Date and Authorship of the Psalms

Although it is impossible to give exact dates for many of the Psalms, the Psalter was in the process of coming into existence from the very beginning of the Israelite nation to the fourth or third century B.C. This means that there are pre-exilic (before the Babylonian Exile in 587 B.C.), exilic (during the Exile, 587-538 B.C.), and postexilic (after the Exile, 538-300 B.C.) compositions. Among Jews in and around New Testament times, David was held to be the author of a large number of the Psalms and the editor of the entire Psalter. For practical purposes, he was considered the author of the Psalms. This same tradition is followed in the New Testament (for example, see Mark 12:36-37; Acts 4:25-26; Rom. 4:6-8). This does not mean, however, that Jesus and the writers of the New Testament were seeking to speak critically on the subject of authorship. They were simply using the common way of referring to the Psalms. Just as all the Law was considered Mosaic and much Wisdom Literature Solomonic, so the Psalter was considered Davidic. The copyright conception of authorship was totally foreign to early Jewish and Christian thinking.

The Davidic tradition, on the other hand, is not without some foundation. David was known as a musician and poet (I Sam. 16: 17-23; II Sam. 1:17-27; 22:1-51; 23:1-7). According to a tradition recorded in postexilic times, he was associated with the organization of choral worship (Ezra 3:10; Neh. 12:24, 36, 45-46; I Chron. 15:16-29). In the Hebrew Bible the word "David" occurs in seventy-two Psalm titles. In the Greek translation it occurs more frequently. No one knows the exact meaning of the Hebrew phrase often translated "A Psalm of David," for the preposition "of" may also be translated "to," "belonging to," or "for." It may indicate a particular collection of Psalms associated in some way with David, just as the phrase, "A Psalm of the Sons of Korah," seems to indicate a collection from which a particular Psalm was taken. Whatever the exact meaning of "A Psalm of David" may be, it bears witness to a tradition which connects David with psalmody. In other words, there is reason to believe that David composed some Psalms and stimulated the composition of others. It is obvious that he did not write all of them. For example, Psalm 137 is a song that came out of the Babylonian Captivity in the sixth century B.C. Some of the Psalms that have "David" in their title specifically refer to the Temple (for example, 5, 27, 138), which did not exist in David's day.

The Titles of the Psalms

The title of the Book of Psalms in the Hebrew Bible is "Praises." In the Greek translation known as the Septuagint it varies in different manuscripts: "Psalms," "Book of Psalms," and "Psalter." Apparently the Greek title is based on the Hebrew word for "Psalm," which occurs frequently to designate individual compositions.

All the individual Psalms bear titles except thirty-four which are known as "orphan" Psalms. It is rather widely held that the titles constitute no part of the original poems but were added later by editors. However, they are pre-Christian since they occur (though with some variations) in the Septuagint. There is considerable uncertainty about the meaning of many of them. These titles may be organized into groups. First, there are those which associate particular Psalms with particular individuals or groups —Moses, David, Solomon, Asaph, the Sons of Korah, Heman the Ezrahite, and Ethan the Ezrahite—but they are not accepted in full by most students of the Psalms as indications of authorship. In some cases they may indicate the collection to which a Psalm belongs. Those Psalms whose titles contain references to episodes in the life of David are laments. It seems that editors found in these Psalms statements which reminded them of sayings or events in the life of David as recorded in the Books of Samuel.

Second, there are titles which designate the kind of composition: Psalm, song, a love song, a song of praise, a prayer, *maskil*, *miktam*, and *shiggaion*. The exact meanings of the last three kinds mentioned are uncertain.

The third group is made up of titles containing musical directions: to the choirmaster, with stringed instruments, and for the flutes. The expression "to the choirmaster" has been interpreted in a variety of ways. It may designate an earlier collection of Psalms bearing the name "Choirmaster," or it may call the choirmaster's attention to musical directions which follow in the title of a given Psalm. While the word "selah" is not a Psalm title, it seems to be a musical direction. It comes from a root meaning "lift up." It may be a direction to the orchestra to play louder during an interlude of the singing, or a direction to the singers to increase the volume of their praise—but no one really knows the meaning of the term.

Group four is composed of titles containing the names of melodies or modes according to which particular Psalms are to be rendered: Alamoth, The Sheminith, The Gittith, Jeduthun, Muthlabben, The Hind of the Dawn, Lilies, The Dove on Far-off Terebinths, Do Not Destroy, and Mahalath. The second half of these names seem to refer to popular tunes, but the first half may refer to modes of rendition.

Finally, there are titles which refer to the liturgical use of specific Psalms: a Song for the Sabbath, for the memorial offering, for the thank offering, a Song at the dedication of the Temple, for instruction, and a Song of Ascents. Psalms 120-134 are known as "the songs of ascents." This expression probably means that these Psalms were sung by pilgrims as they ascended the hill of Zion on the occasion of the great religious festivals.

One Psalter from Several Collections

The Psalter grew into being very much as a modern hymnbook does. As it now stands it is divided into five books: 1-41, 42-72, 73-89, 90-106, and 107-150. At the end of each book except the fifth there is a doxology. However, Psalm 150 in its entirety may be considered a doxology. These divisions are somewhat arbitrarily made, presumably to follow the pattern of the revered "five books of Moses." The numbering of individual Psalms in the Septuagint differs in most instances from the numbering in the Hebrew text, which is followed in English Bibles.

There is evidence for a threefold division of the Psalms prior to the fivefold division already mentioned: 1-41 (Book I), 42-89 (Books II and III), and 90-150 (Books IV and V). These divisions are recognized chiefly on the basis of the use of different divine names. In part one the name "LORD" is used 278 times and the name "God" only 15 times. In Psalms 42-83 the proportion is quite the opposite, "God" occurring 201 times and "LORD" 44 times. Psalms 84-89 revert to the original relationships found in part one, for in these "LORD" occurs 31 times and "God" 7. In part three (90-150) "LORD" occurs 339 times and "God" 6 times. This great difference in the use of divine names is not accidental.

In part at least it is to be accounted for by the work of compiler-editors.

The argument that the Psalter is composed of several collections is well supported by additional evidence. A few Psalms are clearly duplicated: 14 and 53; 40:13-17 and 70; 108:1-5 and 57:7-11; 108:6-13 and 60:5-12. At the end of Psalm 72 this note is appended: "The prayers of David, the son of Jesse, are ended." Yet, Psalms attributed to David are found in Books IV and V. Collections seem to be indicated by some of the Psalm titles, ascribing 72 Psalms to David, 12 to Asaph, and 11 to the sons of Korah, and designating 15 as songs of ascents. It is also possible that the 15 Hallelujah Psalms (104-106, 111-113, 115-117, 135, 146-150) were at one time a separate collection.

The Book of Psalms was informally canonized about the second century B.C. and formally recognized as canonical among the Jews at the Council of Jamnia in A.D. 90. Jesus and the writers of the New Testament accepted the book as authoritative in their day.

The Poetry of the Psalms

Hebrew poetry is always characterized by parallelism and rhythm, and sometimes by strophes (less frequently by stanzas) and acrostic structure. The most important characteristic is parallelism of verse-members. The basic types of parallelism are synonymous, antithetic, and synthetic. In synonymous parallelism the second verse-member repeats the thought of the first.

> but his delight is in the law of the LORD,
>> and on his law he meditates day and night (1:2).

In antithetic parallelism the second verse-member stands in contrast to the first:

> for the LORD knows the way of the righteous,
>> but the way of the wicked will perish (1:6).

In synthetic parallelism the second verse-member continues the thought of the first:

> When my enemies turned back,
>> they stumbled and perished before thee (9:3).

There are several other kinds of parallelism, but for the most part they are developments of these three. Parallelism may be complete or incomplete. In complete parallelism every detail in one verse-member is balanced in the corresponding member (see 83: 14), while in incomplete parallelism this is not the case (see 59: 16). There are many different forms of the latter.

The rhythm of Hebrew poetry is unlike that of Western poetry. It is primarily the rhythm of sense. Parallelism is sense rhythm. Every line of Hebrew poetry is divided into two or more parts, each of which is known as a stich. Every stich contains two to four stressed Hebrew words. It is only the important words that count in measuring Hebrew rhythm. The meter in lines of Hebrew poetry varies: 3+3, 3+2, 2+2, 2+2+2, 3+2+2. Sometimes the Hebrew meter is obvious even in translation:

> The law of the LORD is perfect,
>> reviving the soul;
> the testimony of the LORD is sure,
>> making wise the simple (19:7).

In this verse there are two lines, and each line is composed of two stichs. The meter in both lines is 3+2.

At least some Psalms have strophic or stanza-like structure. This arrangement may be indicated by thought content (107), the occurrence of a refrain (42-43), acrostic structure (119), and perhaps on occasion the presence of "Selah" (46). Technically a stanza is composed of strophes.

Acrostic structure means that each succeeding stich, line, couplet, or strophe begins with the next letter of the Hebrew alphabet. It is found in Psalms 9-10, 25, 34, 37, 111, 112, 119, and 145. Obviously it cannot be recognized in the translations of the Hebrew into other languages.

As a kind of footnote to the poetry of the Psalms it is well to remember that many of the Psalms were sung to the accompaniment of musical instruments. Throughout the ancient Near East songs were sung and musical instruments were played. Israel's music was similar to that of her neighbors. Rhythm was basic and melody present, but harmony was unknown. Percussion, wind, and stringed instruments were all employed in Temple worship, often as an accompaniment to the singing of Psalms (see 33:2-3; 43:4; 71:22; 81:1-3; 150:3-5).

The Theology of the Psalms

Religion has to do with man's response to God in worship and service. The only proper subject of theology, however, is God. Man and the world are theological subjects only by virtue of their relationship to him.

There are serious obstacles to making an adequate statement of the theology of the Psalms. (1) It is impossible to arrange the Psalms chronologically and show the development of doctrine in assured historical sequence. (2) The psalmists were even less systematic and more emotional in their presentation of truth than many of the other writers of Scripture. (3) No one psalmist mentions all aspects of theology, and therefore to speak of the theology of the Psalms is a bit different from speaking of the theology of Paul. Nevertheless, it is possible to speak of a theology of the Psalms in terms of the cross-section of thought represented in them.

The theology of the Psalms centers around the activity and nature of God. God's activity receives even greater stress than his character because it is by what he does that he reveals who he is. God creates, saves, reigns, judges, elects, and reveals. He is holy, righteous, loving, Spirit, and one. Perhaps the word that best helps us to grasp the unity of his activity and character is the word "living." The psalmist cries out, "My soul thirsts for God, for the living God" (42:2).

The Activity of God

God creates. Creation is the activity of God in causing that which exists to exist, and in the passive sense it is that which is caused to exist. In the Psalter as well as in all other parts of the Bible which speak to the subject, God is the Creator of the universe and man. The psalmists do not raise the issue of creation out of nothing; they simply affirm the sovereignty of God in creation.

Creation is continued through God's creative work in nature and history (for example, see Ps. 33). God not only made Israel in the biological sense but also in the sense of electing her to be his special people (95:7; 100:3; compare Deut. 32:6; Isa. 44:2). Furthermore, he made the nations (86:9; compare Deut. 26:19) as historical realities, and formed in advance (ordained) the days of the psalmist (139:16). When the psalmist prays that God will create in him a clean heart (51:10), he uses the same verb as found in Genesis 1:1. Here the creative work of God is clearly saving work and is on a personal scale analogous to the creation of new heavens and a new earth on a cosmic scale (Isa. 65:17).

God saves. The most significant word in the salvation vocabulary of the Old Testament means "to be wide, spacious, or free." Although it basically conveys a positive meaning, the psalmists were greatly concerned with salvation as deliverance from the negative: suffering, sin, and death. However, it is impossible to be delivered from an evil without being delivered to a good. For example, to be delivered from famine is to be blessed with food. Salvation includes what the modern man means by both "material" and "spiritual" blessings. Even in the most pessimistic of the Psalms (44, 88), faith in God is never abandoned. This implies a salvation *in the midst of* suffering as well as a salvation *from* suffering (see II Cor. 12:1-10).

The words for sin in the Psalms are numerous, but the most important are evil, wickedness, missing the mark, rebellion (transgression), and iniquity. However, the psalmists have more to say about sinners than about sin and more about social sins than about religious ones. Yet, in the final analysis all sin is religious because it is opposed to the righteous God. Although all men are sinners, people are divided into two groups, the friends of God and the enemies of God. The enemies of God are also the enemies of his people, and conversely. There is a difference in status between the friends of God who sin and his enemies who sin. The righteous, his friends, are not morally perfect, but they are never said to commit wickedness, do evil, or make trouble. The wicked, his enemies, are guilty of every type of sin, and their sinfulness is characteristic and habitual. They are never said to seek forgiveness. The righteous are forgiven sinners who are committed in Covenant loyalty to God.

The psalmists do not love the wicked man and hate his wickedness; they hate the wicked man and pray for his destruction (see the imprecatory Psalms). The Christian cannot enter into the spirit of the psalmist here, for Jesus said, "Love your enemies" (Matt. 5:44). Of course we must remember that the psalmist lived before the fullness of God's revelation in Jesus Christ. It is sometimes argued that this fact should not carry much weight in the light of certain statements concerning love in the Old Testament (Exod. 23:4-5; Lev. 19:17-18; Prov. 24:17; 25:21). But it must be remembered that all of these statements were understood and interpreted in the context of the thrice-repeated law of retaliation, "An eye for an eye and a tooth for a tooth" (see Exod. 21:24; Lev. 24:20; Deut. 19:21). Jesus' injunction, "Do not resist one who is evil. But if any one strikes you on the right cheek, turn to him the other also" (Matt. 5:39), is far more revolutionary than many are prone to admit. Furthermore, the imprecatory Psalms should be understood in the light of the deep concern of the righteous for the will of God (the psalmists took right and wrong seriously) and their belief (for the most part) that justice must be done in the span of threescore years and ten.

Sometimes the same words used to designate deliverance from other evils are also used to denote the forgiveness of sin. But there are additional expressions: lifting up a burden and removing it, removing mercifully, covering or atoning, hiding sin, cleansing the polluted, not remembering, cancelling a debt, hiding the face from sin, and unsinning the sinner. Forgiveness is rooted in the grace of God, but confession is required before it can be received. It may result in a variety of blessings: deliverance, a sense of security, fellowship with God, joyous praise, and an exhortation to others to repent. Occasionally the psalmists show concern for sin prevention (19:13; 119:11).

Death is a weakened form of life, and one may begin to enter the realm of the dead as his strength ebbs away (30, 40, 69, 88). It is sometimes associated with sin (41; 107:17). Sheol is the dominant conception of existence after death in the Psalms (9:17; 55:15; 86:13) and in the rest of the Old Testament as well. It is thought of as an amoral subterranean abode of shades without meaningfulness. It is a synonym for death (49:14), the Pit (30:3), and Abaddon (88:11). Ordinarily Sheol is thought to make communion with God impossible (6:5; 30:9). However, one psalmist, in proclaiming the omnipresence of God, insists on the presence of God even in Sheol (139:8). In addition, it is possible that a few psalmists anticipated the doctrines of eternal life and the resurrection of the dead (16, 49, 73). It should also be remembered that the perpetuation of one's name in one's posterity is a concept of continuing existence (41:5; 109:13; II Sam. 18:18). It is only in the resurrection of Jesus Christ that the resurrection of believers is made radiantly clear and the hopes of God's people fulfilled. The psalmists' strong faith in God is therefore all the more remarkable.

Positively speaking, salvation is security in God, victory, vindication, prosperity, peace, happiness, and blessing. It embraces all possible goods, material and spiritual, for God is the source of all good things (3:8; 28:9).

God reigns. All of God's deeds manifest his sovereignty. His reign is viewed from the perspective of his past, present, and future activity (see especially 46, 74, 89, 47, 93, 95-100). The God of Israel is never pictured literally as struggling against other deities; he speaks and it is done. He can in no way be controlled by men through magic pantomime. Creation and salvation are embraced by a kingdom whose King is always bringing order out of chaos, but chaos is no monster god who can really threaten Yahweh (see comment on 74:12-17). Sometimes God's kingship is expressed through his Anointed One (see Messianic Psalms below).

There are veiled anticipations of the coming of the Kingdom of God in the Psalms just mentioned. One day the age of peace anticipated by the prophets will come (46:8-11) and the princes of the nations will gather as the people of the God of Abraham (47:9).

God judges. Reigning and judging are inseparable activities. As Judge, God both redeems and condemns, but redemption is his chief objective (see especially 72:1-4). "Judgment" and "justice" are translations of the same Hebrew words. The real purpose of judgment is justice, and justice for the oppressed is a kind of salvation. Condemnation is but the other side of redemption as wrath is love with a backbone. The overwhelming emphasis in the Psalms is upon judgment as salvation (deliverance from various evils). Inasmuch as no man is able to endure the strict justice of God, God's grace is entreated (143:1-2). Ordinances or laws are judgments of God in a derived sense, and their purpose is justice. God's universal judgment upon men and nations will be climaxed at the end of the age.

God elects. Election is Israel's most distinctive doctrine. According to the Psalms, God chose Abraham (47:9; 105:6, 9), Israel (33:12; 105:6, 10; 106:5; 135:4), Israel's inheritance (47:

4), Zion (132:13), Israel's leaders (106:23; 105:26; 78:70; 89:3-4, 20-21), and Judah (78:68). Herein lies the substance of the doctrine of vocation—of the Church and of the individual.

The election of Israel was to privilege, obedience, and service. Election to privilege included redemption from Egyptian bondage, providential care, and the worship of the Lord. Privilege entails responsibility (see Exod. 20:2-18). All of the Psalms are to be understood in the context of the Covenant. Many of them were used as expressions of Covenant renewal at the celebration of the great religious festivals. In the teaching of election to service are found the seeds of the missionary movement. All nations are called upon to praise Israel's God (117), and Israel is to make God's salvation known to the nations (96:1-3; compare Isa. 40-66).

God reveals. God's word and deed are one (33:4-7); his activity is revelatory but must be interpreted by persons. According to the Psalms, God reveals himself' through Israel's history, through law, through nature, and through worship. Prophets, priests, and apocalyptists as well as psalmists were interpreters of history. The Psalms which deal with the history of salvation (for example, 78, 81, 105, 106, 114) lay emphasis upon creation, the Exodus, the Red Sea (Hebrew, "Reed Sea") deliverance, the wilderness wandering, and the entrance into Canaan, but give less attention to the patriarchs, the Covenant at Sinai, and specific events after David. The accounts of the wilderness wandering emphasize God's power and grace in contrast to the sinfulness of the people. God's historical activity in relation to Israel is a means through which he reveals his power, grace, righteousness, and purpose.

Nature is a correlate of creation. God controls both nature and history to serve his purpose of salvation. In three nature Psalms (8; 19:1-6; 104) the general revelation of God's glory, wisdom, honor, and power is set forth—but not the revelation of his moral purpose. His will is revealed through a particular history.

The Nature of God

God is holy. The root meaning of holiness seems to be "separation," and God as the Holy One is in a category by himself. Holiness virtually means "godness"; therefore, all of God's characteristics are embraced in the word. It speaks of that which

God has revealed concerning himself and of that which remains hidden from us. It means that God is far above us but not far from us. That which he sets apart unto himself is made holy. Consequently, he has a holy word, arm, heaven, spirit, throne, name, people, land, city, hill, temple, and sacrifice. The election of a Chosen People is an expression of his holiness.

Sacrifice was offered to secure, maintain, ensure, or express holiness. In the Psalms it is mentioned chiefly as an expression of thanksgiving to God for deliverance from specific evils (for example, 66:13-15; 54:6-7; 107:22). On the surface at least, some psalmists seem to have repudiated material sacrifices altogether (40:6-8; 69:30-31). This attitude may reflect the prophetic condemnation of the abuse of the sacrificial system (see Amos 5:21-24; Hosea 6:6; Isa. 1:11-17; Micah 6:6-8; Jer. 7:21-23), or it may mean that these psalmists considered material sacrifices inadequate for their particular situation.

God is righteous. Just as God makes known his holiness by electing a Holy People, so he makes known his righteousness by judging men and nations in justice (51:4; 96:13). Righteousness ("vindication") appears often in the realm of grace and salvation as God delivers and blesses his people (71:2; 103:6). This same emphasis is made in Isaiah 40-55, for the Lord is "a righteous God and a Savior" (Isa. 45:21). Paul's doctrine of justification in Galatians and Romans is built upon this understanding of the righteousness of God.

God is loving and faithful. The love of God in the Psalter, as well as in the Old Testament as a whole, is expressed by a variety of terms. One of these words is associated with God's choice of his people and their inheritance (47:4; 78:68; 87:2; compare Deut. 7:7-8) and is often referred to as "election-love." God's people love him (31:23; 116:1; 145:20) and that which pertains to him (5:11; 40:16; 26:8; 119).

Another word for "love" is usually translated "steadfast love" in the Revised Standard Version. It is often associated with the Covenant (89:28; 103:17-18; 106:45), which requires steadfastness of the persons bound together by it. It is also closely related to faithfulness (89:1-2, 24, 33-34) and truth (40:10-11). "Faithfulness" and "truth" come from the same Hebrew root and are often synonyms, for they both mean "dependability."

Like righteousness, God's steadfast love is the ground of his saving work (25:6-7; 103:4, 10-12). Also like righteousness, it is sometimes essentially a synonym of salvation (119:41; compare 13:5; 85:7).

The steadfast love of God is associated with other words which emphasize God's mercy and grace (86:15; 103:8; compare Exod. 34:6). Furthermore, it is not shown exclusively to the Covenant people but is over all his creation (33:4-6; 36: 5-10; 145:4-13).

Yet, the adjective which corresponds to the noun "steadfast love" refers to the Covenant people as those who have experienced the steadfast love of God and are devoted to him. It is translated in a variety of ways: "godly" or "godly one" (4:3; 16:10; 86:2), "saints" (30:4; 37:28; 97:10), and "faithful one(s)" (89:19; 50:5) or "the faithful" (149:1).

God is Spirit. Perhaps from the standpoint of the Old Testament it would be more accurate to say God *has* a Spirit. The Hebrew word for "spirit" sometimes means "breath" or "wind." God's Spirit is his power at work in human life and in the natural world. The Israelite saw the evidences of the power of the invisible wind, and therefore thought of the wind as the symbol of the power of the invisible God.

In the Psalms, God's Spirit is associated with power, creativity, guidance, and presence. As the breath of God it is identified with the creative word of God (33:6; compare Gen. 1). It renews and perpetuates life upon the earth (104:30), and guides and teaches God's servant (143:10). It is an omniscient and omnipresent manifestation of God's presence (139:7).

The word "spirit" as used in relation to man may refer to his breath (146:4), his emotional and psychological attitudes (143:4, 7; 106:33), and his expression of will (78:8). Sometimes the spirit of man is the equivalent of the heart of man (77:6; 78:8; 143:4), and the heart of man is his soul inwardly considered. Though soul has varied meanings, it refers chiefly to a person in his total being (103), not to a ghost. The psalmists were concerned about the whole man in relation to God.

God is one. Monotheism is the belief that there is only one God. The Christian doctrine of the Trinity is a monotheistic doctrine—namely, that the one true God has revealed himself to be a tri-unity: Father, Son, and Holy Spirit. Although the intimations of this truth may be seen in the Old Testament through "the eyes of faith," the doctrine as such was made known only in the fullness of time.

Historically speaking, there is a movement in Israel's faith toward an explicit monotheism. Most of the psalmists do not raise the issue of other gods at all; the Lord is their only concern. There are, however, a few Psalms in which are mentioned other "god(s)" (40:4; 77:13; 81:9; 82:1, 6; 95:3; 97:7-9; 136:2; 138:1), "sons of gods" (29:1; 89:6; see margin), "holy ones" (89:5, 7), and "angel(s)" (34:7; 35:5-6; 78:49; 91:11; 103:20). In some cases, at least, it is possible that the psalmist does not mean that he believes in the real existence of other gods, but uses the terminology with the connotation of "so-called gods." However, in other cases this would be a prejudiced interpretation. Nevertheless, in no case is any other divine being a rival of the Lord; all are subject to his will. In other words, they are members of the heavenly council (86:8, 10; 89:5, 7) and are in essentially the same general category as angels—that is, servants of the one true God. A psalmist who believed in the divine council could be a monotheist just as truly as the Christian who believes in angels. When the gods of other nations are specifically referred to, their personal existence is categorically denied (96:4-5; compare 115:3-8).

A Classification of the Psalms

Years ago students of the Psalms concentrated on attempting to determine the authorship, date, and historical background of each of the Psalms. Although some continued this approach, others saw its futility and attempted to assign individual Psalms to specific periods in the history of the People of God. In the best recent research the Psalms are classified on the basis of the situation in life out of which they came and the consequent literary form they took. Perhaps the earliest psalmists composed their Psalms for use in public worship. Then other persons, following the example set in public worship, wrote Psalms of personal devotion and developed yet other types.

The first major classification is composed of *hymns of praise*. (Every Psalm is classified in the Outline that follows this section.) A hymn, as the word is used here, is a Psalm which centers in the praise of God. In its strictest form it is composed of three major parts: introduction, body, and conclusion. The introduction is either a call to praise or a statement of praise. The body is a presentation of the reasons for the praise, which may include some of the acts and attributes of God. The conclusion may be identical with or similar to the introduction. The hymn tends to draw the worshiper out of himself by directing his attention to God, who is usually mentioned in the third person.

The hymns were especially appropriate for the celebration of the great religious festivals, such as Passover, Weeks, and Tabernacles. A few of the hymns are general in nature, while in others emphasis is placed upon creation, history, both creation and history, or Zion. The four Psalms listed under the subtitle "The history of salvation" are rehearsals of God's mighty acts in the history of the Chosen People. They are comparable in content to the Old Testament confessions of faith in Deuteronomy 6: 20-25; 26:5-11; Joshua 24; and Nehemiah 9. However, almost all of the Psalms are rooted in the history of salvation.

The Psalms which emphasize *the kingship of God* are often called "enthronement Psalms." Several closely related theories are held concerning their origin. (1) Some students maintain that as a part of ancient Israel's New Year Festival (the Feast of Tabernacles), the Lord was enthroned yearly through ritual drama in a manner somewhat comparable to the enthronement of an earthly monarch (see I Kings 1:38-40, 45; II Kings 11:12) and the annual enthronement of the god Marduk in Babylon (see comment on 74:12-17). They also maintain that the Psalms of the kingship of God were used in the enthronement ceremony, and translate the expression "The LORD reigns" (see 93:1; 96: 10; 97:1; 99:1; compare 47:6-7; 98:6) as "The LORD has become king." Certain of these students include other Psalms in the category of enthronement Psalms and associate many others with the New Year Festival. No doubt some of the Psalms are to be associated with the various festivals of Israel, but the theory of the Lord's enthronement, as it is often presented, rests too heavily on analogy with Babylonian and Canaanite magical religious practices and too little on the biblical data. Furthermore, it is basically out of harmony with Israel's understanding of the utter sovereignty of God and his revelation through history. (2) The enthronement Psalms are regarded by others as having their origin in postexilic times in connection with the Jewish New Year Festival after that festival became an independent celebration. (3) Still another theory is that there was a Covenant festival at the turn of the year in the autumn in pre-exilic Israel, that centered in God's meeting with his people and the renewal of the

Sinai Covenant, when these as well as other Psalms were used. Whatever may have been their origin, these Psalms proclaim the sovereignty of God.

Closely related to the Psalms which celebrate the kingship of God are those which celebrate *the kingship of his anointed*. These Psalms are sometimes called "royal" or "Messianic" Psalms. The word "messiah" means "anointed one." In one sense all the kings of Israel were messiahs because they were anointed. However, as one after another the kings failed to fulfill the messianic ideal, in time the term "Messiah" came to be applied to the Davidic king par excellence of the future. The royal Psalms are Messianic in the sense that they can best be understood in relation to God's covenant with David (II Sam. 7; compare especially Psalms 89 and 132) and their use in the New Testament. The covenant with David involved a series of kings, but *the* Messiah was Jesus Christ.

Though the royal Psalms are not hymns, it is helpful to study them in relation to the Psalms of the kingship of God. Since the king is God's anointed, Psalms which honor him praise God. The position of the king in Israel was far more significant religiously than most people today realize. He was God's adopted son (II Sam. 7:14; Ps. 2:7) and the representative of all Israel before God. The royal Psalms celebrate his coronation and marriage, and express petition for his guidance and protection. Some of them may have been associated with what has been called the "Royal Zion Festival." This theory is based largely on II Samuel 6 and 7, where the selection of Jerusalem as the Holy City and God's covenant with David are placed side by side. David brought the Ark of the Covenant to Jerusalem, thereby making Jerusalem the religious as well as the political capital of the kingdom. Solomon brought the Ark to the Temple and dedicated the Temple on the occasion of the Feast of Tabernacles. Some of the royal Psalms may have been used on the occasion of Covenant renewal in such a festival.

Several hymns express praise to God as the *Lord of Zion*, for Jerusalem as the City of God plays a distinctive role in them. Sometimes literal Jerusalem is in the poet's thought and at other times the glorified Jerusalem of the future. Jerusalem was so celebrated because the People of God had a vital experience of his presence at the sanctuary there. Some of these Psalms were sung by pilgrims en route to Zion; two celebrate the entrance to the sanctuary; and others look forward to the consummation of God's Kingdom.

In contrast to the hymns of praise are *the prayers in time of trouble*. The People of God in antiquity were no more immune to trouble than the people of God today, and they brought their troubles to God in prayer. These prayers usually are referred to as laments and are divided into two major groups, laments of the community and laments of the individual. *The laments of the community* seem to have originated in connection with the public fasts of the congregation (usually at the sanctuary) in time of national peril. The constituent elements of these laments vary, but frequently they include the lament or complaint proper, an earnest petition for deliverance, and an enumeration of considerations in support of the petition.

The laments of the individual constitute the largest single group of the Psalms, and it is the personal involvement expressed in them that has had much to do with their continuing appeal to this day. Individuals, though always recognizing themselves as members of the Covenant community, faced the trials of sickness, imminent death, false accusation, imprisonment, and personal enemies. It is maintained by some that the personal enemies of the psalmists were primarily sorcerers, but the evidence does not justify so sweeping a conclusion. The individual laments include several subclasses. *Protestations of innocence* are laments in which one seeks to clear himself of false accusation. *Imprecations* are laments in which a curse is pronounced upon one's enemy or enemies. *Penitential prayers* are confessions of sin and supplications for forgiveness and healing. The Psalms thus designated have been known through many centuries of Christian history as "the seven penitentials." Millions of people have prayed these prayers from the heart and have found their sins forgiven.

Although the entire Psalter was written by men of faith, certain of the Psalms may be called *affirmations of faith* in a special sense, because they express so forcibly an unshakable trust in God. They call to mind the quality of faith expressed by Isaiah (Isa. 7:9; 30:15). It is often claimed that these Psalms are a subdivision of the laments of the individual. This is true so far as literary origins are concerned, but they are such moving expressions of deep security in God that they may well be placed in a separate category.

One of man's most significant responses to God is gratitude for his blessings. Hymns express the gratitude of the community in general terms, while *the songs of thanksgiving* express gratitude for specific blessings. A few Psalms may be understood as *thanksgivings of the community*, but most of those in the thanksgiving category are *songs of individuals*. The songs of thanksgiving are actually the counterpart of the laments of the individual, for in them the one whose complaint has been answered in deliverance offers his thanksgiving and pays his vow to God. The same Hebrew word means both "thank offering" and "thanksgiving." On some occasions the worshiper made a literal material offering at the Temple; on other occasions the thanksgiving was altogether spiritual. Ordinarily a Psalm of personal thanksgiving was not used at a public festival. The worshiper, in the presence of relatives and friends, would sing his song of gratitude at the Temple. His song was the telling of his story, frequently composed of the following elements: an introductory statement of the purpose of the Psalm, a rehearsal of his trouble and deliverance, and upon occasion an announcement of a thank offering or thanksgiving.

Wisdom literature has been produced in all ancient and modern societies. Proverbs, Ecclesiastes, and Job are the Wisdom books of the Old Testament. However, several of the Psalms are also placed in this literary category. The wise men of Israel reflected upon the practical affairs of everyday life as well as upon the most profound problems of human experience. They sought to give wise counsel, especially to the young. *The wisdom Psalms* are didactic in purpose. Though wisdom poetry did not originate at the sanctuary, it came to be used there. Some of the wisdom Psalms are most expressive of communion with God. A few of them dwell upon the Law, which means literally "instruction." Retribution and reward are favorite themes of the Psalms of wisdom.

The word "liturgy" is generally employed to mean an order of public worship. It is used in the Outline to refer to those Psalms in which the parts were rendered antiphonally.

Some Psalms are classified as *mixed poems* because they are adaptations of earlier materials. Others are so classified because they are free compositions, in which different literary types are blended.

OUTLINE

In the outline which follows, certain Psalms have been listed in more than one category. Although no system of classification is perfect, anyone who studies the Psalms in groups such as those suggested here will be rewarded many times for the effort put forth. The outline is also designed for quick reference.

Hymns of Praise

In General—100, 113, 117, 145, 150

Praise to the Lord of Creation—8, 19:1-6, 29, 104

Praise to the Lord of History

> The History of Salvation (the mighty acts of God)—68(?), 78, 105, 106, 111, 114, 149 (compare Exodus 15:1-18)

> The Kingship of God (the so-called enthronement Psalms) —47, 93, 96, 97, 98, 99

> The Kingship of God's Anointed (the royal or Messianic Psalms; not hymns, but should be studied with the six preceding Psalms)—2, 18, 20, 21, 45, 61, 63, 72, 89, 101, 110, 132, 144

Praise to the Lord of Creation and History—33, 65, 103, 115, 135, 136, 146, 147, 148

Praise to the Lord of Zion

> In General—46, 48, 76, 87

> Pilgrim Songs—84, 122, 134

> Admission to Zion—15, 24

Prayers in Time of Trouble

Laments of the Community—12, 44, 58, 60, 74, 77, 79, 80, 83, 90, 94, 106, 123, 137

Laments of the Individual

> In General—3, 5, 6, 13, 22, 25, 28, 31, 39, 42-43, 52, 54, 55, 56, 57, 61, 63, 64, 71, 86, 88, 120, 141, 142

> Protestations of Innocence—7, 17, 26, 27, 59 (compare 44)

> Imprecations Upon Enemies—35, 59, 69, 70, 109, 137, 140 (compare the following laments of the community: 12, 58, 83)

> Penitential Prayers—6, 32, 38, 51, 102, 130, 143 (compare 25)

Affirmations of Faith—4, 11, 16, 23, 27, 46, 62, 63, 90, 91, 121, 125, 131

Songs of Thanksgiving

Thanksgivings of the Community—67, 75, 107, 118, 124
Thanksgivings of the Individual—18, 30, 32, 34, 41, 66, 92, 116, 138 (compare Isaiah 38:1-20 and Jonah 2:2-9)

Wisdom Poetry—1, 19:7-14, 32, 37, 41, 49, 73, 111, 112, 119, 127, 128, 133, 139

Liturgies

Liturgies of Instruction—15, 24
Hymn and Priestly Blessing—134
Royal Liturgies—2, 20, 110, 132
Prophetic Liturgies
In General—12, 75, 85, 126
Hymn and Oracle Blended—81, 95
Freer Imitation of Prophetic Style—14 (53), 50, 82

Mixed Poems

Adaptation of Earlier Materials—36, 40, 89, 90, 107, 108, 144
Freer Compositions—9-10, 78 (compare Deuteronomy 32: 1-43), 94, 119, 123, 129, 139

COMMENTARY

BOOK I—PSALMS 1-41

Psalm 1—The Dividing Line

Psalm 1 is an appropriate preface to the Psalter because it presents the two major groups of people mentioned in many of the Psalms. The dividing line between the two is not drawn primarily on the basis of nationality or geography; rather is it drawn on the basis of Covenant relation to God. The righteous are the friends of God and the wicked are the enemies of both God and his true people. The author enunciates the principle that the righteous prosper and the wicked perish. This does not mean that he was unaware of the problems related to such a position as stated in other wisdom Psalms (see Outline). He is only making a general statement without philosophizing about exceptions to the rule.

The Psalm was written after the work of Ezra, under whose leadership the people of God became the people of the Law. At this time the sages of Judah saw God's wisdom in the Law. They were teachers of the Torah (law), the primary meaning of which is "instruction."

The Happiness of the Righteous (1:1-3). The Psalm begins with a beatitude, in which the inward happiness and outward felicity of the righteous man are acclaimed. This man is first characterized negatively. In this negative characterization special attention should be given to three sets of words: (1) "walks," "stands," "sits"; (2) "counsel," "way," "seat"; and (3) "wicked," "sinners," "scoffers." The righteous man does not associate with evil men in such a way as to become progressively one of them. The wicked, the sinners, and the scoffers all belong in the same group as the enemies of God and his people. The word "wicked" calls attention to the fact that they are ungodly and condemned. "Sinners" means that they miss life's goal habitually. And "scoffers" indicates that they ridicule both God and his people (see Prov. 9:7-8; 13:1; 14:6; 15:12; 21:24; 24:9). Of course as Christians we realize that we must have contact with all sorts and conditions of men if we are to win them to Christ (see

Mark 2:15-17), but we are not to imitate the evil in any man, and there are occasions when we dare not join ourselves to the wicked (I Cor. 5:9-13).

The righteous man is then characterized as one who continually delights in God's revealed will. The Law is not a frustration to him but a source of freedom. He is God's man and wants to do God's will. In fact, his blessedness may be likened to that of a small tree which has been transplanted beside life-giving streams of water, which cause it to produce abundantly (see Jer. 17:7-8; Ezek. 47:12).

The Ruin of the Wicked (1:4-6). The wicked do not enjoy the blessedness of the righteous. They are as unsubstantial and useless as the chaff that is separated from the grain by the process of winnowing. In God's judgment they will be cut off from the congregation of his Covenant people. For God approves the way of those who are committed to him, but the way of the ungodly is a dead-end street. In spite of all the psalmist did not say in so short a poem, he has said enough to keep us reminded that a line is drawn between the people of God and the enemies of God (compare Matt. 13:36-43, 47-50; 25:31-46).

Psalm 2—Enthronement of the Lord's Anointed

This Psalm is numbered among the royal Psalms. Its occasion is the enthronement of a new king. Some have identified this king with David, others with Solomon, and still others with Ahaz. The reference to David in Acts 4:25 does not solve the problem, because among the Jews the whole Psalter was thought of in a general way as being Davidic (see Introduction). The Psalm may have come to be used as a part of the liturgy for the occasion of the accession, or anniversary of the accession, of various Davidic kings.

When the message of the Bible as a whole is taken into consideration, it is not difficult to see how parts of Psalm 2 came to be applied to Jesus in many passages of the New Testament, as indicated in the footnotes of the Revised Standard Version. Although David was far from perfect, men of faith, as they thought on him, were led by God to envision the Ideal King of the future. The Kingdom of God cannot be identified with the kingdom of David, but the Messiah of God's Kingdom was to be known as the Son of David.

Conspiracy Against the Lord and His Anointed (2:1-3). Though the Psalm is a dramatic poem with oracles of God included, the king or his representative probably recited it in full. Often subject peoples plotted revolt upon the occasion of the accession of a new king. The revolt in this case is regarded as a revolt against the Lord as well as against his anointed king, for the king was set apart to his task by God himself.

The Heavenly Derision (2:4-6). From the vain plotting of kings on earth the poet moves to a scene in heaven. God is pictured in very human language as mocking the rebels, informing them that he has installed his king on Zion.

The Decree of the Lord (2:7-9). The king repeats the oracle which he has received from the Lord. In the ancient world kings were often thought to be the sons of gods in a literal sense, but this was not the case in Israel. In an adoptive sense Israel was God's son (Hosea 11:1); so was the king of Israel (II Sam. 7:14; Ps. 89:26-27). Verse 7 makes it clear that the king is acknowledged as God's son by adoption on the day of his coronation. "Thou art my beloved Son" (Mark 1:11; Matt. 3:17; Luke 3:22), which is associated with Jesus' baptism, is a quotation from this verse with the word "beloved" added. Furthermore, the full recognition, in the Resurrection, of Christ's inherent Sonship (Acts 13:33; Rom. 1:4) parallels the acknowledgment of the ancient king's adoptive sonship at his enthronement. The vision of world dominion (vs. 8), which goes beyond the actual extent of the realm of any ancient Davidic king, contributed to the eventual Messianic interpretation of the Psalm. Rebels against the Lord's anointed may expect severe judgment (vs. 9).

Exhortation to Submission (2:10-12). All rulers are admonished to submit to the Lord, which includes submitting to his anointed. Those are counted "blessed" or "happy" who find their security in the Lord and his anointed representative.

Psalm 3—A Cry for Deliverance

This is a lament of an individual who cries out to God for deliverance from his enemies and at the same time expresses perfect confidence in God's sustaining help.

The Psalmist's Distress (3:1-2). Here the psalmist pours out his heart to God concerning his numerous foes who are rising against him. Exactly who they are we are not told. He is in some kind of distress which occasions their ridicule: "There is no help for him in God." The word "help" literally means "salvation." The salvation needed in this instance is deliverance from peril.

His Unwavering Trust (3:3-6). In the next two strophes (vss. 3-4, 5-6) the psalmist dwells upon his trust in God. God is his shield which protects him from the weapons of his enemies, whether they be literal weapons or slanderous words and cursings. God is the one who restores his honor and dignity. In the daily routine of sleeping and waking, God is the psalmist's dependable support. This is true whether deliverance comes or not. With such a faith the psalmist is unafraid (compare 23:4), no matter how many enemies should oppose him.

Earnest Petition and Confident Assurance (3:7-8). The thought of the preceding verses is recapitulated here as the psalmist makes a plea for deliverance (literally, "salvation") and expresses the assurance that his prayer is answered in the affirmative. God smites his enemies upon the cheek (see I Kings 22:24; Job 16: 10)—a figure for showing contempt. They are likened to beasts of prey whose teeth are broken (compare 58:6).

In verse 8 the psalmist confesses his membership in the Covenant community. Deliverance of person and people is in the hands of God. The parallelism of this verse indicates that "deliverance" and "blessing" are synonyms.

Psalm 4—Contentment in Whatsoever State I Am

Psalms 3 and 4 are similar, but the latter is more clearly an affirmation of faith.

Prayer to God (4:1). The psalmist is in trouble, but he is not in despair. He addresses God as "God of my right," that is, the one who upholds the rightness of his cause. He grounds his request to be heard in the fact that in past experience God has set him free from distress. This appeal is to the grace or unmerited favor of God.

Counsel to Men (4:2-5). The psalmist's adversaries have dishonored him by bringing false accusations against him (vs. 2). He refers to himself as "the godly" (vs. 3), because he has been the recipient of God's steadfast love (which comes from the same root as "godly") and has committed himself to God in loving steadfastness. God hears his prayer. If his accusers must be angry with him, let them keep their anger and false accusations to themselves rather than adding to these wrongs the sin of unjust public dealings with him (vs. 4). Paul quotes this verse in Ephesians 4:26 as a warning against holding resentment.

Verse 5 is a continuation of the psalmist's counsel to his accusers, but it is very difficult to interpret. He seems to counsel them to offer the sacrifices appropriate to the occasion as they worship at God's house and to trust God to reveal the truth concerning the accusation they have brought.

Joy in the Heart (4:6-8). In contrast to the gloominess of some, the psalmist states that God has given him more joy in his heart than that experienced by those whose harvest has been most abundant (compare 126:6). Here is a man of the Old Covenant who knows the meaning of "eternal life" as a quality of life with God in the present tense. This joy of heart, which is mediated as a gift of God through faith, is more highly treasured than all material prosperity (compare Matt. 6:33; Phil. 4:11). The psalmist's faith is so strong that he is able to sleep in peace without anxiety about tomorrow (see Matt. 6:34; Rom. 8:28).

Psalm 5—A Morning Prayer Accompanied by Sacrifice

Like Psalm 3 this is a lament of an individual, and like both Psalm 3 and Psalm 4 it deals with enemies of the psalmist. Whereas Psalm 4 was offered in the evening (vs. 8), this prayer was offered in the morning along with a sacrifice (vs. 3).

Earnest Appeal to God (5:1-3). The psalmist's urgent appeal is addressed to the Lord as "my King and my God." Of the fixed times for worship, the morning seems to have been the most important (55:17; 59:16; 88:13). The offering of a sacrifice was thought to provide the proper setting for an answer from God (Num. 23:3; compare Luke 1:11). As a separate word, "sacrifice" does not occur in the Hebrew of this verse, but the verb "prepare" is sometimes used in a technical sense with reference to the preparation of the sacrifice itself (Lev. 1:8) and other things associated with it (Gen. 22:9; Lev. 1:7, 12; 6:12; 24:7-8). This is a special sacrifice rather than the continual burnt offering which was made every morning (Exod. 29:39) on behalf of the people of Israel.

God's Hatred of Evildoers (5:4-6). The psalmist's enemies are no amateurs in sin; they are boastful, evildoers, liars, bloodthirsty, and deceitful. The "evildoers" are in the general class of the wicked as the enemies of God and his people. Some claim they are sorcerers. In any case they are always makers of trouble for the People of God. God is not said to love the sinner and hate his sin; he is said to hate both the sinner and his sin. This sounds harsh to modern Christian ears, but there is truth here we dare not overlook. Hate is but the love of God in its judgment upon those who refuse its invitation to Covenant fellowship and obedience (compare Matt. 23:13-36).

The Psalmist's Acceptance with God (5:7-8). In contrast to the evildoers who are morally and spiritually unfit to sojourn in God's house is the psalmist, who upon occasion worships in the Temple and at other times with his face toward it. This access to God is made possible, not through self-righteousness on the part of the psalmist, but through God's Covenant love. The psalmist's worship is offered reverently—"in the fear of thee." He prays that God will lead him, especially as he faces his enemies, and make his way straight in order that he may walk as God wills.

The Psalmist's Enemies (5:9-10). This is a return to the evildoers of the second strophe (vss. 4-6). No dependence can be placed in what they say. Their evil hearts plan destruction. What they say is as dangerous as an unmarked open grave. They say smooth things with their tongue, but they do not mean them.

God's Blessing Upon the Righteous (5:11-12). The psalmist prays for the gift of joy to those who take refuge in God. He further describes the righteous as those who love God's name, that is, those who delight in all for which God's name stands. He asks that God defend them with the shield of his favor.

Psalm 6—The Penitential Prayer of a Sick Man

Through the centuries the Church has regarded Psalm 6 as the first of the seven penitentials (see Introduction). The psalmist regards his sickness unto death as punishment for his sin. It was a common view that a man suffered in proportion to his sin (see the speeches of Job's "comforters"). In spite of the limitations of this view (see John 9:1-3), some suffering is at least in part the consequence of one's own sin.

A Plea for Healing (6:1-5). The psalmist pleads with God to cease his chastisement. He speaks of his bones as being troubled because the bones represent the whole man. In fact, the words

"I," "bones," and "soul" (see John 12:27) are virtually synony-mous since they all stress the psalmist's total involvement in suffering. The psalmist continues his plea for deliverance from sickness and death by appealing to God's steadfast love. He maintains that there is no remembrance of God in Sheol and therefore no praise of God there (compare 30:9; 88:10-12; 115:17; on Sheol, see Introduction).

A Description of Grief (6:6-7). The reference to flooding the bed with tears is a typical exaggeration for emphasis. Such weep-ing affects the eye, and the psalmist's condition is made all the more unbearable by his foes.

Request Granted (6:8-10). Suddenly the tone of the Psalm changes. The psalmist's request has been granted. Did this an-swer come in some direct revelation or through a priestly oracle? He does not tell us. However, he tells his enemies to depart from him (see the use of this verse in Matt. 7:23 and Luke 13:27) and declares that they will be put to shame. These "workers of evil" seem to have called the psalmist's moral and spiritual in-tegrity into question on account of his suffering (compare 35: 21). This Psalm is notable for its implicit confession of sin and assurance of forgiveness.

Psalm 7—The Innocence of a Persecuted Man

This lament belongs in the special category of protestations of innocence. The psalmist has been accused by his enemies and is seeking vindication from God.

Appeal for Deliverance (7:1-2). The appeal begins with a statement of faith in God which occurs frequently at the begin-ning of Psalms (11, 16, 31, 57, 71). This is followed by an appeal for deliverance from pursuers who are likened to a rav-enous lion (compare 10:9; 17:12; 22:13, 21).

The Oath of Clearance (7:3-5). Under certain circumstances a man accused by his neighbors would go to the Temple and take an oath of clearance (I Kings 8:31-32), though the taking of such an oath was not restricted to the Temple (Job 31:5-40). The psalmist has been accused of dealing dishonestly with a friend. In taking this oath of clearance, he calls down God's curse upon himself if he is found guilty.

Petition for Judgment (7:6-8). In verses 4-5 the psalmist refers to his enemy in the singular, but in verses 1 and 6 he speaks of "pursuers" and "enemies." This means that his enemies had a leader who was his chief accuser. Here (vss. 6-8) in pictorial fashion he calls upon God to hold court in which the nations as well as he and his enemies will appear before the Judge.

In the Old Testament, judgment is basically a positive concept, for it is God's activity in establishing justice. The psalmist, therefore, expects to be vindicated by God and expects his enemies to be condemned. The prayer to be judged according to his righteousness and integrity is not a profession of moral perfection but a statement of innocence in the face of false accusation.

The Righteous Judge (7:9-11). The psalmist's prayer that God destroy the wicked and establish the righteous is rooted in his understanding of the righteous character of God and possibly in his belief that justice is altogether a matter of this world (on belief in life after death, see Introduction). God's judgment goes on every day and includes the exercise of his indignation upon the wicked.

The Recoil of Evil Upon the Evildoer (7:12-16). In executing his punishment upon the unrepentant, God is figuratively pictured as using the weapons of a soldier. This is another way of saying that the plots of evil men will boomerang.

Thanksgiving for God's Righteousness (7:17). Assurance of vindication awakens praise for this manifestation of God's righteousness.

Psalm 8—Genesis 1 Set to Music

This is a hymn in praise of the Lord of Creation. Its purpose is to praise the Creator by a meditation upon his creation, especially man. The expression "our Lord" in verses 1 and 9 suggests the congregation at worship, while the "I" of verse 3 implies the personal involvement of the author and each worshiper.

The Majesty of God (8:1a). The first word for "LORD" is the personal name for God revealed to Moses at the burning bush (Exod. 3:13-15). The second word represents an entirely different Hebrew word which bears the meaning of "master" or "sovereign." The majesty of God's name is almost a synonym for the splendor and greatness of his revelation. But it is only the ear of faith that hears the name of God in his creation.

Heavens, Babies, and Enemies (8:1b-2). There is a textual

problem in the beginning of this section which cannot be solved with absolute certainty. The reading given in the Revised Standard Version would have more to commend it if a comma were placed after the word "chanted" and the comma after the word "infants" were omitted. This section of the Psalm would then mean that God, whose glory is praised by the heavenly hosts, has established a stronghold against evil persons through the praise of little children. According to Matthew 21:16 Jesus quoted a part of verse 2 on the occasion of his cleansing of the Temple: "Out of the mouth of babes and sucklings thou hast brought perfect praise." In the Septuagint the word "praise" is found instead of "bulwark." The Hebrew text upon which the Septuagint was based may have read "praise." God has chosen the weak things of the world (such as the praise of children) to confound the mighty (compare I Cor. 1:27).

Man Created in the Image of God (8:3-8). Even in his day the psalmist was impressed with the glory of God in the heavens. In comparison with the greatness and magnitude of the heavens, why should God be concerned about seemingly insignificant man? (compare Job 7:17-18; Psalm 144:3). The expression, "son of man," here is simply another way of referring to "man." In Hebrews 2:5-9 this passage as found in the Septuagint is applied to Jesus as representative man.

In spite of man's apparent insignificance God made him the crowning act of his creation in this world. The word translated "God" in verse 5 may also be translated "gods," "divine beings," or "angels." However, on account of the similarity of the thought here to that in Genesis 1:26-27 and because the psalmist is contrasting man in his smallness with God in his greatness, "God" is the best rendering. This is the poetic way of saying, "God created man in his own image."

Verse 9 is a repetition of verse 1a.

Psalms 9-10—Praise and Lament Combined

Psalms 9 and 10 are really one Psalm. In several ancient manuscripts and versions, they appear as a single composition. The acrostic structure (see Introduction), though incomplete, points to the same fact. Here we have a mixture of literary types: hymn, thanksgiving, and lament, dealing with both domestic and national enemies.

Thanksgiving (9:1-4). The Psalm begins with gratitude to God for all his wonderful deeds. Verses 1-2 set forth God's mighty acts of salvation in behalf of Israel (see 78:4, 11, 32; Exod. 3:20) as a background for verses 3-4, which show that his wonderful deed for the psalmist was vindication against false accusation. The statement of vindication may have been given by a priest or prophet at the Temple (see comment on 7:3-5).

Hymn of Praise (9:5-16). The thought of God as the righteous Judge is related not only to the personal experience of the psalmist but also to God's dealings with nations. God is praised as the King who judges with finality at the end-time (vss. 5-8). This final judgment, which will include the complete destruction of the wicked and their memory, is so certain that it is spoken of as if it were already past (vss. 5-6).

But the praise of God is not to be confined to the anticipation of the future assize, for even now he is a source of strength to those in trouble (vss. 9-10). Those who know his name are those who have received the revelation of himself and have responded to him in faith and obedience. God will not forsake his own. His worshiping congregation is called upon to praise him (vss. 11-12). He is called "the LORD, who dwells in Zion," because the Temple was considered his earthly dwelling place. His deeds are to be proclaimed to the nations. For, as the righteous God, he calls to account those who shed innocent blood and keeps in mind the afflicted.

In the midst of the hymn the psalmist returns to the personal concerns of verses 1-4 (vss. 13-14). As it is translated, verse 13 is a strong personal petition, which seems out of place. However, such an arrangement is by no means impossible. Nevertheless, the context and the evidence of some versions suggest that verse 13 should be rendered:

> The LORD has been gracious to me,
>> he has beheld what I suffered from those
>>> who hate me,
>> lifting me up from the gates of death.

In this case the psalmist has returned to his thanksgiving (vss. 1-4) and appropriately mingled it with the national hymn of praise. Regardless of how verse 13 may be translated, verse 14 strikes the note of thanksgiving. "The daughter of Zion" is a way of speaking of the people of Jerusalem, which is their Mother (see 87:5; Isa. 37:22). Then the writer picks up the theme of the end-time again (vss. 15-16; compare vss. 5-8).

Judgment Upon the Nations (9:17-20). God's judgment is not only an event in the future; it is also a continuing reality. Wicked nations "shall depart to Sheol"; that is, they will be brought to an untimely end. God's people, the poor and needy, will not be overlooked. God's judgment is invoked upon the nations to reveal to them their true identity. They are but "men" (compare Isa. 40:15).

Lament (10:1-11). In Psalm 9 the wicked are hostile nations; in Psalm 10 they are ungodly Jews who persecute their fellow Jews. Although the psalmist was vindicated in a particular situation (9:1-4), this one vindication did not solve the problem of the persecution of the godly by the godless. Therefore, he cries out, "Why dost thou stand afar off, O LORD?" (vs. 1). He further prays that the evil schemes of the godless will boomerang (vs. 2).

Appeal for Divine Intervention (10:12-18). The wicked think that God will not hold them accountable for their behavior (vs. 13), but God takes account of all; the hopeless man places his trust in God who through the years has been the helper of the fatherless (vs. 14). The appeal is made specific; namely, that God will break the power of the wicked and bring their wickedness to an end (vs. 15), for he is King. His kingship will be manifested in a special way when foreign nations are no longer allowed to oppress the land (vs. 16), for the wicked in this Psalm may be those Jews who collaborate with foreign oppressors to their own advantage and the hurt of their fellow Jews. The last two verses (vss. 17-18) are an assurance that God will hear the petition of the meek, who are characterized as the fatherless to emphasize their great need.

Psalm 11—Courageous Faith

Psalm 11 is one of those gems of the Psalter classified as affirmations of faith. In spite of danger to himself, in spite of the advice of friends to flee, and in spite of the seeming hopelessness of his cause, the psalmist affirms his steadfast trust in God.

Faith Against Fear (11:1-3). The Psalm begins with a statement of faith found also in other Psalms (7, 16, 31, 57, 71). But in contrast to the psalmist's faith is the fear of his friends, who counsel him to flee to the mountains because his enemies are seeking his life. They say, "If the foundations are destroyed, what can the righteous do?" In other words, they tell the psalmist he is fighting for a lost cause. Since the moral and theological foundations of society are crumbling under the evil deeds of wicked men, such men as the psalmist are considered helpless. But he is a man with a deep sense of responsibility for his community and an unshakable faith in God.

God Against the Godless (11:4-7). Concentration upon evil has led his friends to despair, but the psalmist's faith in God is the basis of a true optimism. God's presence among his people is symbolized by the Temple and his universal sovereignty by his throne in heaven (compare Isa. 6:1). As a refiner he tests the righteous and the wicked and distinguishes the gold from the dross. He hates the person who loves violence (see comment on 5:4-6). The condemnation of the wicked in the first part of verse 6 ("fire and brimstone") is reminiscent of the destruction of Sodom and Gomorrah in Genesis 19:24. This is a way of saying that the condemnation will be horrible. To say that "a scorching wind shall be the portion of their cup" underscores the devastating judgment to come. The word "cup" is a figurative way of referring to "destiny" (16:5; Matt. 26:39, 42). God's judgment is an expression of his righteous character. He delights in the righteous deeds of his people. The upright enjoy his presence (17:15; 63:2). The Master said it this way: "Blessed are the pure in heart, for they shall see God" (Matt. 5:8; compare Ps. 24:4; Heb. 12:14; I John 3:2).

Psalm 12—Supplication in a Time of Degeneracy

The Psalm is a lament of the community in a time of moral and spiritual bankruptcy, and is also a prophetic liturgy, since in verse 5 God is quoted directly as in the Prophets (compare Isa. 33:10-12).

Appeal for Help (12:1-4). The appeal for God's saving help is made in the face of widespread corruption. The godly and faithful are said to be extinct (compare I Kings 19). Nevertheless, the Psalm is not to be understood in an absolutely literal manner here, for those who offer the prayer are among the godly and faithful (compare similar statements in the Prophets—Hosea 4: 1-2; Micah 7:2; Jer. 5:1). Lying, flattery, and hypocrisy are common. The flatterers and boasters say: "With our tongue we will prevail . . . who is our master?" This implies that these people are persons in power who make their way with smooth talk. They are guilty of practical atheism and say in effect, "What I do is nobody's business but mine."

God's Word of Promise (12:5-6). God responds to his suffering community, the poor and needy, and promises to give them security. God's word is sometimes a promise, as here (119:25, 28, 38; 130:5; 105:42; Gen. 12:1-3). His promises are as pure as silver purified seven times (the number of perfection); that is, in contrast to the insincere words of the flatterers, there is no dross of falsehood in them.

Renewed Appeal (12:7-8). Having been reassured by God's promise, his suffering community renews its appeal by praying for protection from this generation. The word "generation" takes on moral and spiritual significance as it designates people of a particular kind in a given age (see 14:5; Matt. 17:17). Because men of vile character are placed in positions of authority, the wicked have a free rein in society.

Psalm 13—Darkness and Then the Dawn

There is a pattern of negative and positive that runs through the Bible: darkness and light, bondage and freedom, exile and return, crucifixion and resurrection, Armageddon and New Jerusalem. In this personal lament the psalmist moves from sorrow of heart to joy in God's salvation.

Lament (13:1-2). The Psalm begins with a strong lament, in which the expression "how long" appears four times. The translation, "How long must I bear pain in my soul," is based on the Syriac Version and may be correct since it fits the context well. The traditional Hebrew text reads, "How long shall I hold counsels in my soul," that is, in an attempt to find a way out of trouble. In either case the psalmist is suffering; some think he is suffering from illness. Whether or not this is true, he is suffering from enemies (vs. 4), especially from a particular enemy (vss. 2, 4). His emphatic expostulation sounds almost irreverent, but an honest complaint is more acceptable to God than dishonest piety. The psalmist had faith or he would not have prayed in the first place. God works his catharsis in honest souls, not in hypocrites who insist on trying to fool him.

Supplication (13:3-4). After his lament the psalmist implores God's consideration and help. He prays that God will lighten his eyes, in which his weakened condition is reflected (see 6:7; 38:10; Lam. 5:17; compare I Sam. 14:27, 29; Ezra 9:8). If his present situation continues, there is danger of his sleeping the sleep of death (for death as a sleep, see Job 3:13; Dan. 12:2; I Thess. 4:14). Moreover, if he dies his enemies will interpret his death in such a way as to mock his trust in God.

Grateful Faith (13:5-6). In spite of the darkness of the hour, the psalmist anticipates the dawn of a new day. He has placed his confidence in God's Covenant love, and he promises to rejoice and sing about God's bountiful dealings with him (compare 116:7; 119:17; 142:7). God's people have always lived in the faith that God has the last word and that that word is good.

Psalm 14—Corruption Denounced

See comment on Psalm 53.

Psalm 15—Qualifications for a Guest in God's House

This Psalm was probably used liturgically by pilgrims who asked their question concerning qualifications for admission to God's house (vs. 1) at the Temple gates and received the answer from attendants within (vss. 2-5). Though strictly speaking it is not a hymn, on account of its association with the Temple it is classified with the hymns of praise to the Lord of Zion. It is more technically classified as a liturgy of instruction (see Introduction), in which the qualifications for worship at the Temple are stated in the form of a decalogue.

The Pilgrims' Question (15:1). The pilgrim is considered a sojourner or guest who enjoys the hospitality of God as his host. The question is, What kind of person must this guest be?

The Priests' Answer (15:2-5ab). The answer is one that stresses the ethical imperatives of the Law and the Prophets. No ceremonial qualifications are mentioned. Yet, the guest in God's house made use of ceremonies in worship. This means that the ceremonies of worship, to be acceptable, must come from lives that are ethically akin to God, and this kinship to God is demonstrated in one's treatment of others (compare I John 4:20). The requirements in this decalogue are typical, not all-inclusive.

The man worthy to be God's guest does not seek the hurt of his neighbor by word or deed. Nevertheless, he refuses to applaud a scoundrel and shows him the disapproval he deserves. On the other hand, he loves those who serve the Lord. When he makes a promise, he will keep it even if it is to his disadvantage to do so. He is no money lover (see I Tim. 6:10), for persons and principle are of greater importance than things. The Law forbade the taking of interest from a brother in the Covenant community (Exod. 22:25; Lev. 25:37; Deut. 23:20) because borrowing took place only in the case of dire need and the rates of interest were exorbitant. Therefore, to take interest would be to profit out of a brother's tragedy. Borrowing for investment as in the modern world was largely unknown. Though the economic and social structures of life change from age to age, the theology behind this law does not change, namely, that God's people are to use things in the service of persons (see Matt. 12:12). God's true worshiper will show no partiality to the man who offers him a present to betray the cause of justice.

The Divine Reward (15:5c). The reward of godliness is security in God (compare Matt. 7:24-27).

Psalm 16—Joy in the Presence of the Lord

This is an affirmation of faith in God as refuge, portion, counselor, and the giver of joyous life. It contains a reminiscence of lament (vs. 1) and thanksgiving (vss. 7, 9), but its characteristic mood is joyous trust.

No Good Apart from God (16:1-4). There is no indication that the psalmist is in peril; therefore, his petition for preservation is to be understood in a general sense. He says to the "LORD" (Yahweh, the personal name of God), "Thou art my Lord [sovereign]; I have no good apart from thee" (vs. 2). But he is not alone, for he is a member of the true Covenant community, "the saints in the land." The word "saints" means "holy ones," for they have been set apart by God unto himself and in them the call of God to the nation to be holy (Exod. 19:6) is being realized.

Over against God's holy ones are those who choose another god and thereby multiply their troubles. The psalmist will not participate with them in their rituals of worship. In fact, in obedience to the Law (Exod. 23:13; compare Hosea 2:17; Zech.

13:2) he will not even take the names of the pagan deities upon his lips, for to do so would be to pay them homage.

The Lord My Portion and Counselor (16:5-8). The Lord is the psalmist's portion and cup. The word "portion" ordinarily refers to an allotted share of property, but is here used metaphorically (compare 73:26; 119:57; 142:5). The figurative meaning of "cup" in this context is destiny (compare 11:6; Matt. 26:39, 42). All that the psalmist cherishes is in God's hand, and no one can snatch it from him. Still another figure is used (vs. 6). God is to the psalmist as the choicest lands which have been lined off and assigned to him. The psalmist is also grateful to God for the counsel he gives at night through the still, small voice within. He deliberately practices the presence of God that he may not fall, for with God at his right hand he is truly secure (see 15:5c).

The Joy of Life with God (16:9-11). The use of the words "heart," "soul" (literally, "glory" or "liver"), and "body" (literally, "flesh") emphasizes the response of the psalmist's whole being to God as the source of his joy and security. Verses 10-11 may be interpreted to mean that God will preserve the psalmist from a premature death and grant him the continuing joy of his presence and blessing throughout the length of his days. On the other hand, it is possible that this psalmist is standing on the threshold of belief in eternal life not only as a present reality but also as a future hope. At Pentecost, Peter saw a deeper meaning in verses 8-11 (from the Septuagint) in relation to Jesus' resurrection (Acts 2:25-33; compare Acts 13:35). Certainly it is only in the resurrection of Jesus Christ that the hope of God's people finds its center.

Psalm 17—A Cry for Vindication

Psalm 17 is closely related to Psalm 16 in thought and expression. In both Psalms there is a profound sense of communion with God. However, Psalm 16 is primarily an affirmation of faith and Psalm 17 a protestation of innocence in the face of false accusation.

The Lamenting Appeal (17:1-2). This is the psalmist's initial cry for vindication. The word translated "vindication" is literally "judgment." Here, as so often in the Old Testament, God's act of judgment is viewed as a saving act.

The Declaration of Innocence (17:3-5). If God examines the

psalmist, especially at night when communion with God is unin-
terrupted, he will find no dross of wicked purpose in him. He has
not transgressed God's commands by sins of the tongue. He has
avoided the violence of such crimes as robbery and murder. He
has known the security of those who follow God's direction.
These declarations are not expressions of what we mean today
by self-righteousness, but an oath of clearance at the Temple as
provided for in I Kings 8:31-32.

The Appeal Continued (17:6-9). As the psalmist continues his
prayer for vindication, he appeals to the Covenant love of God
who has time and again revealed himself as Savior of those who
have sought refuge from adversaries. He prays that God will
keep him as the pupil of the eye because that is the part of the
body most carefully guarded (compare Deut. 32:10; Prov. 7:2;
Zech. 2:8). "Hide me in the shadow of thy wings" is another
way of praying for protection from the enemies who threaten
his life. The figurative expression, "shadow of thy wings" (36:7;
57:1; 61:4; 63:7; 91:4), is of uncertain origin. It may have been
prompted by the winged solar disk of the Egyptian sun-god
Horus, or by the care of a mother bird for her young, or by the
wings of the cherubim in the Temple.

The Psalmist's Enemies Described (17:10-12). The enemies
are heartless, arrogant, cruel, and beastly (for evil men compared to a lion, see also 7:2; 10:9; 17:12; 22:13). There is no
hope in appealing to them for compassion.

A Curse Upon These Men and Their Descendants (17:13-14).
The petition to overthrow the psalmist's enemies is essentially
the same as the petition to deliver him, for in the view of his
day he cannot be vindicated unless they are overthrown (see I
Kings 8:31-32 again). What appears on the surface as a blessing
(vs. 14) is really a curse upon his enemies and their descendants
to the third generation ("them," "their children," and "their
babes"; compare Exod. 20:5). (For a discussion of the Christian's approach to imprecation in the Psalms, see the Introduction.)

The Assurance of Vindication (17:15). The psalmist seems to
be spending the night in the Temple precincts (vs. 3). When he
awakes in the morning, God will reveal himself to him in righteousness, which in this case is vindication. To behold God's
"form" is to have an intimate vision of his presence (see Num.
12:8). The quality of fellowship envisioned by the psalmist is of

a piece with Christian experience. However, the psalmist does not draw out the implications of his faith, for he is concerned about deliverance from death, and therefore about life in this world.

Psalm 18—A Thanksgiving of the Lord's Anointed

The text, authorship, date, and composition of this Psalm are warmly debated. II Samuel 22 is identical with Psalm 18 except for minor variations. In its original form it may have come from David, but its present form gives evidence of later editing. Regardless of debate about details, Psalm 18 is a thanksgiving of David or a king of David's line for deliverance and victory. It was probably used by various Davidic kings in public worship at the sanctuary to celebrate their victories.

A Prelude of Praise (18:1-3). The Psalm is introduced by a brief statement of praise, in which the Lord's relation to the king is expressed by a series of metaphors. The first verse is not found in II Samuel 22. The word for "love" denotes very tender affection.

The King's Distress (18:4-6). With a variety of figures the king describes how he was almost taken by death. He cried out in his distress to God, who answered him from his heavenly temple.

The Lord's Response (18:7-19). The Lord's response to the king's prayer is first set forth in terms of a theophany, that is, an appearance or coming of God. His coming to help the king is likened to his coming in judgment, revealing his power through volcanic eruption, earthquake, smoke, and storm. Of course many of the expressions are not to be taken literally—for example, riding on a cherub (vs. 10). The Lord's response is then set forth in a more direct way (vss. 16-19). He delivered the king from his enemies and gave him a new freedom.

The King's Reward (18:20-24). This section of the Psalm sounds like Deuteronomy. In any case, the king interprets God's goodness to him as a reward for his faithfulness. He has obeyed the Law and kept his hands morally clean.

A Generalization (18:25-30). In the manner of a wisdom teacher the king now generalizes on his experience, maintaining that God rewards the loyal, blameless, pure, and humble but punishes the crooked and proud (vss. 25-27). Although this is not a statement of the whole truth (see Matt. 5:43-48), there is truth in it (see Matt. 7:21; 12:50; 25:31-46). The king reverts to his own experience in verses 28-29 and again generalizes in verse 30.

God the Source of the King's Victory (18:31-45). The king confesses gratefully that the source of his strength and victory over his enemies is the Lord (vss. 31-42). He could not have succeeded alone. As a consequence of his victory other peoples submitted themselves to his sovereignty (vss. 43-45).

The King's Grateful Praise (18:46-50). The king reiterates the fact that the Lord has been his rock, God, and savior (vss. 46-48). Therefore, he will praise him among the nations (vs. 49). Paul quotes this verse in Romans 15:9 along with other passages from the Old Testament to show God's purpose of salvation for the Gentiles. The Psalm is Messianic in the sense that it reflects God's Covenant with David and his descendants (II Sam. 7:12-16). These rulers were "messiahs," for they were the anointed of the Lord, and from their line the Messiah of messiahs would come and invite all men to accept his dominion.

Psalm 19—God's Word Through Nature and Law

Psalm 19 is composed of two originally independent poems, one presenting the revelation of God through the heavens (vss. 1-6) and the other the revelation of God through the Law (vss. 7-14). The differences in point of view, subject matter, poetic meter, and the names of God point to this conclusion. Whoever formed Psalm 19 by combining two other Psalms, whether he was the author of verses 7-14 or an editor, was surely inspired to do so; for verses 1-6 are incomplete as an expression of Israel's faith. What the Jew heard God say through nature was conditioned by what he had seen God do in Israel's history.

The Glory of God in the Heavens (19:1-6). The heavenly anthem is unheard by the outer ear, but what marvelous harmony it brings to the inner ear! From the beginning of creation the choirs of day and night in antiphonal fashion have proclaimed the glory of their Creator. The day impresses men with certain of the wonders of creation and the night with others. Such proclamation of God's glory is world-wide (see Paul's use of verse 4 in Rom. 10:18).

The psalmist calls special attention to the sun, the most prominent member of the daytime choir (vss. 4c-6). It is pictured as having a tent in the heavens or in the sea ("in the sea" is preferable to "in them," vs. 4c). It is likened to a bridegroom in his radiance and vitality, and to an athlete in his eagerness to demonstrate his strength and endurance. Its light and heat are universal blessings.

The psalmist may have been acquainted with Babylonian and Egyptian hymns to the sun, but his theology is fundamentally different from that of the authors of these hymns. To them the sun was a deity; to the psalmist it is a creation of God, set in the heavens to reveal his glory.

The Will of God in the Law (19:7-14). We have been out of doors looking at God's world with one of the two psalmists as our guide; the other now leads us inside, picks up a scroll, and tells us the wonders of the Law of the Lord. The name of deity in verses 1-6 is "God" (El), a word denoting power; this is an appropriate word to use for God in association with his creation. His name in verses 7-14 is "the LORD" (see Exod. 3); it is appropriately used in connection with the Law that was given to Israel. The Law is also known by different names: law, testimony, precepts, commandment, fear, and ordinances (vss. 7-10). Although these words as used here are virtually synonyms, they do have distinctive shades of meaning. As Torah the "law" is instruction; as testimony it is a witness to God's will and man's duty; as precepts it is a collection of specific injunctions; as commandment it is that which expresses the will of the personal God; as fear it is that which enjoins reverence for God; and as ordinances it is a group of divine judgments. It is flawless, dependable, right, pure, clean, and true. It has not yet been made the occasion for legalistic self-righteousness or burdened with the minute interpretations of scribes. It refreshes the inner man, makes the simple wise, brings joy to the heart, and sheds light on the way of life. It is more desirable than the finest gold and the best honey—in other words, it is better than all the things money can buy.

The praise of God through the admiration of his Law leads the psalmist to self-examination and prayer (vss. 11-14). He looks upon himself as God's servant who is warned by God's laws and is rewarded in keeping them (compare Matt. 16:27; 10:42). Yet, he realizes that no matter how hard he may try to obey, he sins inadvertently. He also realizes that only God enables him to avoid the more heinous sins. The aim of his life is to be blameless and free of great transgression (compare Matt. 5:48). For

sins of inadvertence the Law provided an atonement (Lev. 4-5;
Num. 15:22-29), but for sins committed with a high hand no
animal sacrifice was provided (Num. 15:30-31); in such a case
a man could cast himself directly on the mercy of God.

The psalmist's concluding petition is that what he has thought
and said in his Psalm may be received by God as an acceptable
offering. He addresses God as his rock, who gives him strength
and security, and as his redeemer, who sets him free from the
tyranny of sin.

Psalm 20—God Save the King

This Psalm is a royal liturgy (see Introduction), sung by different voices in the Temple as the king prepares for battle. This
means that the Psalm is pre-exilic and that the king is a Judean
of Davidic descent (vs. 2). The king has already prayed, and
sacrifices are being offered by the priests on his behalf (compare
I Sam. 7:9; 13:9).

The People's Prayer for Their King (20:1-5). The congregation or a choir on its behalf prays that God will grant the king's
request for victory in battle. God's help is thought of as coming
from the Temple which is his dwelling in the midst of his people.
The people pray that he will accept the king's meal offerings and
whole burnt offerings, which are expressions of his devotion.
They anticipate waving their banners after victory is won.

Assurance of Victory (20:6-8). A priest or prophet, who identifies himself with his people, proclaims the message of assurance. He knows that God will give saving help to his anointed
king. The fact that the answer is said to come from heaven this
time rather than from Zion (as in vs. 2) simply reflects Israel's
faith that God is sovereign over all as well as present among his
people. Israel's enemies place their confidence in military equip-
ment, but Israel places her confidence in the name of the Lord
(see Deut. 20:1; Isa. 31:3).

The Concluding Prayer of the People (20:9). In this one verse
the theme of the entire Psalm is recapitulated. "Give victory to
the king, O LORD," is literally "Save the king, O LORD." This
ancient prayer, like its modern counterpart, "God save the king,"
is also a prayer for the nation, since its well-being inheres in its
ruler.

Psalm 21—A Celebration for the King

As Psalm 20 is a royal Psalm accompanying the sacrifice of the king before battle, Psalm 21 may be a Psalm accompanying the king's thank offering after battle. However, it is possible that Psalm 21 celebrates the anniversary of the king's coronation (vs. 3).

Thanksgiving for Past Mercies (21:1-7). Although Psalm 21 is not as obviously liturgical as Psalm 20, it may have been sung by alternating voices. Verses 1-7 may have been sung by the congregation or a Temple choir. The king rejoices in God's strength and help. The word "help" is literally "salvation," and may refer to victory granted in answer to the petition for victory in Psalm 20 (compare 20:4-5 and 21:1-2). In addition to granting the king saving help in answer to prayer, God has confirmed his coronation; given him the assurance of long life (the meaning of "for ever and ever"); bestowed upon him regal glory, splendor, and majesty; and made him glad with his presence. The king trusts God, and God makes the king secure in his Covenant love.

Anticipation of Future Victories (21:8-12). Here it seems that a prophet or priest assures the king of future victories. God's ancient people lived in a situation in which war was considered inevitable, and quite naturally they turned to God in prayer for victory. The desire to cut off the descendants of their enemies arose in part from their fear of threats in the future.

Concluding Prayer of the People (21:13). The people pray that God will exalt himself by blessing the king with victory again, and they pledge themselves to renewed praise.

Psalm 22—The Passion Psalm

This has been called "the Passion Psalm" because Jesus quoted its opening words in the agony of the Cross (Mark 15:34; Matt. 27:46) and the Gospels record the parallels between his sufferings and those of the psalmist (vs. 7—Matt. 27:39; Mark 15:29; vs. 8—Matt. 27:43; vs. 18—Matt. 27:35; Mark 15:24; Luke 23:34; John 19:23-24). It is the greatest of the personal laments in the Psalter, having affinity with the Book of Job (30:9-11) and with passages depicting the Servant of the Lord in Isaiah 40-55.

My God, Why? (22:1-21). The psalmist feels utterly forsaken
by God, yet even in his forsakenness he cries in faith, *"My* God."
It seems to him that God has ignored his unceasing cry for help
in the midst of enemies and illness. He appeals to the saving acts
of God in the history of Israel: "In thee our fathers trusted . . .
and thou didst deliver them." But in contrast to the situation of
the Israelite fathers is his present predicament. He feels as insignificant as a worm and is scorned and despised by men (compare Isa. 41:14; 49:7; 52:14; 53:2-3).

Then he appeals to God as the one who has been a Father to
him since birth (vss. 9-10). His tormentors are likened to the
bulls of Bashan (a Transjordanian territory) and to an attacking
lion (vss. 12-13). He gives a vivid description of his symptoms
as he begins to enter the realm of death (vss. 14-15), and pictures his enemies as a company of evildoers who gloat over his
declining condition and divide his clothes among them in eager
anticipation of his death (vss. 16-18).

Throughout the lament he is concerned about God's distance
from him. In the very first verse he questions, "Why art thou so
far . . . ?" In verse 11 he pleads, "Be not far from me." And in
verse 19 he begs, "But thou, O LORD, be not far off!" A man who
has known the presence of God can endure anything better than
his absence. The psalmist prays for deliverance from violent
death and from his enemies, who are described as a dog, a lion,
and wild oxen (vss. 20-21).

I Will Praise Thee (22:22-31). The mood of the psalmist suddenly changes from painful lament to exhilarating praise and
thanksgiving. What has happened is spiritually and psychologi-
cally sound. God has used the psalmist's honest uncovering of
his sorrow to work such a catharsis that he now knows whom he
has believed.

The psalmist vows to praise God for his deliverance in the
midst of the assembled congregation, and calls upon the Covenant community to join him in thanksgiving (vss. 22-24). God
is the author of his praise (vs. 25). When the psalmist pays his
vows by the presentation of his thank offerings at the Temple,
he will invite the afflicted (poor) to eat as much as they desire
and will pronounce upon his guests a blessing, "May your hearts
live for ever!" (vs. 26).

The psalmist began with a concern for himself and then
moved in an expanding fashion to a concern for the hungry and

the poor within the congregation of his own people. But now with prophetic insight he envisions the Kingdom of God (vss. 27-31). He sees the conversion (vs. 27) of people from the ends of the earth to the worship of Israel's God (compare Isa. 43:8-13; 45:22-23; 49:1-6; 56:7). The proud and even the dead shall bow down in worship before him (vs. 29; compare Phil. 2:9-11). The good news of God's salvation shall be proclaimed to generations yet unborn.

No wonder Jesus turned to this Psalm in the hour of bitterest anguish, for through his suffering and death, which are too deep for our complete understanding, he was making possible the consummation of that Kingdom for which he had lived. And as we read it, we cannot help thinking of him as he preached and taught the gospel of the Kingdom, counseled the proud, blessed the poor, fed the hungry, suffered, and died. The "why" of the psalmist and the "why's" of all our hearts are caught up into the "why" of Jesus and are answered in his resurrection from the dead.

Psalm 23—The Psalm of Psalms

This Psalm has sung its way into more hearts than any other part of the Bible except the Lord's Prayer. Its message has been grasped by young and old alike. The tiny tot memorizes it before he can read, and the old man dies with it upon his lips. It is a personal confession of faith in the God who cares. The psalmist asks for nothing; he affirms his faith without reservation: "The LORD is my shepherd"; "I fear no evil"; "I shall dwell in the house of the LORD for ever."

The Lord Is My Shepherd (23:1-4). Various metaphors are used throughout the Old Testament to express the Covenant relation between God and his people, and one of the most beautiful and meaningful is that of the shepherd and his sheep. The appropriateness of this figure is at once obvious when it is remembered that Israel was a seminomadic people. The patriarchs had flocks and herds. God called Moses from keeping the flock of Jethro, his father-in-law, to become the shepherd who would lead his people out of bondage. David, the shepherd lad, became the shepherd king of Israel (II Sam. 5:2; 7:7; Ps. 78:70-72), a man after God's own heart. All the kings of God's people were supposed to be shepherds, and the Messianic king of the future, of

whom David was a type, was to be the shepherd par excellence
(Ezek. 34:23).

God is often referred to directly or indirectly as the shepherd
of Israel (74:1; 77:20; 78:52, 70-72; 79:13; 80:1; Micah 7:14;
Isa. 40:11), but infrequently as the shepherd of an individual
(Gen. 48:15). This Psalm is, therefore, all the more remarkable
for its emphasis upon God's care of an individual sheep. Sometimes the most valuable gifts are wrapped in the smallest pack-
ages. The little word "my" is not even a whole word in Hebrew;
it is only a suffix on the noun "shepherd"—but what an important suffix! To say, "The LORD is my shepherd," is to say, "The
LORD is my pastor," for "pastor" is simply the Latin word for
"shepherd." To say, "The LORD is my shepherd," is also to say, "I
shall not want." This does not mean that I shall have everything
I desire, but that I shall not lack that which the Shepherd knows
I need.

The oriental shepherd guides and provides for his sheep. He
makes his sheep lie down in pastures of tender green grass,
which is often hard to find in some parts of the Near East. He
leads them beside waters of rest. Through rest and life-giving
water he restores the sheep's life ("soul" often means "life"), and
it is ready to travel again. He leads his sheep in the safest paths
for the sake of his name. As a shepherd he has a name or reputation based on a dependable record, and this he will not violate.

As God's people we have our green pastures and still waters:
the daily bread, family prayers and Bible study, worship in the
sanctuary, service in the market place, in fact, all the blessings
of God. God's blessings—material and spiritual—bring renewed
vitality for the tasks ahead. He leads each of us in paths of
righteousness. If we choose, instead, the paths of sin, we cannot
accuse him of leading us there. He will not betray his name as
the righteous God.

The shepherd is not only guide and provider, he is also com-
forter. "The valley of the shadow of death" should probably be
rendered "the valley of deep gloom." The shepherd must often
lead his sheep through deep and dark ravines where wild beasts
and robbers may lurk to pounce upon the sheep. But the presence of the shepherd banishes fear. With his rod the shepherd
can ward off an attacker and with his staff rescue a sheep that
has fallen into a pit.

In verses 1-3 the psalmist has addressed God in the third person. When he begins to speak of the dangerous experiences of life, he changes to the more intimate second person, "thou." In some of life's hard experiences friends and loved ones go with us a long way, but only the Heavenly Pastor can go all the way. This is notably true when we pass through the literal valley of the shadow of death. The presence of the Shepherd banishes fear.

The Lord Is My Host (23:5-6). Most interpreters of the Psalms feel that the figure of the shepherd gives way at this point to that of the gracious host. Though this interpretation is not certain, it is probable. The host is a "sheik" to whose tent the psalmist has fled from his enemies. Once he has reached the tent, he is safe from his pursuers. His host prepares a banquet for him, and his enemies can but watch him enjoy this gracious hospitality. He is anointed, in accordance with oriental custom, with perfumed oil (Amos 6:6; compare Luke 7:46). He says, more literally, "My cup is overflowing abundance," for his host is most generous.

Whether God be thought of as the shepherd or as the gracious host in verse 5, the message of the verse is the same: God cares for his people as individuals and provides abundantly for their needs.

The word usually translated "follow" does not mean to tag along but to pursue with the intention of overtaking. God is so eager to bless the psalmist that his goodness and Covenant love are pictured as ministering spirits seeking to overtake and bless him. "The house of the LORD" is probably the Temple in Jerusalem. The Christian worshiper very naturally tends to read the meaning of life after death into the expression "for ever" or "length of days," but for the psalmist it meant, "as long as I live." He does not mean that he wants to live in the Temple for the rest of his life, but that he wants to have, all the time, the quality of fellowship with God which he has found in the Temple.

As the Christian reads this Psalm, he thinks of the Good Shepherd who lays down his life for the sheep (John 10:1-30), for in Jesus Christ the Shepherd-God became incarnate. In his vision on Patmos, John looked for the Lion of the tribe of Judah to open the scroll of destiny, but as he looked he saw, not a Lion, but a Lamb standing as though it had been slain (Rev. 5:1-14). The Good Shepherd is the Lamb of God. "The Lamb in the midst of the throne will be their shepherd" (Rev. 7:17).

Psalm 24—The King of Glory

This Psalm is composed of three distinct parts: verses 1-2, 3-6, and 7-10, which may have originated independently. However, in its present form, the Psalm found its unity in some festal celebration. Interpreters have associated it with a variety of occasions: David's bringing up the Ark to Jerusalem (II Sam. 6:12-19), the pre-exilic Feast of Tabernacles, the postexilic New Year Festival, and others. The reflection of prophetic thought in verses 3-6 is too clear to permit a Davidic date for the composition as a whole. It is a hymn of Zion, which may be subdivided into a hymn of creation (vss. 1-2), a liturgy of instruction (vss. 3-6), and an antiphonal song (vss. 7-10).

The Earth Is the Lord's (24:1-2). Verses 1-6 were presumably sung as the procession of worshipers was approaching the hill of Zion. Verses 1-2 may have been sung by the whole group of pilgrims. Both the Feast of Tabernacles and the later New Year Festival were closely associated with the creation of the world. The thought of the earth's being established on waters is a part of ancient Near Eastern views of creation. In the Psalm there is an allusion to God's bringing order out of chaos (Gen. 1:2).

Who Shall Ascend the Hill of the Lord? (24:3-6). As the pilgrims reach the foot of the hill, they stop and a priest intones the question of verse 3. Another priest gives the answer (vss. 4-6). His answer should be compared with Psalm 15:2-5. The person who worships God in the Temple must be innocent of violence or other wrongdoing, and pure in the intentions and desires of the heart. Both outward act and inward motive must be right. He must not give his allegiance to idols or anything else that is false or empty, and he must not perjure himself. Such a person will receive God's blessing and righteousness ("vindication" is a free translation of the word for "righteousness" in verse 5). As shown by the parallelism, God's blessing is God's righteousness, for it is as the righteous God that God will deal with his worshiper. The priest regards the group of pilgrims before him as meeting the requirements set forth (vs. 6). Therefore, the procession continues.

Who Is the King of Glory? (24:7-10). At the Temple gates the procession stops again, and a choir addresses the Temple gates as though they were persons. It calls upon them to be lifted up in order to let the King of glory in, for something representing the presence of the Lord (perhaps the Ark of the Covenant or some other object) seems to be leading the procession. The fact that the gates are called "ancient doors" means that the Temple has been standing for a long time.

Then voices from within reply, "Who is the King of glory?" And those outside the gates cry out, "The LORD, strong and mighty, the LORD, mighty in battle!" A second time the group outside calls upon the gates to be lifted up, and the voices within ask the same question again. Then comes the answer that unlocks the gates: "The LORD of hosts, he is the King of glory!" The gates are opened and the procession enters. Thus the glory of God as the King of creation and King of his people is dramatized.

Psalm 25—An Alphabetical Lament

In most cases each succeeding verse of this Psalm begins with the next letter of the Hebrew alphabet. This acrostic structure makes for limited freedom of expression, though the psalmist achieved a remarkable degree of freedom in this case. Lament, wisdom teaching, and intimate fellowship with God are blended together.

Prayer for Protection, Guidance, and Forgiveness (25:1-7). First, the psalmist commits himself to God in prayer. Then he prays that God will not let him and others who hope in God be put to shame by their enemies. His enemies gloat over his predicament but are not the primary cause of it. His prayer continues with a petition for guidance in keeping with the truth revealed in the Law (vss. 4-5). In the third part of the prayer (vss. 6-7) he throws himself as a sinner on the mercy (literally, "tender feelings") and steadfast love of God, which have been revealed in God's dealings with his people since the beginning of their history. The word for "sins" designates those inadvertent failures and lapses so characteristic of youth, and the word for "transgressions" means those more serious acts of deliberate rebellion.

God's Dealings with His People (25:8-15). Because God is good and upright he instructs sinners in his way. The sinners in this case are not the habitually wicked but the humble, among whom the psalmist numbers himself. God's true people are not sinless, but they do not place themselves in the category of the wicked by refusing to seek God's forgiving grace. God's faithfulness and

Covenant love are available for those who take seriously the
Covenant relation as expressed in the Law (vss. 8-10).

In the midst of setting forth God's revealed character, the
psalmist repeats his prayer for forgiveness, recognizing the greatness of his guilt (vs. 11; compare 32:2, 5). Then he returns to his
wisdom teaching (vss. 12-15). God will instruct his true worshiper (one who fears him) in the way he should choose. He will
remain prosperous and his descendants will continue to possess
the land (compare 37:11; Deut. 4:40; Prov. 2:21-22). God's
friendship also belongs to his true worshipers. The word translated "friendship" signifies secret counsel, intimate fellowship,
familiar converse.

Renewed Prayer for Protection and Forgiveness (25:16-21).
The answer to the psalmist's prayer has not yet come. He is
lonely and feels that his sufferings are the consequence of his
sin. The word translated "forgive" signifies the lifting up of a
burden. If God's help does not come, the ridicule of the psalmist's enemies will but increase. His final petition is that his integrity and uprightness will preserve him, not as self-righteous vir-
tues, but as characteristics which come from dependence on God
(compare Eph. 6:10-17).

Verse 22 is outside the alphabetic scheme mentioned above
and seems to have been added to adapt this individual lament to
public worship. It is a recognition of God as the Redeemer of the
nation as well as of the individual.

Psalm 26—I Wash My Hands in Innocence

This Psalm belongs in the category of the protestations of innocence. In such a composition the person who has been falsely
accused goes to the Temple and seeks vindication as provided
in I Kings 8:31-32. He does not maintain that he never sins,
but that he is innocent of the accusation brought against him.

Plea for Vindication (26:1-3). "Vindicate" is literally "judge."
The suppliant wants to be judged by God because in the light
of his integrity and faith such judgment can only issue in vindication. Three different verbs are used to request God to make a
thorough examination of his inner being. "My heart and my
mind" is literally "my kidneys and my heart." The expression refers to the total inner man as he feels, thinks, and wills. The
ground for making his plea is the suppliant's faith in God's stead-

fast love and faithfulness. The marginal reading in the Revised Standard Version, "in thy faithfulness," is much to be preferred to the reading in the text, "in faithfulness to thee" (vs. 3), for "faithfulness" is parallel to "steadfast love" and virtually synonymous with it.

The Suppliant's Protestation (26:4-7). The suppliant vows that he does not consort with hollow men, pious frauds, evildoers, and the wicked. All of these categories belong in the general category of the wicked or ungodly (compare Ps. 1).

This petitioner along with others in his situation may go through the ritual of washing his hands to reinforce his oath (compare 73:13; Deut. 21:6; Matt. 27:24), or he may indicate that he does in spirit what the priests do ritually (see Exod. 30: 17-21). He processes around the altar (compare 118:27) as he sings a song of thanksgiving telling of God's wonderful deeds.

Renewed Plea for Vindication (26:8-12). The suppliant renews his plea for vindication as one who loves God's house, the place where his glory dwells. The glory of God is his revealed presence, of which the Ark was a symbol (see Exod. 33:18-22; I Sam. 4:21-22). The suppliant prays that he may not be taken away by premature death along with men who are guilty of violence, evil schemes, and bribery. After protesting his integrity once more, he prays for redemption (deliverance from false accusation) and grace. Through faith there comes the assurance that his prayer has been granted. His standing on the level ground of the Temple area is symbolic of his newly found security. In the great congregation he will bless God for his deliverance.

Psalm 27—Trust and Lament Combined

An affirmation of faith (vss. 1-6) and a lament (vss. 7-14) seem to have been combined to form Psalm 27. The contrasting moods, however, may be the expression of a unified experience.

Trust (27:1-6). God is the psalmist's "light," "salvation," and "stronghold." As light, God dispels the darkness of trouble and gives life, joy, and guidance (compare 36:9; 43:3). With such a God there is no reason for fear.

The psalmist's one consuming desire is that he may have the privilege of dwelling in God's house as a guest over and over again throughout his life (compare 23:6), for the purpose of enjoying the beauty of God's gracious presence as symbolized in the sanctuary, and of seeking God's guidance (see 73:17). God's protection of him is imaginatively described as a shelter or tent and as a rock fortress high on a hill (vs. 5). He fully expects to be victorious over his enemies and vows to express his gratitude by presenting thank offerings and hymns of praise in the Temple ("tent" is an archaism for "Temple," associating it with the more ancient Tabernacle).

Lament (27:7-14). Here the mood of the Psalm changes abruptly from victorious faith and thanksgiving to lament and earnest petition. For the psalmist to seek God's face is for him to seek his favor. In times past God has been his help, and he prays that God will not forsake him in his present trouble (vs. 9). It is possible that his father and mother have literally forsaken him, or verse 10 may be a proverbial way of saying that all those one would expect to be helpful and understanding have deserted him in his time of need. But God is superior to all relatives and friends. God will take him up. Not only have loved ones and friends proved faithless, but the psalmist is confronted by false witnesses who endanger his life (vss. 11-12). In this context he prays for divine guidance along a safe path.

By faith he anticipates a favorable reply to his prayer. He is assured that he will see the goodness of the Lord in this present world of living men (vs. 13), and he calls upon himself to place his hope in God and take courage (vs. 14). Thus both parts of the Psalm bear testimony to a vital faith.

Psalm 28—A Cry for Help

This is a lament of an individual to which an appendix (vss. 8-9) has been added, adapting it to use by the congregation.

The Appeal (28:1-5). The psalmist appeals to God as his rock (compare 18:2, 31; 19:14; 73:26, margin), who gives support and protection. If God does not hearken to his prayer, he is in danger of going down to the Pit (a synonym for Sheol; see Introduction). He lifts up his hands in supplication (see 63:4; Neh. 8:6) toward the Holy of Holies (vss. 1-2). He is in danger of losing his life along with the wicked in some calamity or pestilence which is regarded as a judgment of God. The wicked are troublemakers who say one thing but plan another. Therefore, he prays God to give them their just deserts. This is not so much vindictiveness as a concern for the moral government of society. The wicked are practical atheists (see Pss. 14, 53), who will be destroyed on account of their disregard for God's works of creation and providence.

The Assurance (28:6-7). The psalmist receives assurance that his prayer has been answered, and he expresses his faith *in* and gratitude *to* God.

A Liturgical Appendix (28:8-9). These verses apply the thought of the Psalm to the whole nation, for the Lord is the strength of all the people and the saving refuge of the king in particular. God is implored to save and bless his people, and to play the role of a shepherd on their behalf forever. His saving work is for the nation as well as for the individual.

Psalm 29—Peace in the Midst of Storm

This is a majestic hymn in praise of the Lord of creation. The poet, however, concentrates upon one aspect of creation, the thunderstorm. The Psalm was probably written for use at the beginning of the rainy season in the autumn.

To some degree this Psalm rests upon Canaanite literary forms. But its theology is Israelite, not Canaanite. The expression "heavenly beings" in verse 1 is literally "sons of gods" in both Canaanite and Hebrew. In Canaanite terminology it means "gods," but in Hebrew "stars" (Job 38:7) or "heavenly beings" in the same general category as angels. Thunder is regarded as "voice" in the Canaanite literature of Ras Shamra (in Syria) as well as in this Psalm; but here it is the voice of the Lord.

Summons to the Heavenly Beings (29:1-2). The psalmist, who worships along with other Israelites in the Temple on earth, thinks of the heavenly host as worshiping God in a temple in heaven (compare Heb. 8:1-7; 9:24). Therefore, he calls upon these heavenly servants of God to ascribe to the Lord glory and strength, and to bow down in worship before him in the garments appropriate to the heavenly setting (see Exod. 28:2).

The Voice of the Seven Thunders (29:3-9). God's voice is identified with the thunder of the storm (see 18:13), and the phrase "the voice of the LORD" occurs seven times (compare Rev. 10:3). The psalmist writes as one who has witnessed such a storm as he describes. The storm clouds gather over the waters of the Mediterranean and move eastward until the storm breaks in crashing fury over the mountain ranges of Lebanon and snow-

capped Hermon (Sirion; see Deut. 3:9). Even the mighty cedars
of Lebanon are broken, and the mountains themselves skip like
a calf and a wild ox. The lightning flashes and the thunder shakes
the wilderness of Kadesh.

"The voice of the LORD makes the oaks to whirl" (vs. 9a) is
a possible translation of the Hebrew text without the vowel
points. It may be correct, because "oaks" are a part of the "forests" mentioned in 9b. However, "The voice of the LORD makes
the hinds to calve," which is found in the margin, is a preferable
rendering for the following reasons: (1) it is an exact translation
of the Masoretic Hebrew text; (2) the Septuagint (Greek translation) reads "hinds" not "oaks"; and (3) this rendering continues the interest in animals already begun in verse 6. The interest in trees is continued by the word "forests." In other words,
the female deer, as typical of various animals, goes into labor on
account of the storm (medically we would probably say, on account of the change in barometric pressure accompanying the
storm), and the trees are stripped of their leaves and branches.
The worshiping congregation in the Jerusalem Temple joins the
heavenly congregation in the cry, "Glory!" These verses (3-9)
are a theological and poetic interpretation of a storm as a revelation of the glory of God.

The Blessing of the Heavenly King (29:10-11). The storm is
glorious to God's people because it means the end of drought
and brings the gift of water of life for another season. Israel's
Lord is the one true King of heaven and earth. He is enthroned
as King over the primeval waters above the firmament (Gen.
1:7) and is therefore able to send the life-giving rain in due time.
It is he who gives strength and blessing to his people. "Peace"
includes every possible blessing, material and spiritual, which
contributes to the well-being of his people.

While the psalmist of necessity has expressed himself in the
thought forms of his own day, he has left us a poem of beauty
and truth for all time. God still reveals himself in the majesty of
the storm, and we are dependent upon him for every good and
perfect gift.

Psalm 30—Mourning Turned to Dancing

Here we have one of the best illustrations of a thanksgiving
of an individual. The psalmist's prayer for healing has been

granted, and he thanks God for his restoration. The part of the title which reads, "A Song at the dedication of the Temple" (literally, "house"), shows that the Psalm came to be used on the anniversaries of the rededication of the Temple in 164 B.C. by Judas Maccabaeus. The Jewish community thought of itself as repeating the experience of the psalmist in its suffering under Antiochus Epiphanes and its deliverance under the Maccabees.

The Occasion for Thanksgiving (30:1-5). The psalmist was about to die with a serious illness. His death would have pleased his enemies, but God heard his cry and brought him up from the realm of the dead into which he was already sinking as his life ebbed away.

He calls upon other saints to join him in his thanksgiving. They are persons who are the recipients of God's steadfast love and respond to that love in devotion to God and his people. God's anger which brings weeping is short-lived, but his favor which brings joy is enduring.

Autobiographical Rehearsal (30:6-12). In his prosperity the psalmist was guilty of self-sufficiency and a false sense of security. Yet it was God who had established him. Then, as a result of his self-sufficiency and perhaps other sins as well, God removed his favor and the psalmist was sorely troubled (compare Deut. 8:10-20). In his illness he cried to God for help. With childlike simplicity he reminded God that his death would mean that he could not praise him further, since those in the Pit could not praise God (on Sheol and the Pit see Introduction). But God has granted his petition and turned his mourning into dancing (compare 26:6-7; 118:27-28; Lam. 5:15), the sackcloth of sorrow into the festal garments of praise. Faith in God, communion with God, and joyful thanksgiving to God are the keynotes of this Psalm.

Psalm 31—Into Thy Hand

According to Luke 23:46 the last words of Jesus from the cross were taken from this Psalm (vs. 5a). This fact has endeared the Psalm all the more to Christian people. As it now stands, it appears to have been composed of two originally independent laments, the one a petition to be delivered from impending danger (vss. 1-8), the other a plea to be delivered from illness and enemies (vss. 9-24).

Deliverance from Danger (31:1-8). The psalmist is threatened in some way by enemies. He confesses his faith in God and seeks deliverance from the net which is hidden for him. His enemies are likened to hunters who set snares to catch animals (see 9:15; 35:7; 57:6; 140:5). He entrusts to God's care the life ("spirit") which was the gift of God in the first place, and he is assured that God has redeemed him from the threat of his enemies. As used in Luke, verse 5a is Jesus' commitment of himself to the Father when his enemies have done him to death.

The psalmist continues his assurance of deliverance (vss. 6-8). His enemies are idolaters, but he trusts in God and rejoices in his Covenant love. "Adversities" in verse 7 means those things which cramp a person in a narrow place. In contrast to former adversities is the "broad place" in which God has set the psalmist's feet.

Deliverance from Sickness and Enemies (31:9-24). The psalmist is now in "distress" (this is a form of the word "adversities" in vs. 7) and pleads God's grace. Verses 9-10 are a vivid description of his progressive disintegration. His suffering is increased by the reaction of his adversaries and acquaintances (vss. 11-13). People shun him as an object of dread. He is forgotten by many as if he were dead, and is cast aside like a potsherd. His enemies carry on a slanderous whispering campaign against him and even plot to take his life (on vs. 13 see Jer. 6:25; 20:3-10; 46:5; 49:29). He confesses his faith in God, seeks deliverance from his enemies, and prays for their premature death (vss. 14-18). "My times are in thy hand" means that God controls the events in his life and determines his destiny. "Let thy face shine on thy servant" is a prayer for a favorable response (compare 67:1; 80:3, 7, 19; 119:135; Num. 6:25).

Thanksgiving for Deliverance (31:19-24). In his gratitude the psalmist generalizes on his experience, affirming that God's goodness and protecting presence are available to all who commit themselves to him in trust (vss. 19-20). He then returns to his own experience in thanking God for his deliverance (vss. 21-22). Finally he calls upon all the saints to love God and take courage (vss. 23-24; compare 27:14; Deut. 6:5).

Psalm 32—A Beatitude of Forgiveness

A beatitude is an expression of happiness. The beatitudes par excellence are the statements of Jesus found in Matthew 5:3-12 and Luke 6:20-23. This Psalm is an expression of the happiness of a forgiven sinner. Traditionally it has been classified as one of the seven penitentials (6, 32, 38, 51, 102, 130, 143), because as a part of his composition the psalmist narrates his confession of sin. It is also classified as a song of thanksgiving because the outlook of the psalmist is one of gratitude. In addition it is a wisdom poem, since the author seeks to instruct others on the basis of his experience.

The Happiness of the Forgiven Sinner (32:1-2). Chronologically speaking the beginning of the Psalm is its end, for it is the conclusion to which the psalmist came as a result of the experience which he later narrates. Actually he is so athrill with his message that he begins both verse 1 and verse 2 with the equivalent of an exclamation. Here he universalizes his experience of soul-joy by applying it to everyone who receives God's forgiveness. In this first section of the Psalm three of the most important general words in the sin vocabulary are used, together with a fourth word which designates a particular sin. "Transgression" refers to willful disobedience to God's command and therefore involves rebellion. "Sin" means basically "to miss the mark." It is an all-inclusive word, for it may refer to sins committed in ignorance as well as to any kind of sin committed willfully. Every kind of sin involves missing the goal God has set for us. "Iniquity" is a word which combines the ideas of wrong (Jer. 11:10; Isa. 43:24), guilt (Exod. 34:7), and punishment (Gen. 4:13), but usually in a given passage the accent is on one of the three ideas. In verse 2 the accent is on guilt. "Deceit" refers to insincerity, which makes forgiveness and its consequent blessedness impossible.

Set over against the three general words for sin are three expressions of forgiveness. "Forgiven" refers to the "lifting away" of a burden. "Covered" refers to the act of the Judge in putting the sin out of his sight. "Imputes no iniquity" means that God has canceled the debt from his ledger. Paul quotes verses 1 and 2 in Romans 4:7-8 in order to undergird the doctrine of justification by faith.

The Burden of Unconfessed Sin (32:3-4). The psalmist's refusal to confess his sin resulted in what we would today call a psychosomatic illness. The guilty conscience and its consequences, physical and spiritual, were God's hand in judgment upon him. His vitality was consumed as he suffered from a high fever. But the hand of God in judgment is the hand of God in mercy.

Confession and Pardon (32:5). Under the hand of God the psalmist was brought through the struggle of the soul to the moment of transforming decision. When he laid his heart bare before God, God forgave him and his burden was gone (compare I John 1:8-9).

A Witnessing Faith (32:6-9). The psalmist is not content to let his experience die with him. Therefore, he gives a witness which grows out of his experience. He calls upon everyone who is dedicated to God to pray in time of difficulty. God will not permit such a person to be overwhelmed in the floods of calamities, for he is man's security. A sense of guilt produces a sense of insecurity, but forgiveness brings a sense of at-home-ness with God.

In verses 8 and 9 the psalmist passes on to others the oracle of instruction which he received from God through his experience. Everyone is encouraged to learn the lesson of the psalmist's mistake, for he had been like an animal which was brought to do the master's will only under the pressure of suffering.

The Call to Thankful Joy (32:10-11). Here the psalmist contrasts the experience of the wicked and the righteous. The wicked, in the Psalter as a whole and in this Psalm in particular, are the habitual enemies of God and his people. Their wickedness is characteristic, and they are not given to repentance. God's judgment rests heavily upon them. On the other hand, God's steadfast or Covenant love encompasses the one who has faith in God. In the light of this love and in the light of all that has been said in the Psalm, the psalmist calls God's people to rejoice in the Lord. The righteous or upright in heart are not perfect people, but rather are those who live in the Covenant of their God. It is they who confess their sins and acknowledge their membership in the household of faith.

Psalm 33—The Word and Work of God

Psalm 33 is a hymn which brings together the work of God in creation and the word of God in history. Some number it among the Psalms sung at the New Year Festival.

The Call to Worship (33:1-3). Joy, praise, music, and song are all united in this call to worship. The "righteous" or "upright" are not the morally perfect but are the worshiping congregation who acknowledge themselves to be God's Covenant people. The expression "new song" refers to the Psalm itself because it is a fresh composition for a particular occasion.

The Word of God (33:4-9). God's word and work are one in creation and history. For God to speak is for him to accomplish. For God to work is for him to speak. In the parallelism of Hebrew poetry, to say "the word of the LORD is upright" is to say "all his work is done in faithfulness." This is in accord with Hebrew psychology. All of God's activity in creation and history is characterized by uprightness, faithfulness, righteousness, justice, and steadfast love.

Verses 6-7 are a poetic reflection of Genesis 1. "The breath of his mouth" is another way of denoting God's word. The "bottle" in which the waters of the sea are gathered is thought of as a bottle made of skin. The power of God manifested in creation is sufficient cause for all men to reverence God (vss. 8-9).

The Purpose of God (33:10-12). Up to this point the psalmist's concentration has been largely upon God's work in creation. He now begins to concentrate upon his work in history. The word "counsel" means "purpose." God's purpose is set over against the purpose of the nations. He rules and overrules in individual and national affairs. The Chosen People are counted happy, the reason being their participation in the privilege of election.

The Providence of God (33:13-19). The phrase in this section of the Psalm which best expresses the meaning of providence is "the eye of the LORD" (vs. 18). God sees the deeds of all men, who in some way serve his purpose (vss. 13-15). Physical might is not the ultimate security (vss. 16-17), for the destiny of men and nations is in the hands of God (vss. 18-19), who provides food and saves from premature death.

The Ground of Hope (33:20-22). The Psalm begins on the note of joyous praise and ends on the note of joyous expectation, composed of quiet waiting, simple trust, and persistent hope. The ground of hope is the sovereign Lord of creation and history (compare Rom. 8:25).

Psalm 34—An Alphabetical Thanksgiving

This Psalm may be regarded as a companion piece to Psalm 25. Both Psalms are acrostics; that is, each succeeding verse be-

gins with the next letter of the Hebrew alphabet. The sixth letter
has been left out in Psalm 34. In both Psalms the final verse
goes beyond the last letter of the alphabet and begins with the
seventeenth letter, which corresponds to our letter "P." Furthermore, both Psalms reflect the wisdom teaching of Proverbs.
Psalm 25 is an alphabetical lament, and Psalm 34 an alphabetical
thanksgiving.

An Invitation to Praise (34:1-10). The psalmist will not confine his praise of God to special times; it will be continual. His
boast is not in wealth, wisdom, or power (49:6; Jer. 9:23-24),
but in the Lord (compare I Cor. 1:31; II Cor. 10:17). He calls
the afflicted to be glad and to join him in ascribing greatness to
God's name.

Then he gives his personal testimony of what the Lord has
done for him (vss. 4-10). His personal experience is the basis for
his invitation to others to praise God with him. When he sought
the Lord, the Lord delivered him from all his fears. Therefore,
other poor people should look to God in such confidence that
their countenance will light up with joyous expectation. The
angel of the Lord (see 35:5-6; Exod. 23:20; II Kings 6:17) protects God's reverent servants. Others are invited to learn by experience ("taste and see") that the Lord is good. Though the
mightiest beasts of prey experience hunger, God's saints will lack
no good thing (compare 23:1). The psalmist surely knew of
exceptions, but they do not concern him here. The word for
"saints" in verse 9 is different from the word often so translated
in the Psalms. It means "holy ones" (see 16:3); that is, those
separated unto God, who by their lives are fulfilling God's call
to the nation to be holy (Exod. 19:6; Lev. 11:44-45).

Invitation to Learn (34:11-22). At this point the psalmist assumes the role of a wisdom teacher and addresses his companions as sons (compare Prov. 1-9). The content of his teaching
is the fear of the Lord (see Prov. 8:13; 9:10), which is a reverence before God that expresses itself in godly conduct. In verses
12-14 the psalmist summarizes this fear. The man who desires
to live a long, happy life shall not sin in word or deed; he shall
do good and seek peace (the well-being which God grants; compare Rom. 14:19; Heb. 12:14). Verses 12-16 are quoted from
the Septuagint in I Peter 3:10-12.

The Lord cares for the righteous but cuts off the remembrance
of the wicked (vss. 15-22). The righteous are the brokenhearted

and crushed in spirit (vs. 18), those whose suffering has issued in humility. They have many afflictions, but God delivers them out of all of them (again the psalmist does not mention exceptions).

Psalm 35—Threefold Trouble

Psalm 35 is a threefold lament, each section of lament being concluded with a brief vow of thanksgiving for the anticipated salvation. In part one, the psalmist's enemies seek his life and possessions (vss. 1-10). In part two, persons whom the psalmist befriended in their sickness, turn against him and bear false witness against him (vss. 11-18). In part three, the psalmist's enemies claim to be eyewitnesses of wrong committed by him (vss. 19-28). Three originally independent compositions may have been united to form this Psalm, or the three divisions may be three different ways of describing the same enemies.

Contend, O Lord (35:1-10). The psalmist begins his plea for help by picturing God as a soldier (vss. 1-3; compare Exod. 15:3) who battles in his behalf. Then he prays for the repulsing of those who seek his life (vss. 4-8). Let them be disgraced before men. Let them be put to flight like a defeated army, driven like chaff by the wind (compare 1:4; 83:13), pursued by the angel of the Lord (see 34:4-7; I Chron. 21:15-20) in dark and slippery paths, caught in their own nets, and brought to ruin unexpectedly—for they have sought the psalmist's life without justification. When God grants his request, the psalmist vows that he will thank him for his deliverance (vss. 9-10).

How Long, O Lord? (35:11-18). In the second lament wicked witnesses rise up against the psalmist and accuse him of crimes of which he has no knowledge. Such accusation is base ingratitude, for he had prayed and mourned for his accusers when they were sick. When trouble came his way, they rejoiced and tore his reputation with slander as wild beasts tear flesh. Therefore he cries out, "How long?" and pleads for deliverance. Again he vows to thank God as a member of the Covenant community in the Temple when his petition is granted.

Vindicate Me, O Lord (35:19-28). In the third lament the psalmist prays that God will not permit his enemies to rejoice over him. They "wink the eye" in contempt and they hate him without cause (see 69:4; John 15:25). In fact, they are enemies of all the saints or the "quiet in the land." Therefore the psalmist prays for vindication (literally, "judge me") as an expression of God's righteousness (vss. 22-25). Such vindication will of necessity involve the discrediting of his enemies (vs. 26). But he is not only interested in what happens to himself and his enemies, he is also concerned that those who desire his vindication (literally, "righteousness") shall join in thanksgiving to God for his deliverance (vs. 27). For the third time he vows to praise God (vs. 28).

Psalm 36—Wicked Man and Righteous God

This is a reflective Psalm in which various literary types are mixed—wisdom, lament, and hymn. The character of God (vss. 5-12) is set in contrast to the character of the wicked man (vss. 1-4).

The Character of the Wicked Man (36:1-4). In the Psalter, only here is transgression (or "rebellion") personified as an evil spirit who speaks in oracular fashion to the heart of the wicked man, thereby filling him with evil. This man has no dread of God's judgments for sin. Paul quotes the latter part of verse 1 in Romans 3:18 as the last item in his summary of human depravity. The wicked man deceives himself into thinking that God cannot discover his wickedness and punish him. Verses 3-4 describe the behavior that issues from such self-deception.

The Character of the Righteous God (36:5-12). In contrast to the wicked man, God is characterized by steadfast love, faithfulness, and righteousness—terms used almost synonymously. These attributes of God characterize him not only in his relationship to his Covenant people but also in relation to the universe (vss. 5-6), to animals (vs. 6), and to all men (vs. 7). "The mountains of God" may be an allusion to the ancient Near Eastern idea that the abode of the gods was in the mountains, but the psalmist does not accept the polytheistic theology associated with the expression. He is saying that God's righteousness is dependable. The expression of his righteousness in judgment is unfathomable like the great deep (see Gen. 1:6; 7:11; compare Rom. 11:33). God reveals his attributes in saving man and beast alive (vs. 6). He protects men under the shadow of his wings (see comment on 17:8; compare 57:1; 63:7). "The abundance of thy house" and "the river of thy delights" are figures to describe God's provision for man's needs (compare 65:9-13). God is the source of life (see Jer. 2:13) and light (see 27:1); to have one is to have the other. As the Christian reads verse 9, he thinks of the life-light of the Incarnation of Jesus Christ: "In him was life, and the life was the light of men" (John 1:4).

The psalmist concludes with a prayer that God continue his steadfast love and salvation to his true people, and that he protect him from wicked men (vss. 10-12). To know God (vs. 10) is to commit oneself to him in steadfast love and faithfulness (see Hosea 4:1-6; 6:6; Isa. 1:1-4).

Psalm 37—The Wicked and the Righteous

This is a wisdom acrostic, in which an old man counsels younger men concerning the prosperity of the wicked. Every other line begins with the succeeding letter of the Hebrew alphabet. The central thesis of the sage is that the righteous are rewarded and the wicked are punished (compare 49; 73; Prov. 10:24; Job). When circumstances do not bear this out, they are considered to be only temporary.

Counsel of Calm Faith (37:1-11). The theme of these verses is stated in the first line, "Fret not yourself because of the wicked" (see also vss. 7 and 8). The righteous man is not to get heated in anger at the prosperity of the wicked, for his prosperity is short-lived. He is to trust God to answer prayer, to grant vindication, and to give such people as himself possession of the land. Anger, wrath, and fretting may lead to a denial of God's care (vs. 8). The meek (vs. 11)—that is, those who wait for the Lord (vs. 9)—shall ultimately possess the land (compare Matt. 5:5).

Reflections on the Righteous and the Wicked (37:12-22). Here the psalmist contrasts the welfare of the righteous with that of the wicked. The plots of the wicked man will recoil upon himself (vss. 12-15). The little of the righteous is better than the abundance of the wicked because the power of the wicked will be destroyed (vss. 16-17; compare Prov. 15:16; 16:8). The heritage of the righteous is stable and they have plenty even in famine (vss. 18-19), but the wicked are like pastures which are verdant today and gone tomorrow (vs. 20). The wicked man comes to poverty and debt and stands under God's curse; the righteous man is generous and stands under God's blessing (vss. 21-22).

Reward and Retribution (37:23-40). The psalmist continues his theme in a slightly varied manner. A righteous man may be down, but he is not permanently out (vss. 23-24). In all his long experience the psalmist has not seen the righteous permanently forsaken or his children begging bread (vss. 25-26). Some of us have seen exceptions to the second part of this statement, but it is true that, in the over-all picture of life, there are relatively few beggars among the members of the Covenant community. The righteous will be preserved through their offspring and thereby possess the land in perpetuity, but the posterity of the wicked will be cut off (vss. 27-29; compare vs. 38). The righteous man is a wise man, who speaks justice and obeys the Law (vss. 30-31). The Lord will not abandon him to the wicked but instead will destroy the wicked (vss. 32-34). The Hebrew of verses 35-36 is somewhat uncertain. It is sufficiently clear for us to know that the psalmist is citing an illustration of the downfall of a wicked man. God takes care of his own (vss. 37-40).

Psalm 38—The Prayer of a Suffering Sinner

This is one of the seven Psalms that have been regarded by the Church as penitential (6, 32, 38, 51, 102, 130, 143). The psalmist is suffering from a painful and loathsome disease as well as from the plots of enemies and the indifference of friends. In accord with the thought of his time, he considers his sickness the punishment of his sin. This may have been the literal truth in his case, but it is by no means always true (see Job; Isa. 53; John 9:3).

The Introductory Appeal (38:1-2). Verse 1 is a negative way of appealing for God's grace (compare 6:1). God's anger against the psalmist on account of his sin is expressed here by two figures: arrows that penetrate (see Deut. 32:23; Job 6:4; Lam. 3:12-13) and the blow of God's hand (see 32:4; 39:10).

Suffering from Sin (38:3-10). The psalmist confesses that his illness is the consequence of his own sin (vs. 3). One meaning of "iniquity" is "punishment for iniquity" (Gen. 4:13). Therefore, the punishments for the psalmist's wrongdoings are first pictured as an overwhelming flood (see 69:2, 15; 124:4-5) and then as a heavy burden (vs. 4). His wounds inflicted by God smell and run with pus on account of his "foolishness" (see 69:5), which is sin viewed as opposition to wisdom. He is bent by pain and goes about in the garb of a mourner (see 35:14). His flesh is filled with fever and inflammation; and the anguish of his heart is expressed by audible groaning (vss. 5-8). God knows his longing and sighing. His heart throbs, his strength fails, and his eyes have become dim and dull on account of exhaustion and weeping (vss. 9-10; compare 6:7; 31:9; Job 17:7).

Suffering from Friends and Enemies (38:11-16). Friends and kinsmen treat him as an untouchable (vs. 11; compare 31:11-13; 69:8; 88:18; Job 19:13-22; Isa. 53:3). His enemies are encouraged to plot his death (vs. 12). Yet, like a deaf and dumb man, he attempts no rebuttal (compare Isa. 53:7; I Peter 2:23); rather does he leave his cause in the hands of God (vss. 13-16).

The Concluding Appeal (38:17-22). The psalmist cannot endure his pain much longer. Again he confesses his guilt and anguish for his sin (vss. 17-18). His adversaries have no grounds for hating him. In fact, they are returning evil for the good he has formerly done them (vss. 19-20; compare 35:12-14). Therefore, his final plea is for the presence and help of the Lord, who is his only salvation (vss. 21-22; compare 22:19; 40:13). Many a man in his utter helplessness has found God the only reality of any value.

Psalm 39—Faith Without Assurance

The author of this Psalm has faith in God, even though he has no expectation of meaningful life after death or any assurance that his prayer for healing will be granted. The Psalm should be studied in connection with Psalm 38, because the two compositions are similar in expression and thought at several points.

Self-Imposed Silence (39:1-3). The psalmist tells how he kept silent during his brooding over his predicament in order to avoid giving the impression to his godless visitors that he was irreligious himself. This fed the pent-up emotional fire within him which could be smothered no longer. It broke into open flame.

The Transitoriness of Life (39:4-6). However, he speaks to God, not to the wicked. He is sick unto death and asks God to tell him how frail and fleeting his life is. But he answers the question himself. His life is but a few handbreadths (a handbreadth is four fingers) and therefore as nothing. He then universalizes his experience and views human life as a phantom-like existence without meaning. The turmoil of life and the striving after wealth are futile. The similarity of the psalmist's thought to that of Ecclesiastes is apparent. He is seeking for meaning in life and seems to be on the verge of laying hold on belief in eternal life, but he remains a child of his own age.

Enduring Faith (39:7-13). Regardless of the seeming meaninglessness of life, he turns to God in faith and hope. He prays for forgiveness, which includes healing in this case (vs. 10), that the cynic may have no ground for mocking him. He is silent in that he does not accuse God of injustice in dealing with him. Again he universalizes his experience: when God corrects a man for his sin (literally, "iniquity"), he consumes what the man holds dear, as a moth eats up clothes (see Hosea 5:12; Job 13:28; Isa. 51:8).

In one last effort the psalmist pleads with God to grant his request, regarding himself as a temporary resident in the earth (compare I Chron. 29:15; I Peter 2:11; Heb. 11:13). "Look away from me" is another way of saying, "Remove thy stroke from me." Even if God grants his request, he assumes that his gladness will be only a brief respite, for soon or late he will depart and be no more. Unlike most laments this one does not end on a note of assurance, yet the psalmist's faith endures and puts to shame many who live in the light of the Christian hope.

Psalm 40—Thanksgiving and Lament Combined

Two originally independent Psalms were combined to form Psalm 40. Verses 1-11 are the thanksgiving of an individual who has been delivered from illness, and verses 13-17 are a lamenting appeal for deliverance from enemies, which occurs later as Psalm 70. Verse 12 was written to form a transition from the first part to the second part. The two parts may be thought of as constituting a psychological unity, because past deliverance is a ground of hope for the future.

Thanksgiving for Past Deliverance (40:1-11). The psalmist bypasses the usual introduction found in songs of thanksgiving and proceeds immediately to the narration of his testimony. He had to wait a considerable time before God answered him. But God brought him out of the realm of the dead into which he had already begun to sink on account of severe illness. By this new act of salvation God put a new song (40:1-11) in his mouth

which he sings in the great congregation (vs. 9) as a witness
that will lead many others to put their trust in God.

Now the psalmist pronounces a beatitude upon the man who
trusts the Lord and refuses to join those who go astray after
false gods (literally, "lies"). He is so much a part of the congregation of God's people that he recalls God's wondrous deeds
and thoughts toward "us." These mighty acts and purposes are
so numerous that it is impossible to enumerate them (compare
John 21:25).

Ordinarily a person who had been so signally delivered would
make a thank offering in the Temple. But this psalmist has been
influenced by the prophets (see Amos 5:21-24; Hosea 6:6; Isa.
1:11; Jer. 7:22-23), and feels that God does not desire any kind
of material offering in his case (compare 51:16), for it would not
adequately express the depth of his relationship to God. He has
an ear open to the word of God. In the sacred scroll (a part of
the Bible-to-be) God speaks to him of his will, and he responds
with joyful obedience. In other words, he offers himself to God.
It is this emphasis upon self-offering which the author of the
Letter to the Hebrews picks up from the Septuagint to interpret
Christ's offering of himself upon the cross (Heb. 10:5-20). The
psalmist has proclaimed the gospel of his deliverance (literally,
"righteousness") as a manifestation of God's faithfulness, salvation, and steadfast love (vss. 9-10). He concludes his thanksgiving with a prayer that God will continue such wondrous care
of him as he has just experienced in deliverance from his illness
(vs. 11).

Petition for Future Deliverance (40:12-17). Verse 12 is loosely
connected with what precedes and what follows. The psalmist is
in trouble on account of his iniquities. The remainder of the
Psalm (vss. 13-17) is a plea for deliverance from enemies who
seek the psalmist's life. He prays that they may be dishonored
as a defeated army. On the other hand, he prays that those seeking the Lord may rejoice in him. He himself is poor and needy
but God will take care of him. (Verse 17b does not occur in
Psalm 70.)

Psalm 41—A Beatitude for the Merciful

The happiness of the righteous man is celebrated in Psalm 1,
the happiness of the forgiven sinner in Psalm 32, and the happi-

ness of the compassionate man in Psalm 41. If the time sequence were reversed, the Psalm might be considered a commentary on one of Jesus' beatitudes: "Blessed are the merciful, for they shall obtain mercy" (Matt. 5:7). It is the thanksgiving of a man who has been delivered from a critical illness and from the reproach of malicious enemies.

The Blessedness of the Merciful (41:1-3). The heart of the psalmist's teaching is found in these verses, for they are the conclusion at which he arrived as a result of the experience he later narrates (compare 32:1-2). The blessedness of the man who considers the poor (see 35:13-14; James 1:27) consists in deliverance from trouble, preservation of life, esteem in the community, protection from enemies, support in illness, and healing of disease.

Narrative of Past Distress (41:4-10). The psalmist reconstructs his past distress so vividly that he seems to be passing through it as he writes. He appeals to God's grace for healing and, by implication, for forgiveness, since he considers his illness the punishment for sin (vs. 4). His enemies speak of him maliciously, desiring his death and the obliteration of his name. Even when one of them visits him, his words are empty, for all the while he is plotting mischief to spread abroad when he leaves. In fact, all the psalmist's enemies carry on a whispering campaign against him and imagine the worst with uncharitable satisfaction (vss. 5-7).

They say a magical curse ("deadly thing") has been fastened upon him by a sorcerer, so that he cannot get well. Even the psalmist's "bosom friend" (literally, "man of my peace"), who is bound to him by the tie of hospitality, has turned against him (compare 55:12-13). Verse 9b is quoted by Jesus in John 13:18 as being fulfilled in the treachery of Judas. Again the psalmist prays that by God's grace he may be healed, and gives as a reason for his healing that he may requite his enemies. We may understand his feelings, but we can hardly share them, for vengeance belongs to God alone (Lev. 19:18; Deut. 32:35; Rom. 12:19).

Request Granted (41:11-12). The psalmist knows that God is pleased with him because he has healed him and thereby prevented the triumph of enemies over him. God has vindicated him and placed him in his abiding presence on account of the psalmist's undivided commitment to his will. In the light of verses 1-3

this means among other things that the psalmist ha[?]
mercy to the poor and weak. It does not mean [?]
less, for he has already appealed to God to be
as a sick sinner (vs. 4).

Verse 13 is the editorial doxology which closes Book 1 c[?]
Psalter; it is not a part of Psalm 41.

BOOK II—PSALMS 42-72

Psalms 42-43—Homesick for God's House

Psalms 42 and 43 are one composition. The thought of 42 is
continued in 43; in the Hebrew text 43 has no title; and the
same refrain occurs in both parts. It is one of the most beautiful
and appealing of the laments of the individual. The author is
a musician (43:4) who formerly led pilgrims in procession to
God's house, but he is now in serious trouble, exiled from Jerusalem and the Temple and tormented by enemies.

Thirsting for the Living God (42:1-5). As the deer longs for
flowing streams in the dry season, so the psalmist longs for God
(compare 63:1). God is "living" as the source of all life and
as One who does things, in contrast to so-called gods or idols who
can do nothing (compare Jer. 10:1-16; Isa. 44:9-20). The
psalmist wants to behold the face of God; that is, he wants to
go to the Temple and be admitted as a worshiper to the presence
of God as it is known in sacramental, corporate worship. He
does not mean that he lacks fellowship with God in his present
condition, for he addresses God directly in prayer (42:1, 7, 9;
43:1, 2, 3). Man needs to meet God face to face in the closet
(Matt. 6:6), but he needs also to meet him face to face in corporate worship (Matt. 18:20; Acts 2:1-4) and in that which is
sacramental (Acts 2:41-42; I Cor. 11:24-25). Because of his
inability to visit God in the Temple, tears are the psalmist's constant diet. Those who do not share his faith, ridicule him with
the words, "Where is your God?"

The remembrance of happier days makes the present distress
all the more unbearable. He remembers how he used to lead the

ilgrims in procession to the Temple to participate in the great festivals (vs. 4).

No doubt every person talks to himself at times. The psalmist does this in the refrain. Throughout the Psalm he speaks of himself as "soul." In the refrain the stronger self reproves the weaker self, "Why are you cast down, O my soul?", and calls it to a hopeful waiting upon God and to an assurance that God will make praise at the sanctuary possible again.

Exiled and Overwhelmed (42:6-11). The author is exiled in the territory where the Jordan has its origin, to the north of the Hermon range. The exact location of Mount Mizar is uncertain. As he contemplates the antiphonal thunderings of the mountain cataracts, he feels that he is being overwhelmed by the waters of the underworld ("deep"). Perhaps he is sick; we do not know. In poetic metaphor he expresses the idea that he is near death. Yet, even in the midst of the waves and billows, God grants him his steadfast love and makes possible a song and a prayer. Nevertheless, his soul struggle continues as he expostulates with God concerning the oppression of his enemies, and as the stronger self chides the weaker self in the refrain.

A Prayer for Vindication (43:1-5). Now the psalmist prays in deep supplication that God will vindicate him by removing his trouble and restoring to him the privileges of pilgrimage to Zion. He prays that God will send out his light and his truth, which are personified as ministering spirits, to lead him to the Temple where in public worship he may see God, the joy of his life. He will express his joy in God by praising him with the lyre. The presence of the living God calls forth music from the heart of man. When the refrain is repeated this time, the accent is on the second part.

Psalm 44—The Cry of a Defeated Nation

The armies of the nation have been defeated; many of the people have been slaughtered; others have been scattered among the surrounding nations as slaves; God's Covenant people are being ridiculed; and the psalmist and his fellow worshipers do not know why God has permitted all these things to happen. The author of the Psalm may be the warrior who leads the community in lament (vss. 4, 6, 15) and who identifies himself with his people.

John Calvin and many others have dated the Psalm in the Maccabean period (second century B.C.), but this is too late in the light of recent Psalm study. It is probable that it was composed at some earlier time in the postexilic period.

God's Mighty Deeds of Old (44:1-3). The Psalm begins with a brief recollection of God's mighty acts in behalf of his people in the days of old. The Israelite fathers were faithful in telling the story to their children as they had been commanded to do (see Exod. 12:26; Deut. 6:20; Joshua 4:6, 21). The deeds upon which the psalmist concentrates are those recorded in the Book of Joshua. God drove out the nations of Canaan and established Israel in the land. It was not the skill of Israel's swordsmen that won the victory, but God's power and his selection of Israel for his own purpose (compare Deut. 4:37-39; 8:17-18; 9:4-6).

The People's Trust in God (44:4-8). The warrior who leads his people in worship recognizes God as his own King and the King of Israel ("Jacob"), for whom upon occasion he ordains victories, enabling his people to overcome their fear. The warrior's trust (and the trust of his people) is not in bow or sword but in God alone (compare 20:7; 33:16; I Sam. 17:47). On the basis of God's saving deeds in the past, his people have boasted in him and are resolved to thank him perpetually.

Faith and Fact in Conflict (44:9-22). But the facts of the immediate past and the present seem to contradict the faith just expressed. Military defeat and all that goes with it are the facts of the present situation. God is even pictured in very human terms as a shepherd who has sold his sheep to the butcher for a trifle. The psalmist employs a varied vocabulary to express the shame and disgrace of his people (vss. 13-16).

The conflict between faith and fact is seen most sharply in verses 17-22, for the people maintain that their tragedy is undeserved. They have not been false to the Covenant in forgetting God or departing from his way as made known in the Law. Yet God has crushed them and placed them in desolation ("the place of jackals") and death ("deep darkness"). In fact, for his sake they are slaughtered as martyrs. Paul quotes verse 22 in Romans 8:36 to help the Roman Christians see that, like the saints of the ancient People of God, they may have to face persecution and even death for their faith.

The conflict between faith and fact arises for the psalmist and his people from a literal understanding of the dogma of retri-

bution (see especially Deut. 28). This means that they think God
blesses in exact proportion to obedience and curses in exact proportion to disobedience (contrast Job; Isa. 53).

An Urgent Plea for Help (44:23-26). God is addressed as
though he were sleeping, and is called upon to awake and deliver his people. Some have felt that the psalmist's language here
is especially unseemly (compare vss. 12, 17-19). However, he
and his people are accustomed to bold figures of speech (see 7:6;
59:4; 78:65; Isa. 51:9-10). Nevertheless, it is helpful to remember that Jesus did not and Christians do not pray, "Rouse thy-
self! Why sleepest thou, O Lord?" The psalmist can teach us of
the providence of God in history, of faith in God when the facts
seem to contradict it, of loyalty to our Covenant with God and
his people, and of praying with importunity (compare Luke
11:8); but we must learn from Another how to pray, "Father,
if thou art willing, remove this cup from me; nevertheless not
my will, but thine, be done" (Luke 22:42).

Psalm 45—A Song for a Royal Wedding

This is a song composed and presented by a court poet upon
the occasion of the marriage of his king to a foreign princess.
At a much later time Jewish interpreters allegorized it and identified the king as the Messiah and his bride as Israel. In the
Letter to the Hebrews (1:8-9), verses 6-7 are used to describe
the kingship of Christ.

Address to the King (45:1-9). The poet bubbles over with his
theme, and addresses himself directly to the king. He feels that
his tongue is as fluent as the pen of a ready scribe. First, he calls
attention to the king as a man (vs. 2). He is handsome, his
speech is gracious and winsome, and the blessing of God rests
upon him. In the second place, he celebrates the abilities of the
king as a warrior (vss. 3-5). Thirdly, he gives the king assurance
of a stable government (vss. 6-7a). Although verse 6a may be
rendered, "Your divine throne endures for ever and ever," the
Hebrew is more naturally rendered, "Your throne, O god, endures for ever and ever." In other words, the poet uses the word
"god" as he addresses the king in grandiose style, since the king
is regarded as the adopted son of God (see 2:7; II Sam. 7:14).
This does not mean that the poet regards him literally as God.
However, the king's dynasty will continue since he seeks to rule

in equity and righteousness. Finally, the poet announces that God has made the king supremely happy on his wedding day (vss. 7b-9). He has anointed him with "the oil of gladness," a pleasantly scented oil used on occasions of festivity (see 23:5; Isa. 61:3). Furthermore, the king's clothes have been prepared with expensive perfumes from distant places: myrrh, a resin from East Africa or Arabia; aloes, an aromatic wood from India; and cassia, a kind of cinnamon found in warm climates. From the royal palace decorated with inlaid ivory paneling comes the festive music. Kings' daughters are in the bridal party, but it is the young queen who takes her place at the king's right hand (the place of honor) bedecked in the celebrated gold from Ophir (see I Kings 9:27-28; Job 22:24; 28:16).

Counsel to the New Queen (45:10-13a). The poet turns to the young queen and counsels her to forget her people and her father's house (thus indicating that she is probably from a foreign country), and to yield herself with complete devotion to her husband. The people of Tyre and other nearby places will send her appropriate gifts.

The Bride and Her Attendants (45:13b-15). The princess, dressed in the most beautiful and costly robes, processes with her attendants to the palace of the king.

A Look to the Future (45:16-17). In the lofty manner of the Orient the poet now anticipates the blessings of the future: many sons of renown who will bring honor to their father.

Psalm 46—The City of God

Some have connected this hymn with the deliverance of Jerusalem from the invasion of Sennacherib's army in the time of Isaiah (II Kings 18:13—19:37). Although an emergency seems to be reflected, it is impossible to determine just what it is. Others have associated the origin of the Psalm with the celebration of the New Year Festival. It is the kind of Psalm that would be appropriate for the celebration of any of the great religious festivals. Without using the word "faith," the Psalm is one of the most magnificent expressions of faith ever penned. Strength for the present is found not only in God's creative power and control of history but also in the assurance that he has the *final* word. The theme of the Psalm is carried by the refrain (vss. 7, 11). In the text, as it has come down to us, this refrain is found only after the second and third strophes. A careless scribe was probably responsible for dropping it out after the first strophe, where it fits just as perfectly as it does in the other two places.

God Our Refuge in the Midst of Chaos (46:1-3). Throughout their history God has been the refuge and defense of his people. Even if the primeval chaos (Gen. 1:2) should return, God's people will not be afraid. As God manifested his sovereign power in the beginning by bringing order out of chaos, so at the end of the age there will be a new beginning.

God Our Help in the Midst of the City (46:4-7). Here past history, present experience, and future hope converge. Through many years Jerusalem was thought of as "the city of God," the religious and political capital of the nation where the Temple was located. There was not a literal river in literal Jerusalem. However, there was the river of God's life-giving presence (36: 8-9; Jer. 2:13). God's presence in the midst of his people brought security and much-needed help. But the language of the Psalm and of this strophe in particular also points to the New Jerusalem with its life-giving stream (Isa. 33:20-21; 54:11-15; Ezek. 40-48; compare Rev. 21:1—22:5). The new City of God is symbolic of the consummation of God's saving purpose. Whereas the chaos mentioned in the first strophe is in the natural world, here it is in rebellious nations. God has but to speak in judgment for the earth to dissolve (compare 76:8; Jer. 25:30-31; Joel 2:11; 3:16). Regardless of what the situation may be, Israel's God, who is also Lord of heaven and earth, is with his people.

God Our Hope in the Midst of the Nations (46:8-11). This last strophe in a special way looks to the future with such assurance that in the worshiping community the future is present (see Heb. 11:1). As in the prophets, so in this Psalm, judgment and salvation go together. God will bring desolation to his enemies and establish the New Age of universal peace (compare Isa. 2:4; Micah 4:3). All peoples and nations are called upon to desist from opposing God and to be willing to accept him as their exalted Sovereign.

Psalm 47—The Kingdom of God

Psalm 47 is one of the hymns of the Psalter which exult in the kingship of God (see Introduction). Sometimes these Psalms are called "enthronement Psalms"; that is, it is claimed that they were used on the occasion of the Jewish New Year Festival to celebrate God's re-enthronement over creation and history in a ceremony comparable to that used on the occasion of installing an earthly monarch. Certainly God is thought of as King of Israel and of the universe. Too, this Psalm has been recited on New Year's Day in the synagogue through many centuries. But the language of the Psalm may be metaphorical rather than literal. In no sense is God thought to be enthroned by man through magic ritual. His sovereignty is acknowledged and proclaimed, not created. In the so-called enthronement Psalms the accent is upon the coming reign of God, and the thought may be compared to the phrase of the Lord's Prayer, "Thy kingdom come." New Year's Day suggested the creation of the world and the end of the created world, which was not to be a dead end but a new beginning, a manifestation of the kingship of God. Through worship at the sanctuary, God's people as a corporate unity were caught up by faith into that future consummation.

Although it is possible to divide the Psalm into three major divisions (1-4, 5-7, 8-10), two are more in keeping with the literary form and thought content (1-5, 6-10). As in the case of Psalm 100 there are two calls to worship (1 and 6) and two sets of reasons for worship (2-5 and 7-10). In other words, this structure gives the effect of a double hymn.

The Nationalistic Outlook (47:1-5). Clapping the hands and shouting were a part of the ceremony of the installation of an Israelite king (II Kings 11:12; 9:13; II Sam. 15:10). All peoples are called upon to join in these expressions of praise to God as King of all the earth, who is "terrible" in the sense that he inspires fear or reverence. In times past God showed his sovereign power by subduing the nations of Canaan and giving their land to Israel. Israel was both a Church and a state, which means that a nationalistic outlook was inevitable until Church and state should be separated. As the earthly king was installed with "shout" and the sound of the "trumpet" (I Kings 1:38-40), so at the Festival, God is acknowledged as King.

The Missionary Perspective (47:6-10). The second call to praise refers to God as "our King." Yet the reasons for praise by the Covenant people include the fact that God is King over all the earth. His reign, though real in every generation, will one day be consummated when the rulers of all peoples gather "as

the people of the God of Abraham"—the fulfillment of the
promise made in Genesis 12:3, "in you all the families of the
earth will be blessed" (margin).

According to Paul, men become sons of Abraham by faith in
Jesus Christ (Gal. 3:6-29). Verse 10 finds the Christian counterpart in Revelation 11:15, "The kingdom of the world has become the kingdom of our Lord and of his Christ, and he shall
reign for ever and ever."

Psalm 48—The City of the Great King

This is one of the songs of Zion (see 137:3), which celebrate
Jerusalem as the Holy City to which the people of God make
pilgrimages for the great religious festivals. It is very closely
related in thought to Psalm 46.

Mount Zion in the Far North (48:1-2). Ultimately a song of
Zion is always a song in praise of the God of Zion, for he gives
the city its significance, and his people worship him there. Jerusalem is thought of as God's holy mountain and as a source of
joy to the Jewish people scattered in so many lands. It is identified as "Mount Zion, in the far north." Of course Jerusalem
is not geographically in the far north. The phrase "in the far
north" is a reference to an ancient Babylonian and Canaanite
idea that the gods assembled on a mountain in the far north (see
Isa. 14:13; Ezek. 38:6, 15; 39:2). The psalmist throws the pagan
mythology out the window and, by his use of the expression, says
that Zion is God's mountain. In other words, "in the far north"
gives Jerusalem its theological location. Jerusalem is also called
"the city of the great King" (see 95:3; Matt. 5:35). "The great
king" was a title used of the kings of Assyria (see II Kings 18:
19, 28; Isa. 36:4), but to the psalmist there is only one Great
King.

God's Defense of His City (48:3-8). In time past God has revealed himself as the defender of his city. Attacking kings have
become panic-stricken. Probably the psalmist has in mind God's
deliverance from Sennacherib in the time of Hezekiah (Isa. 36:1
—37:38) and other less spectacular events. God's delivering
power is comparable to the destructive east wind as it demolishes
the sturdiest vessels which sail the Mediterranean, namely, the
Phoenician ships that make the journey to Tarshish in Spain. The
enthusiastic reports which the pilgrims have received about Jeru-

salem from others are now confirmed by a visit to the Holy City. Past deliverance is a token of future security.

God's Steadfast Love (48:9-14). The pilgrims, as a part of their worship in the Temple, have meditated on the ways in which God has shown his Covenant love to his people. God's praise extends to the ends of the earth, at least in part through the pilgrims who tell their story when they return home. It is God who has given his people victory in times past. Jerusalem and her daughter towns and cities throughout Judah are called upon to rejoice on account of his judgments that have brought deliverance to his people. The pilgrims make a tour of the city in order that they may the better tell their children not only of the city itself but of the God of the city. "He will be our guide for ever."

Psalm 49—The Destiny of the Wealthy and the Wise

The psalmist is concerned with the inequalities of life (compare 37, 73), especially between the rich and the poor. His theme may be stated in the words of Jesus: "A man's life does not consist in the abundance of his possessions" (Luke 12:15; compare Luke 16:19-31).

A Universal Invitation (49:1-4). The wise man summons all men to listen, whether they be Jew or Gentile, rich or poor. Through a special revelation he has received wise instruction ("a proverb") on a hard problem ("riddle"), which he will solve for his hearers to the accompaniment of the lyre (compare I Sam. 10:5; II Kings 3:15). This hard problem concerns the rich and the righteous.

The Inadequacy of Wealth (49:5-12). The wise man does not say that all rich people are evil, but that those about whom he speaks are iniquitous persecutors, who trust and boast in their wealth. But no man can pay a big enough price to ransom himself from death (compare Exod. 21:30 with Num. 35:31). Both the wise and the stupid die and leave their property to others. There is nothing in the pomp of men to make them different from the beasts. Their graves are their permanent homes in spite of the fact that they leave landed estates bearing their names.

Death and Destiny (49:13-15). Those who put their confidence in wealth are appointed for Sheol, where "Death shall be their shepherd." The text of the remainder of verse 14 is very uncertain, as can be seen from the footnotes in the Revised Standard

Version. The text of verse 15 is easily read, though it has been variously interpreted. Some have maintained that the verse was added, but there is no adequate evidence for this position. Others have insisted that the writer is saying that the haughty rich will be cut off prematurely and the psalmist will be delivered from an early death. But the psalmist nowhere claims this; he acknowledges that death comes to all alike. He is saying that God will ransom him (and other godly persons) from the power of Sheol after death. Perhaps he thinks that his case is similar to that of Enoch, who "walked with God; and he was not, for God took him" (Gen. 5:24). The psalmist makes one of the few Old Testament confessions of faith in a meaningful afterlife (compare 16:10; 73:24; Job 19:25-27; Dan. 12:2-3; Isa. 26:19).

The Limitation of Worldly Success (49:16-20). Here the psalmist returns to his theme of the inadequacy of wealth. Regarding wealth and prestige he says in effect, "You can't take it with you."

Psalm 50—Before the Judgment Bar of God

This is a prophetic liturgy (see Introduction), composed of an introduction (vss. 1-6), two testimonies of God against his people (vss. 7-15, 16-21), and a conclusion (vss. 22-23). In dependence upon the teaching of the prophets the psalmist pictures a court scene, in which God is both plaintiff and judge (compare Isa. 41:1, 21; 43:8-13). The thought of the Psalm has two foci, the institution of sacrifice and the moral law.

The Convening of the Court (50:1-6). God's coming to the trial is set forth in language reminiscent of the giving of the Law at Sinai (Exod. 19). This time God appears from Zion rather than from Sinai. Lightning and storm dramatize the awesomeness of the occasion. The heavens and the earth are summoned as God's associates, because they are the constant observers of the behavior of his people (compare Deut. 4:26; Isa. 1:2). Further, they are called upon to gather the saints ("faithful ones"), who first made a Covenant with God by sacrifice at Sinai (Exod. 24:3-8) and have renewed that Covenant in the same manner through the years. The heavens call the court to order and present God as the righteous Judge.

God's Testimony Concerning Sacrifice (50:7-15). God does not reprove his people for failure to offer enough sacrifices but for their assumption that he needs such gifts for food and drink. What he wants is sacrifice that consists of thanksgiving offered from the heart and of trusting prayer in the day of trouble.

God's Testimony Concerning the Wicked (50:16-21). God now testifies against the wicked man, who is guilty of hypocritical externalism. This man can say the Ten Commandments by heart without making a mistake, and he can profess the Covenant as he offers his sacrifices. But his religion is only so much external ceremony, for he consorts with the thief and adulterer and uses his tongue for deceit and slander (compare Hosea 4:1-2; Rom. 2:17-24). Because God did not earlier confront him with his sin, he thought God was wicked too; but now God calls him to judgment in unmistakable terms.

A Final Warning and Promise (50:22-23). God warns both the morally wicked who forget God and the formalist who is content with offering a material sacrifice; and promises his saving help to those who are true to the Covenant.

Psalm 51—The Penitential of Penitentials

This is the greatest of all penitential prayers, biblical and extrabiblical. Through the centuries men with a burden of guilt have been led to the very throne of grace by its words. The author is not only conscious of being a sinner in general, he is also conscious of being a heinous sinner in some specific way. Yet, he is not one of the habitually wicked who refuse to repent. The saint is the sinner who repents; the wicked man is the sinner who refuses to throw himself upon the mercy of God. It is no wonder that in tradition the Psalm was associated with David in his deep sin and soul-searching repentance (II Sam. 11-12).

A Plea for Mercy (51:1-2). God's mercy is his grace or unmerited favor on which the supplicant throws himself with abandon. "Steadfast love" usually refers to God's Covenant love. This plea for mercy is a plea for forgiveness. The second word for "mercy" comes from the Hebrew word for "womb," and the writer may be suggesting that the mercy of God is comparable to the love of a mother for her child (compare Isa. 66:13).

Sin is designated by three different words: "transgressions," "iniquity," and "sin." "Transgression" is rebellion or willful disobedience. To use a present-day metaphor, it is the private slapping the general in the face. "Iniquity" tends to combine three meanings: crookedness (Jer. 11:10), guilt (Exod. 34:7), and punishment (Gen. 4:13)—though the emphasis may be first on one meaning and then on another. "Sin" literally means to miss the mark which God has set. Perhaps the writer of Psalm 51 is using all three words (transgression, inquity, and sin) as synonyms to describe his predicament from different points of view.

The psalmist also describes forgiveness by three different terms: "blot out," "wash," and "cleanse." "Blot out" refers to removal from a record of some kind (compare Isa. 43:25). "Wash" calls to the mind's eye the washing of clothes by treading (Exod. 19:10). "Cleanse" is used of removing dross from metals (Mal. 3:3) and of ceremonial purifications (Lev. 14:11; 16:19). Sin leaves a bad record, makes a person dirty, and contaminates morally and spiritually.

Confession of Sin (51:3-5). No one has to prove to the psalmist that he has sinned. The fact is that his sin is like a haunting specter that will not let him rest. His sin is against God, but this does not necessarily mean that he has not wronged his fellow man, for sin is sin because God is God. If a person does not believe in God, he may recognize the category of "crime," but he cannot recognize the category of "sin" in its theological dimension. Because he has sinned, the psalmist accepts the fact that he deserves the judgment of God (see Rom. 3:4). In connecting sin with his birth he is not speaking of the sex act or of the ceremonial uncleanness associated with conception and birth (Lev. 12:2). Rather is he confessing that he is a sinner born of sinners. This is not an attempt to avoid personal responsibility for his transgressions, but to acknowledge his solidarity with others in the human predicament (compare Isa. 6:5). All men stand in the need of a salvation which they themselves cannot provide.

Petition for Forgiveness and Renewal (51:6-12). At the very outset of this petition there is the recognition of the necessity of truth as wholehearted sincerity in approaching God. Only God can impart the kind of wisdom or fear of the Lord which makes such wholeness of the inner man possible. "Purge" is a weak rendering of the Hebrew word which means literally "un-sin." Hyssop was used in the ceremonial purification of persons healed of leprosy (Lev. 14:1-9) or from pollution caused by contact with a dead body (Num. 19:14-19). But the cleansing of which the psalmist speaks is not a ceremonial affair; therefore, the language is figurative. The desire to be "whiter than snow" is similar to Isaiah's expression in 1:18. Sin introduces discord into the music of life, but the establishment of right relations with God brings back the joy of living. The figure of broken bones may indicate mental anguish or both mental anguish and physical illness. The hiding of God's face from sin is an expression for forgiveness not mentioned in the introductory plea of the Psalm.

But renewal from the inside out (vss. 10-12), as well as forgiveness, is needed. The verb used here for the creation of a clean heart is the same verb that is used in Genesis 1:1 for the creation of the heavens and the earth. The same Power at work in the creation of the universe is at work in the re-creation of a human heart. In Scripture only God is ever said to be able to "create" in the sense of this word. He can give his people a new heart (Jer. 24:7; Ezek. 11:19; 36:25-27). The psalmist helps to pave the way for the New Testament doctrines of the new creation (II Cor. 5:16-21) and the new birth (John 3:1-16). To pray for a "right spirit" is to pray for emotional and spiritual stability. The context suggests that God's Spirit is the source of both the right spirit (vs. 10) and the willing spirit (vs. 12) in man. A willing spirit is a bent of disposition that wills to do God's will (compare John 7:17). "Salvation," as used here, is virtually a synonym for joyous fellowship with God. It is bound up with deliverance from sin, the creation of the new heart, and moral victory.

Commitment to Witness (51:13-17). Forgiveness and renewal issue in commitment to witness, which includes grateful praise to God (vs. 15). In spite of the suggestion by some that the vowels of the word translated "bloodguiltiness" be changed and the word translated "silence," the traditional rendering is preferable. In either case the penitent is praying to be delivered from death as punishment for his sin. If God will give him the opportunity, he will sing of his deliverance. "Deliverance" is the translation of the Hebrew word for "righteousness." Both in this verse and sometimes elsewhere (for example, 98:2; Isa. 45:8; 46:13), "righteousness" (vindication or deliverance) is essentially a synonym for "salvation." It sets forth God's saving character and activity as a unity.

The psalmist's praise to God cannot be expressed acceptably through animal sacrifice. Some have interpreted verses 16 and 17 as well as statements by the prophets (Amos 5:21-22; Hosea

6:6; Isa. 1:10-17; Micah 6:6-8; Jer. 7:21-23) as being a repudiation of the whole sacrificial system. This is not necessarily true.
The prophets condemned that separation of ritual from righteousness which placed ritual on the plane of magic. Even in the
laws of sacrifice in the Old Testament there is no sacrifice for
sins committed with a high hand. This means that for the one
who was guilty of such willful disobedience there was no sacrifice. He must throw himself directly on the grace of God. Since
this was true, it also stands to reason that no one of the legal
sacrifices was adequate to express the psalmist's heartfelt thanksgiving and praise for so great a salvation. The only sacrifice
known to him under such circumstances was his broken and con-
trite heart.

An Editorial Addition (51:18-19). It is evident that these
verses were added by a later hand to prevent the interpretation
of the Psalm as a repudiation of all sacrifice.

Psalm 52—Contrasting Commitments

This is a remarkable lament. Without the usual appeal to be
heard and the earnest petition for deliverance, the psalmist immediately launches into an attack on the wicked man whose ultimate commitment is to his wealth (vss. 1-7), and then sets forth
the happy status of the righteous whose ultimate commitment is
to God (vss. 8-9).

The Commitment of the Wicked (52:1-7). The wicked man
addressed here seems to be typical of a religio-political party to
which the psalmist and his party are opposed. This man is particularly guilty of sins of the tongue (vss. 1-4). He may appear
to be mighty (vs. 1), but God will break him down, tear him
from his home, and cut off his posterity (vs. 5). The righteous
shall hold him in contempt, because he made wealth rather than
God his ultimate security (vss. 6-7; compare 49:6-12, 16-20).

The Commitment of the Righteous (52:8-9). The psalmist
(and by implication others like him) flourishes under God's
blessings as a green olive tree located in the general area of the
Temple. He will thank God for his blessings and proclaim his
revealed character ("name") in the congregation of those ("the
godly") who like himself have received and trust in God's steadfast love.

Psalm 53 (14)—Human Depravity

For the most part Psalms 53 and 14 are the same Psalm. The differences in these compositions are minor except that 53:5 and 14:5-6 are almost totally different. The Psalm is classified as a prophetic liturgy (see Introduction). It is possible to regard verses 1-5 as a prophetic oracle, delivered by a prophet, and verse 6 as a prayer, sung by the Temple choir. The theme of the Psalm is the depravity of mankind.

Practical Atheism and Its Consequences (53:1-5). The fool who says, "There is no God," is not a speculative atheist who denies the existence of God, but one who denies God's moral control of the world. He represents a whole group of persons who are morally perverse and impious toward God and his people (see 74:18, 22). The psalmist sees people all about him acting like fools. When God looks down from heaven upon men, he, too, sees that they have all played the fool. In verses 1-3 it seems that the psalmist has all mankind in mind (see Rom. 3:10-12).

However, he is primarily concerned about those who oppress God's people (vs. 4). Some translators have rendered this verse in such a way as to identify the oppressors as corrupt priests who eat the "bread" of God (sacrificial offerings) but are not really godly men. Others claim that the oppressors are Jewish nobles. And still others maintain that the reference is to foreign oppressors. A dogmatic statement on this matter cannot be justified. These foolish oppressors should understand that God's judgment upon them is certain (vs. 5). Their bones will be unburied, and they will be put to shame.

Prayer for Restoration (53:6). The Psalm ends with a prayer for God to deliver his people from all evils and restore to them the happy times enjoyed in the past.

Psalm 54—God Is My Helper

The detailed background of this personal lament is difficult to reconstruct. Apparently the psalmist's life is in danger from false accusation, and he is seeking God's vindication at the sanctuary (see I Kings 8:31-32). In any case, he is seeking God's intervention on his behalf.

Appeal for Vindication (54:1-2). The Psalm begins with the appeal typical of laments. The parallelism between "save" and "vindicate" in verse 1 shows that the salvation for which the psalmist prays is vindication. The parallelism between "name" and "might" suggests that God's name is mighty to save.

The Reason for the Appeal (54:3). The reason for the appeal is that ruthless men are seeking the psalmist's life. These men "do not set God before them" in terms of doing his will or fearing his judgments. They are practical atheists (see 10:4; 53:1).

Assurance and Petition (54:4-5). Because God is his helper, the psalmist feels assured that God will vindicate him by causing their plotted evil to recoil upon his enemies, and in this confidence he petitions God to destroy them.

A Vow to Thank God (54:6-7). In response to God's deliverance of him the psalmist promises to make a freewill offering to God, accompanied by thanksgiving. A freewill offering was a kind of peace offering for which there was no binding legal requirement (Exod. 35:29; 36:3-5; Lev. 7:16); it was a free expression of gratitude. Vengeance upon his enemies, which the psalmist heartily desires (vss. 5, 7) at the hand of God, is not primarily a matter of personal animosity but would be understood by the psalmist and his contemporaries as a manifestation of God's righteousness and faithfulness within the proverbial "threescore years and ten."

Psalm 55—Wings Like a Dove

Some interpreters think that this lament is a product of composite authorship, but they do not agree perfectly on how to divide the material between the two authors. One theory is that verses 12-14, 20-21, 22 are fragments of a lament which have been united with the main body of the Psalm. However, the change from "enemies" in the plural to "enemy" in the singular in these verses offers no insuperable barrier to regarding the Psalm as a unity. One enemy stands out above all others.

Appeal to God Because of Oppression (55:1-3). The psalmist is utterly distraught on account of the trouble brought upon him by his enemies, and therefore makes an urgent appeal to God for an answer.

The Psalmist's Inner Turmoil (55:4-8). He feels that the agonies of death have already fallen upon him and are overwhelming him. He wishes for "wings like a dove" that he might fly far away from the storm of party strife in which he finds himself. It is possible that he has been falsely accused and is praying for vindication.

Earnest Petition for Destruction of Enemies (55:9-15). This earnest petition for the destruction of the psalmist's enemies is tantamount to a petition for deliverance. The prayer that God will confuse their tongues may reflect the account of the confusion of tongues at Babel (Gen. 11:9). "Violence" and "strife" are personified as watchmen who patrol the walls of the city (Jerusalem) day and night; within are mischief, trouble, and ruin; and oppression and fraud are constant occupants of the market place. In other words, this is a time of moral anarchy in Jerusalem (vss. 9-11).

But what disturbs the psalmist most is not the general condition of moral anarchy; it is the fact that one of his most intimate friends has turned against him, one with whom he used to hold sweet converse and worship in God's house (compare 41:9). It is no wonder that many have recognized the likeness of this man to Judas (see also vss. 20-21). Suddenly the psalmist returns to the whole group of the wicked and, in words reminiscent of the fate of Korah and his fellow rebels (Num. 16:30-33), prays that they may go down to Sheol alive (vs. 15; the verb "destroy" in vs. 9 means "swallow up").

Conviction That Petition Is Granted (55:16-23). Verses 17-23 are an elaboration of verse 16. Saving the psalmist includes humbling his enemies (vs. 19), who are godless. The treachery of his erstwhile friend is so disturbing that he returns to it again (vss. 20-21). The traitor has also dealt treacherously with other "friends" (literally, "those at peace with him"). His talk was smooth but his heart was evil.

Verse 22 is a statement of comfort for the psalmist and all of God's people who feel the burden of life's load (see I Peter 5:7). In contrast to the security of the righteous is the insecurity of their enemies, men of blood and treachery, who shall die prematurely (literally, "they shall divide their days in half").

Psalm 56—God Is for Me

Such outcries as this lament keep us reminded that life in biblical days was not easy. The keynote of Psalm 56 is trust in God, twice repeated in almost identical words (vs. 4 and vss. 10-11).

Appeal to the God of Grace (56:1-4). The psalmist makes no claim upon God; he simply pleads his unmerited favor. The oppression of enemies is the occasion of his appeal. He places his trust in God, whose word of assurance in trouble is the ground of his praise. With God as his God, what can weak, frail, transient human flesh do to him? (compare 78:39; Isa. 40:6).

The Psalmist's Enemies (56:5-7). The psalmist's foes are diligent in their attempt to injure him and his cause. They pool their efforts and spy on him. Therefore, he prays that God will repay them for their evil and adds a petition for judgment upon the nations.

The Psalmist's Faith (56:8-11). The psalmist is confident that God keeps a record of his sleepless tossings, and he prays that God will treasure his tears in a bottle. The word translated "bottle" is the usual Old Testament word for a large bottle made from the skin of an animal. Some think it may be a reference to the kind of tear bottles found by archaeologists. In any case, "bottle" and "book" are used metaphorically in a request that God remember the psalmist's troubles. The psalmist is satisfied that God will defeat the purpose of his enemies. Like Paul, he is assured that God is for him (vs. 9; compare Rom. 8:31).

Vows of Thank Offering (56:12-13). Before his deliverance the psalmist vowed that he would make thank offerings to God when his petition was granted. He now fulfills his vow at the sanctuary. By preserving him alive, God has given him the opportunity to walk before him in the world of light and life in contrast to the world of the dead. (For a richer meaning of "the light of life" see John 8:12.)

Psalm 57—The Psalmist in the Lions' Den

The psalmist, like Daniel (Dan. 6:16-24), finds himself in the midst of lions (vs. 4), but the lions in his case are men. Moreover, like Daniel he shows great faith in the presence of great danger. As it now stands, the Psalm is a lament of an individual. However, it may have been composed of earlier materials: verses 1-4 and 6 coming from one source and verses 5 and 7-11 from another. With only minor differences verses 7-11 constitute Psalm 108:1-5. Psalm 57 is characterized by the repetition of certain words (see vss. 1, 3, 7-8) and lines (see vss. 5 and 11;

compare 56:4 and 10-11; 59:9 and 17; 62:2 and 6) for emphasis.

Appeal to the God of Grace (57:1-3). The psalmist finds refuge under the shadow of God's wings (see comment on 17:8; compare 36:7; 61:4; 63:7; 91:4; Matt. 23:37). The psalmist's confession that God fulfills his purpose for him reminds the Christian of Romans 8:28. God will send forth his steadfast love and faithfulness as ministering spirits of deliverance.

The Psalmist's Enemies (57:4-6). His enemies are as dangerous as lions. As lions destroy with their sharp teeth, his enemies destroy with sharp words—slander and false accusations. Even in the midst of describing his enemies, he lifts his eyes heavenward (vs. 5) to the sovereign Lord of heaven and earth. Then he returns to his enemies who are this time likened to hunters that set nets and dig pits in which to catch wild animals. Through the eyes of faith he sees the hunters themselves caught in their own traps (compare 7:15; 9:15).

A Brief Song of Thanksgiving (57:7-11). Although these verses may originally have had a different setting, here they form an integral part of this Psalm as the joyous response of gratitude for deliverance. The psalmist has a new security about which he must sing. He calls upon himself and the Temple musicians to awake and join in praise, because the revelation of his deliverance came during the night. Ordinarily the dawn awakens him, but on this occasion he is so exuberant that he gets up before daybreak and summons the sun to rise. He will not confine his thanksgiving to God to the Jewish Temple but will sound it abroad to the nations, for God's steadfast love and faithfulness are over all his creation.

Psalm 58—There Is a God Who Judges

In this lament of the community, wicked divine beings and wicked human beings are called into judgment. A belief in subordinate divine beings or angels did not compromise the faith of Israel, for such beings were regarded as subject to the one true God (see 29:1; 82:1-8; Job 1:6; Introduction). In a time of moral anarchy the psalmist announces in no uncertain terms: "There is a God who judges on earth" (vs. 11).

Divine Judges Called Into Judgment (58:1-2). The word translated "gods" (vs. 1) is sometimes translated "congregation." The meaning "gods" is almost certainly correct. While it is possible to understand this word to mean "mighty lords" or "chief men" (see II Kings 24:15; Ezek. 17:13; 32:21), the literal meaning is probably intended. These subordinate heavenly creatures are thought of as exercising responsibilities delegated to them by God (compare Dan. 10). The ones addressed by the psalmist have been perverted in their administration of justice on the earth and therefore stand under the judgment of God (compare 82:7; Isa. 24:21-23).

A Description of Wicked Men (58:3-5). The psalmist now describes the wicked (especially the wicked rulers of vs. 1), who are the human tools in the hands of the perverted "gods." They are estranged from justice and given to oppression from infancy (compare Gen. 8:21). They are like a snake which is so deaf to the charmer's voice that it injects its deadly poison without fail. Their venom appears to be a mixture of cursing, slander, and lying (especially perjury).

A Sevenfold Curse Upon the Wicked (58:6-9). The psalmist prays that God will execute a sevenfold (seven is the number of perfection) curse of destruction upon the wicked (on imprecation, see Introduction): (1) break their teeth; (2) tear out their fangs; (3) let them vanish like water, (4) like grass, (5) like a snail that seems to dissolve as it crawls, (6) like a miscarriage, and (7) like thorn bushes placed under a cooking pot and blown away by a whirlwind. (On the use of the curse in Israel, see Numbers 5:21-31; Deuteronomy 27:14-26.)

The Gratitude of the Righteous (58:10-11). The righteous man will rejoice when he sees God's vengeance upon the wicked. Imaginatively he will bathe his feet in their blood. While the Christian cannot share the feeling of the psalmist toward other persons, he can share his real concern—namely, that the righteous God judge on earth.

Psalm 59—Deliverance from Howling Dogs

Although this is a lament of an individual with the usual themes of deliverance, faith, imprecation, and gratitude, it also contains elements of national interest (vss. 8b, 11, 13cd). The Psalm is characterized by the repetition of themes and verses (see especially vss. 6 and 14, 9-10 and 17).

Appeal for Help (59:1-5). By the use of different verbs the psalmist prays that God will deliver him from those who seek his life (vss. 1-2). The attack of these men is unwarranted, for the psalmist is not guilty of any sin against them. He is falsely accused (vss. 3-4a). Therefore, he prays that God will rouse himself and come to his aid (compare 44:23). Here the personal appeal moves into an appeal for the protection and deliverance of the nation (vs. 5).

Enemies of the Psalmist and the Nation (59:6-15). In this section of the Psalm there is a mingling of description of enemies (vss. 6-7, 14-15), assurance of triumph over them (vss. 8-10), and imprecation upon them (vss. 11-13).

A Vow to Praise God (59:16-17). The psalmist is confident that during the night God will in some way clear him of false accusation. Therefore, he vows to offer a song of thanksgiving in the morning.

Psalm 60—The Nation's Cry for Help

The setting of this lament is some military defeat in the history of God's people. Opinions concerning the date of composition range all the way from that found in the superscription (see II Sam. 8; I Chron. 18) to the time of the Maccabees in the second century B.C. The compiler of Psalm 108 quotes 60:6-12 as 108:7-13.

Prayer of the Congregation (60:1-5). Because they have suffered defeat, God's people feel that God has rejected them. Their disaster is likened to an earthquake. The hard things which they suffer are the wine of God's wrath (compare 75:8; Jer. 25:15; Isa. 51:17, 21-23). They maintain that God has set up a banner for them, not to serve as a rallying point of attack, but as a rallying point for flight from the bows of professional soldiers. In face of this predicament they cry out for deliverance and salvation ("victory").

A Prophetic Oracle (60:6-8). This oracle is a quotation from an earlier prophecy (compare II Sam. 7:9-17). It promises a reunited kingdom and subjugated neighbors, as in David's day. Shechem and its environs, which became the center of the Samaritan community after the downfall of the Northern Kingdom in 721 B.C., and the Valley of Succoth in the territory of the Jabbok River east of the Jordan, will be redistributed among the People of God. Gilead and Manasseh, east of the Jordan, will again be parts of Israel's dominion. Ephraim (Northern

Israel) as helmet will be the chief protection of the reunited nation, and Judah will be the royal tribe through which the sovereignty of the Davidic line will be exercised. Moab, Edom, and Philistia will be subdued. Moab, as the land of the Dead Sea, will be the basin in which God washes his feet, after he has taken off his shoe and cast it upon nearby Edom, thereby symbolizing his taking possession of that land (see Ruth 4:8-9). Over the Philistine Plain bordering on the Mediterranean, God will shout in triumph. The great spiritual understanding of God's Kingdom which transcends military victories is set forth in the New Testament.

Prayer of a Leader (60:9-12). Here a military leader, perhaps the psalmist, prays for himself and his people. He asks in effect: "Who will bring me to Petra [Sela], the rock city of Edom?" This may mean that he is praying that God will give him victory over Edom, or it may mean that he and others of his people desire to flee to Petra for safety. Because they have been defeated in battle he feels that God has rejected him and his people (compare 44:9), and pleads for divine help since human help cannot avail. God communicates a favorable reply, and the Psalm ends on the note of anticipated victory.

Psalm 61—A Royal Lament

The most reasonable approach to this Psalm is to consider it a lament of a king who is sorely troubled. The king's prayer is interrupted by the intercession of the people on his behalf (vss. 6-7).

Petition for Security (61:1-4). Half of the Psalm is a petition for security. The king calls to God "from the end of the earth" when his heart is faint. This expression does not mean that he is exiled from Jerusalem and the Temple. Rather does it mean that he is at the end of the earth and the beginning of the world of the dead. He is probably suffering from sickness as well as from enemies. By the use of various figures he prays for security in God. He wants to be a priest in God's tent forever; that is, he wants to have permanently the same sense of security that he has in the Temple ("tent" is an archaic name for "Temple"). (On the expression, "shelter of thy wings," see comment on the synonymous expression, "shadow of thy wings," in Psalm 17:8.)

Petition Granted (61:5). The king has been assured that God has heard his vows of thanksgiving and granted his request (reading "request" instead of "heritage"), as he is accustomed to do for those who revere his name.

Intercession for the King (61:6-7). Here the people, or a choir on behalf of the people, intercede for their king. They pray that his life may be prolonged (compare II Kings 20:6), that his reign may always be carried out in the presence and under the direction of God, and that steadfast love and faithfulness may watch over him like guardian angels.

A Promise to Keep (61:8). Repeatedly the king will sing God's praise and pay his vows of thanksgiving. Gratitude is a royal emotion for all God's people.

Psalm 62—Waiting Upon God

This is an affirmation of faith which reflects the kind of distress normally found in a lament. The psalmist's political enemies try to throw him down from his high position, but he waits confidently upon God. Verses 1-2 and 5-6, which are almost identical, state the theme of the Psalm.

The Psalmist's Adversaries (62:3-4). The psalmist accuses his enemies of continuing to hit him when he is already tottering. It is their intention to shatter him as a wall or fence, made of brick or stones, is shattered when it falls. By falsehood and duplicity they plan to depose him from his position of political leadership.

The Psalmist's Trust in God (62:1-2, 5-7). Out of deep struggle the psalmist has reached his present confidence. He now waits upon God quietly, for God alone is his true security.

The Psalmist's Counsel to His People (62:8-12). As a wise teacher the psalmist calls upon his followers to trust God under all circumstances, and to pour out the anxieties of their hearts to him. For men, with or without prestige, are but "a breath" and "a delusion." They are lightweights, for when they are weighed in the balances they are found wanting. The psalmist further admonishes his followers to put no confidence in extortion and robbery. By implication, his enemies put their trust in unjust gain.

On two occasions God has revealed to the psalmist the fact that power and steadfast love belong to God. The punishment of the wicked and the reward of the righteous both witness to these attributes (compare Jer. 17:10; Rom. 2:6; Rev. 2:23; 22:12).

Psalm 63—Thy Steadfast Love Is Better Than Life

This Psalm has some of the characteristics of a lament and some of an affirmation of faith. It may have been prepared by the king himself or by a poet under the direction of the king, and verse 11 was probably sung by a Temple choir in behalf of the king.

The King's Faith (63:1-8). With his whole being ("soul" and "flesh") the king longs for God as though he were thirsting for water in a dry land. Verse 1 is similar to 42:1, but, unlike the author of Psalm 42, the king is not exiled from Jerusalem. His troubles accentuate his feeling of need for God. In the sanctuary he experiences the presence, power, and glory of God by participation in worship and through the sacramental drama and symbolism of the Temple. Many psalmists consider long life as the chief evidence of God's favor, but this one can say, "Thy steadfast love is better than life" (compare 73:25-28). In other words, the Covenant relation with God is superior to mere biological existence. For this reason, the king will praise God as long as he lives. To sing God's praise is to the inner man what eating the choicest foods is to the outer man—it is feasting on God. This feasting is especially memorable when the king spends the night in the Temple and meditates upon God throughout its three divisions or watches. Thus he has found God's help and assurance for deliverance from his enemies (see vss. 9-11). The wings of the cherubim located in the Holy of Holies here symbolize God's protecting care (see comment on 17:8). The king clings to God, and God upholds the king.

The King's Future (63:9-11). Through his meditation the king has received assurance that the mouths of the liars who seek his life shall be stopped, that the liars shall be put to death by the sword, that their carcasses shall be unburied and be eaten by jackals, and that they themselves shall go down to the lowest depths of Sheol (compare Deut. 32:22). The death of the king's enemies means brighter days ahead for the king. Grammatically the word "him" in verse 11 may refer to the king or to God. It is probable that the psalmist refers to God. Those who swear by him are his true worshipers who glory in the deliverance of their king as God's representative.

Psalm 64—The Arrow of the Lord

In this personal lament the psalmist prays that God will preserve his life from the secret plots of evil men, is assured that his
request will be granted, and therefore calls upon the righteous
to rejoice in the Lord.

Petition for Preservation (64:1-6). The psalmist specifically
calls his prayer a "complaint" (or "lament"). His enemies are in
the category of the wicked. They "whet their tongues like swords"
(compare 55:21; 57:4) and "aim bitter words like arrows" (compare 7:12-13; 11:2), shooting suddenly from ambush at the
blameless. Some interpret these words as references to the cast-
ing of curses or spells by those who practice black magic. Others
hold that they refer to malicious slander. The troublemakers may
be guilty of both. They hold fast to their evil purpose as they talk
of laying snares secretly, and think that no one knows their
schemes.

Petition Granted (64:7-9). Some interpreters, especially those
who see the evildoers as sorcerers that cast magic spells, understand these verses as a countercurse uttered by the psalmist.
However, it is preferable to accept the translation of the verbs
as statements of fact, for verse 10 shows that the psalmist is certain that his petition has been granted. God will recompense the
evildoers "suddenly" (vss. 4, 7) with their own weapons, ar-
row(s) and tongue(s) (vss. 3, 8). The psalmist's deliverance will
cause even those outside Israel to fear God, to tell what he has
wrought, and to ponder what he has done.

The Rejoicing of the Righteous (64:10). The psalmist calls upon
all those in Covenant relation with God to rejoice and take refuge
in the Lord and to glory in his triumph over evildoers.

Psalm 65—Praise to God in Zion

This is a hymn of praise and thanksgiving to God as the Lord
of creation and history. Verses 9-13 suggest that the worshiping
congregation is gathered at the Temple in the spring after the
results of the autumn rains can be seen in the promise of a
bountiful harvest.

The Goodness of God's House (65:1-4). After the finding of
Deuteronomy or a part of it in the Temple in 621 B.C., Zion be-

came *the* place of public worship among the Jews (see Deut. 12).
The psalmist is conscious of the need of his people to come to
God as sinners seeking forgiveness of sins, since it is God who
atones for them (literally, "covers them"). That person is happy
whom God elects to dwell in his courts, for the goodness of God's
house embraces the satisfactions of security, thanksgiving, prayer,
forgiveness, festal meals, and fellowship with God and man.

God's Dread Deeds (65:5-8). God's awe-inspiring deeds (see
106:22; II Sam. 7:23; Isa. 64:3) of deliverance (literally, "righteousness") on behalf of his Chosen People invite other peoples
from the ends of the earth to put their hope in Israel's God (see
also vss. 7-8). This note of missionary outreach is found also in
other Psalms (for example, 22:27-31; 47:9-10; 67:1-7) and
Isaiah 40-66. The inhabitants of the earth everywhere respond to
God's mighty acts in creation with awe and joy. The stilling of
the roaring seas (vs. 7) is an allusion to the ancient story of the
dragon (see comment on 74:12-17; 89:9-10).

God's Material Blessings (65:9-13). God's people were acutely
aware of the fact that "every perfect gift is from above" (James
1:17). From his river above the firmament (an ancient Near
Eastern conception; see also Gen. 1:7; Job 38:25) God has sent
showers of "blessing" which are making possible a bountiful harvest. "The tracks of thy chariot drip with fatness" is a metaphorical allusion to an ancient story which expresses the fact that God
makes the soil fertile. The verdant meadows are filled with flocks,
especially the newborn lambs and the kids. Pastures, hills, meadows, and valleys all together seem to join in the doxology of
God's people.

Psalm 66—The Witness of Gratitude

Psalm 66 is composed of two major parts: Israel's grateful witness to the nations (vss. 1-12) and an individual's grateful witness to all who fear God (vss. 13-20). The strophes of part one
were probably sung by antiphonal choirs, and those of part two
by an individual. The Psalm was composed to be sung on the
occasion when a particular man paid his vows in the Temple
(see vss. 13-15). The similarity in missionary thought between
this Psalm and Isaiah 40-66 suggests a postexilic date for the
Psalm.

Israel's Witness to the Nations (66:1-12). Israel's witness to the nations is so presented as to be a hymn of praise and thanksgiving to God. In the first strophe (vss. 1-4) all the peoples of the earth are invited to praise God (compare 22:27; 98:4). In verses 3-4 the psalmist places a song on their lips. They are to proclaim that God's deeds are awesome, and that his enemies, out of fear, yield at least feigned obedience to him. Their announcement that "all the earth worships thee" is more prophetic anticipation than literal fact (compare Isa. 49:6).

In the second strophe (vss. 5-7) the nations are invited to take cognizance of the mighty acts of God in the history of the Chosen People. The two acts which stand out conspicuously are the crossing of the Red Sea (Exod. 14) and the crossing of the Jordan River (Joshua 3). In these and subsequent events God has shown that he keeps watch over the nation; therefore, "let not the rebellious exalt themselves." Although the Psalm was written centuries after the Exodus and the entrance into Canaan, the psalmist and his people could say, "There did we rejoice in him." They were present at the Exodus and entrance to Canaan as the Church of today was present at the crucifixion and resurrection of Jesus Christ.

In the third strophe (vss. 8-12) the choir calls the nations to bless God for his preservation of Israel through many trials. This invitation rests upon the thought that because of Israel's survival she as God's missionary will bring God's saving light to the nations and she and they together will be God's people (see Isa. 60:1-7; 61:9; 66:18-21). Israel's trials at God's hands are likened to the refining of silver (see Isa. 48:10; Zech. 13:9) and ensnaring in a net (see Lam. 1:13; Job 19:6). God let men trample over his people with horses and chariots (compare Isa. 51:23) and caused his people to go through fire and water (compare Isa. 43:2). Yet he has brought them to a new freedom. While many experiences of affliction are in the psalmist's mind, the Babylonian captivity is paramount.

The Individual's Witness to God-fearers (66:13-20). The hymn of the community has prepared the way for the psalmist to pay his vows and give his testimony. First, he pays his vows (vss. 13-15). However, in addition to the votive offerings promised when he was in trouble, he offers burnt offerings of various kinds. The large number of sacrifices offered by this man indicates that he was a person of wealth and position. It also indicates his gratitude.

The second strophe (vss. 16-19) of this part of the Psalm is testimony to what God has done for the psalmist. He is so grateful, he cannot contain himself. Such grateful testimony is often a means used by God to strengthen the faith of others. This individual worshiper knows that God would not have listened if his heart had been filled with hypocrisy (compare Luke 18:9-14).

Psalm 67—A Harvest Thanksgiving

Verses 6-7 are the key to understanding this Psalm. They show that it was used in celebrating a bountiful harvest. In Psalm 65, the People of God at a spring festival anticipate the *harvest yet to come;* here they thank God at the Feast of Tabernacles for the *harvest that has come.* The refrain, which is found after the first strophe as verse 3 and after the second strophe as verse 5, was probably lost after the third strophe through the carelessness of a copyist.

God's Grace Upon Israel (67:1-3). Although this Psalm is primarily a song of thanksgiving for blessings that have already been granted, these verses show that God's people realize that they are dependent upon him for future blessings as well. Verse 1 reflects the wording of the Aaronic benediction (Num. 6:24-26). "Make his face to shine upon us" is a prayer in metaphorical language for God's favor (compare 4:6; 44:3; 89:15). The reason given for this petition is that God's way and works of salvation may be made known through Israel to all nations. The refrain picks up this missionary prayer.

God's Rule of the Nations (67:4-5). The nations are called upon to "be glad and sing for joy," and the reason for such rejoicing is that God governs (judges) them with equity and guides them.

God's Earthly Blessings (67:6-7). Through the yield of the harvest God has blessed his people. "Man shall not live by bread *alone*" (Matt. 4:4), but in this world he cannot live without it (Matt. 6:11). The Psalm ends on the note of missionary concern, that all peoples to the ends of the earth may be reverent worshipers of Israel's God (compare 65, 66). As Christians we do well to base our missionary concern and activity on gratitude to God.

Psalm 68—A Liturgical Anthology

Of all the Psalms this one is the most difficult to interpret. It does not fit into any of the literary classifications listed in the Introduction, though it is closely akin to the hymn. It is best classified as a collection of songs and poetic fragments for use in a dramatic procession celebrating the kingship of God (see vss. 24-25; comment on Ps. 47). Each part of the Psalm was presumably sung in relation to a specific act of the sacred ritual. Some parts may date as early as the thirteenth or twelfth century B.C., while others may date considerably later. No one knows when the parts were put together. Canaanite poetry and the Song of Deborah (Judges 5) are two of its sources. Throughout the centuries it has been a favorite of those who have felt that they were fighting God's battles—for example, Savonarola, the Huguenots, and Cromwell.

A Processional Invocation (68:1-3). These verses constitute an invocation by which the processional was begun. "Let God arise . . ." (vs. 1) is almost an exact quotation of the words used by Moses when the journey in the wilderness was to be resumed (Num. 10:35). Inasmuch as the Ark represented God's presence at the head of the procession in the wilderness, it is possible that some symbol represented his presence in the procession mentioned in the Psalm. The invocation includes a prayer for the destruction of God's enemies and the joyous triumph of his people.

God's Action in History (68:4-14). In anticipation of the recital of God's mighty acts in the history of his people, there is an invitation to sing his praises (vs. 4). "He who rides upon the clouds" is an appellation of Baal in Canaanite literature. The Hebrew poet took over the expression to show that Israel's God, not Baal, is the Lord of nature (compare Deut. 33:26).

In Canaanite poetry Baal was also known as "the one who judges the case of the widow, adjudges the cause of the fatherless." In the Psalm, God is presented in somewhat the same way (compare Exod. 22:22; Isa. 1:17), and as the liberator of captives (vss. 5-6).

Verses 7-10 recall the Exodus from Egypt, the march through the wilderness, the Covenant at Sinai, and the preparation of a well-watered Canaan for God's people. Verses 7-8 are based on Judges 5:4-5.

God enabled his people under Joshua and the Judges to win and retain the land of Canaan (vss. 11-14). The defeat of Sisera is typical of a whole series of victories (Judges 5:31). "The wings of a dove covered with silver" describes a valuable item of booty.

Verse 14 seems to be a reference to a victory on Mount Zalmon in the vicinity of Shechem (see Judges 9:48).

God's Selection of Zion (68:15-18). Instead of many-peaked Mount Hermon in the territory of Bashan, God chose Zion as his dwelling. This is significant because Mount Hermon was associated with Canaanite Baalism. With his heavenly hosts (see Deut. 33:2) God came from Sinai to Zion. In doing this he led captives in his train and received gifts from men, even the rebellious (vs. 18). This seems to refer to the conquest of Canaan and the subsequent taking of Jerusalem by David. In Ephesians 4:8, Paul interprets verse 18 with reference to the victorious Christ who "gave gifts to men."

God the Savior of His People (68:19-23). God is the source of Israel's salvation in every sense of the word. He sustains his people day by day and preserves them alive. His salvation for them includes his judgment upon their enemies. "The hairy crown" is an allusion to the practice of letting the hair grow until the warrior had fulfilled his vow in fighting the enemy to the death. Israel's enemies took their vows in the names of pagan gods. But God will not permit his enemies to escape, though they flee to Bashan or take refuge in the sea. The spirit of vengeance in verse 23 is similar to that in 58:10.

God's Solemn Processions (68:24-27). These verses are a description of the festal procession into the sanctuary. Some symbol representing the presence of God as the King of his people may be in the lead. Then come the singers, next the maidens playing timbrels, and last the minstrels with their instruments. They call upon all those who are descendants of Jacob ("Israel's fountain") to bless God. These are representatives of Benjamin and Judah from the South and of Zebulun and Naphtali from the North.

God's Universal Dominion (68:28-35). To some extent these verses look to the coming of God's Kingdom in its fullness (see Zech. 14:18-19). The kings of the nations will bring gifts to Jerusalem. Egypt, as Israel's typical enemy, is referred to as "the beasts that dwell among the reeds" (crocodile and hippopotamus). Egypt and Ethiopia will recognize the Lordship of Israel's God. All nations are summoned to sing praises to him as the Lord of all creation.

Psalm 69—Not Guilty as Charged

In this imprecation the psalmist seeks deliverance from sickness and premature death, forgiveness of sin, and salvation from false accusers. For the seventeen references to this Psalm in the New Testament, see the footnotes in the Revised Standard Version.

The Opening Appeal (69:1-3). The opening appeal is that God will save the psalmist from death. He is sick and already feels that he is sinking in the quicksand of the underworld. He is exhausted waiting for God's answer.

The Psalmist's Predicament (69:4-12). Since the psalmist's enemies are numerous, he is probably a prominent leader. They have falsely accused him of stealing and have taken his illness as evidence of the truth of their accusation (vs. 26). He confesses his folly to God, but he is not guilty of theft (vss. 4-5). If he is not vindicated, others will be brought to shame. It is for God's sake that he is bearing reproach. This reproach includes alienation from his closest relatives (vss. 6-8). Because he has interfered with misbehavior in the Temple (compare John 2:17), the insults of God's enemies have fallen on him. As a result of his fasting and mourning for the wrongs committed in the Temple by these persons, he has become an object of ridicule.

Petition and Imprecation (69:13-29). The psalmist petitions God for deliverance from death, enemies, sickness, and shame (vss. 13-21). The appeal is based on God's steadfast love and abundant mercy (vss. 13, 16). The psalmist's enemies reveal their duplicity by giving him poison instead of food, and vinegar to make him all the more thirsty (vs. 21).

Therefore, in the light of the religious outlook of his day (see Introduction on imprecation), the psalmist feels justified in retaliating with a prayer of cursing (vss. 22-28). He prays that God will do to them what they have tried to do to him, namely, poison their sacrificial food and thereby bring darkness to their eyes and trembling to their loins; so add up their guilt and punishment that they can never be justified; and exterminate them so thoroughly that no one will dwell in their tents and their names will be blotted out of the book of the living.

Praise to God (69:30-36). The psalmist is assured that God will grant his request for salvation (see vs. 29) and vows to thank him (vss. 30-33). Animal sacrifice is inadequate to the occasion (see comment on 40, 50, 51).

All creation is called upon to praise God, who will save Zion and make it a dwelling for all who love him (vss. 34-36). In these verses there is a social concern for all God's people.

Psalm 70—Make Haste to Help!

This Psalm is identical with 40:13-17 except for minor variations. See the comment on that Psalm.

Psalm 71—Do Not Cast Me Off in Old Age

An old man who has been faithful throughout his life, seeks deliverance from enemies, sickness, and shame. The Psalm is a lament but with considerable variation from the norm. Because of its dependence on other Psalms a postexilic date is probable.

Appeal Mingled with Gratitude (71:1-21). The aged saint begins his appeal with words borrowed from another (31:1-3). He then prays for rescue from his wicked enemies and uses as a basis of his petition the fact that he has belonged to God since his birth (vss. 4-6). Many have regarded him as a "portent" (a typical example of divine punishment), but he maintains his trust in and praise to God, expressing his supplication in deeply moving words (vs. 9). His enemies interpret his weakened condition as a sign that God has forsaken him and they seek to take advantage of him (vss. 7-11). As other psalmists do, he prays for the divine vengeance upon his enemies (vs. 13). He praises God for his many deeds that reveal his righteousness (vss. 15-16). From youth God taught him to sing his praise, and this he has continued to do. Therefore, he prays that God will not forsake him now in old age, in order that he may proclaim God's might to the younger generations who in turn will carry on the witness (vss. 17-19). He is assured that God will again bring him back from the depths of Sheol into which he feels that he is sinking (vss. 20-21).

A Vow to Praise God (71:22-24). He vows to pay his thanksgiving to the accompaniment of stringed instruments. He addresses God as the "Holy One of Israel," a title made famous by Isaiah (see also 78:41; 89:18). He has been rescued and his enemies disgraced (compare vs. 13).

Psalm 72—A Prayer in Behalf of a King

This prayer was written by a court poet for the celebration of some festive occasion in a king's life. While it is not Messianic in the strict sense and is never quoted in the New Testament, its idealization of the king eventually came to point beyond the king for whom it was originally composed.

Petition for a Just Rule (72:1-4). The poet's first petition is that his king may rule in accord with God's justice and righteousness. "The king" and "the royal son" refer to the same person. In other words, the king is the son of a previous king, and not a usurper. He is probably of Davidic descent. The word translated "prosperity" in verse 3 is the same as that translated "peace" in verse 7. It includes the total well-being of the nation. "Defend" in verse 4 is literally "judge." Judgment is basically a saving work of God, administered in this case through his representative, the king.

Petition for a Long Life and a Beneficent Reign (72:5-7). Here begins the grandiose language typical of ancient Near Eastern courts. It is a court poet's way of praying that his king may have a long life and that he may be as great a blessing to his people as the rain is to the soil.

Petition for World-Wide Dominion (72:8-14). The poet now prays that his king may have world-wide dominion. "From sea to sea" may mean from the Mediterranean to the Persian Gulf; "from the River to the ends of the earth" may mean from the Euphrates to some undefined limit in the southwest. On the other hand, both of these quotations may refer to an all-encompassing yet invisible sea which was thought to nourish Jerusalem. In either interpretation these phrases express the king's universal sovereignty. The poet prays that the king's enemies may submit to him ("lick the dust"). Tarshish is in Spain; Sheba in southeastern Arabia; and Seba probably in Ethiopia. The poet bases his petitions for his king on the king's deeds in behalf of the needy, the poor, and the weak (vss. 12-14). It is expected of any man who rules by God-inspired righteousness (vs. 1) that he champion the just cause of those in need.

Petition for Abundant Life (72:15-17). The petition for the abundant life of the king includes (1) long life, (2) continual intercession on his behalf, (3) plentiful harvests, (4) a reproductive population, (5) an enduring name (compare 45:17), and (6) his being a means of happiness to others. "Lebanon" is probably a reference to Mount Lebanon, noted for its luxurious forests; however, it may be a reference to a sweet-smelling tree from whose leaves incense was made. The king, like Abraham (Gen. 12:3), is considered a channel of blessing to all nations.

Verses 18-19 are not a part of the Psalm but are the doxology which closes Book II of the Psalter. Verse 20 is a comment by an editor in whose collection there were no more Davidic Psalms.

BOOK III—PSALMS 73-89

Psalm 73—A Skeptic Becomes an Evangelist

Here is one of the most profound expressions of personal communion with God in the Psalter. The author's religious pilgrimage moves from skepticism to faith, to communion, to witness. His chief problem is the prosperity of the wicked (compare 37, 49), and his Psalm falls into the category of wisdom poetry.

A Statement of the Theme (73:1-3). In verse 1 the psalmist states the conclusion to which God had led him through his testing (compare 32:1-2), and in verses 2-3 he gives a brief introduction to his problem. Verse 1 is better read, "Truly God is good to Israel, to those who are pure in heart." That is, God is good to the true Israel (compare 24:4; Matt. 5:8; Rom. 9:6-7). But this conclusion was hard to come by, for the psalmist almost lost his faith through jealous envy of the prosperous wicked.

The Dark Night of Doubt (73:4-14). The wicked are not in trouble as other men. Yet, they are guilty of pride, violence, scoffing, malice, oppression, and irreverence (vss. 4-9). Many people are led astray by their example and become practical atheists themselves (vss. 10-11). What is more, the psalmist is tempted to give up his faith and join the ranks of the wicked who are wealthy and at ease. He feels that his godly life has been in vain, since he has faced continual chastisement at the hands of God (vss. 12-14).

The Bright Day of Faith (73:15-20). Fortunately the psalmist did not parade his doubts in the presence of others; for if he had, he would have been a traitor to God's children. He was not able to find a solution to his wearisome problem until he went to God's house, where through the experience of worship his perspective was transformed and faith conquered doubt. He then saw that the wicked and their prosperity are transitory and that they live in a dream world of counterfeit securities.

The Continual Grip of God (73:21-26). The psalmist confesses that his former bitterness was an evidence of his sinful stupidity, culpable ignorance, and degenerate beastliness. But now he knows that he is continually with God, who grips his right hand. He has experienced the love that will not let him go. God guides him now and will afterward receive him to glory. In spite of all arguments to the contrary, this seems to mean a fellowship with God that death cannot overcome (compare 49:15). God is the psalmist's highest good. Presumably the psalmist is just as poor as ever, but another's prosperity is no longer a problem for him. Flesh and heart may fail, but it does not matter, for God is his security (compare II Cor. 4:16-18).

The Grateful Response of Witness (73:27-28). Ultimately those who are false to God (literally, "all who go a-whoring from thee") shall perish, but the highest good in life is to be near God. The psalmist has made God his refuge that he may bear grateful witness to his works. He has made a pilgrimage from skepticism to evangelism.

Psalm 74—The Destruction of God's House

In this Psalm the congregation laments the desecration and destruction of God's house. It is impossible to be certain of the event to which the psalmist refers. The three most popular identifications are the destruction of Jerusalem and the Temple by Nebuchadnezzar in 587 B.C. (II Kings 24), the suppression of a Jewish insurrection by the Persian King Artaxerxes Ochus in 351 B.C., and the profanation of the Temple by the Syrian Antiochus Epiphanes in 167 B.C. The first of these is the most likely. However, the Psalm may have been reworked to apply it also to a subsequent event.

The Complaint of God's People (74:1-3). God's people, the sheep of his pasture, expostulate: "O God, why dost thou cast us off for ever?" They implore him to remember the congregation which he redeemed at the Exodus (see Exod. 15:13, 16), and

Mount Zion which has been his earthly dwelling since the days of King David. The ruins of the Temple are called "perpetual" because they have been standing a long time.

The Destructive Work of the Enemy (74:4-8). The enemies roared with shouts of victory in the place where God's people had offered their praise. Then they set up either their military standards or pagan symbols. They hewed down those parts of the woodwork which were overlaid with gold, and set fire to the whole. Furthermore, they burned all other places of assembly in the land.

The Complaint Renewed (74:9-11). "Signs" in verse 9 may refer to such symbols as the Sabbath and the great festivals, or to portents of the future. The prophetic voice has ceased and no one knows how long the sanctuary will be desecrated. Therefore, the congregation renews its complaint: Why does God not take action?

The Saving King (74:12-17). In spite of the present calamity, God is Israel's King who has manifested his sovereignty in his creative and redemptive activity. Verses 13-17 are a combined reference to the Babylonian story of creation and the Canaanite story of Baal. According to the Babylonian story the god Marduk conquered the "dragon" goddess Tiamat and from her divided carcass made heaven and earth. According to the Canaanite story Baal crushed the sea-dragon Yam, also called Tannin, Lotan (Leviathan), "the winding Serpent" (see Isa. 27:1), and "Shalyat of the seven heads." The Babylonians and Canaanites believed their myths to be literally true, but the Hebrew poet did not. He uses some of their language in referring to the Lord in order to state symbolically his power as the one true God in creation (compare Gen. 1:1—2:4a; Job 26:12-13) and history (compare Isa. 51:9-11). In other words, God's mighty acts in creation seem to be combined with his mighty acts of dividing the Red Sea, overcoming the Egyptians, providing food and water for his people in the wilderness, and creating a dry place in the Jordan for his people to pass over. In any case, the psalmist's primary interest is in God's power and his desire to save his people under the present circumstances.

The Final Appeal (74:18-23). The congregation petitions God to remember how irreverent people revile his name, and it beseeches him to protect the remnant of his own people. The Covenant people refer to themselves as God's "dove" (thereby indi-

cating defenselessness), "poor," "downtrodden," and "needy."
"The dark places of the land" (vs. 20) may refer to the hiding
places of the Jews in Palestine where their enemies tracked them
down and slaughtered them. God's people regard their cause as
God's cause.

Psalm 75—Thanksgiving for Judgment

Psalm 75 is a thanksgiving of the community in the form of
a prophetic liturgy. Verse 1 is rendered by the congregation,
verses 2-5 by a prophet speaking for God, and verses 6-10 by
another individual.

The Wondrous Deeds of God (75:1). God's people are especially grateful for a recent deliverance and recall the many other
wondrous works he has wrought.

The Word of God (75:2-5). God speaks through his prophet
and announces that he judges at the time which he himself sets.
He it is who holds the physical and human worlds steady. That
the earth was founded on pillars was a part of the ancient Near
Eastern world view (see Job 9:6; compare Pss. 18:15; 82:5;
104:5). "The boastful" and "the wicked" are the same people,
and God's warnings, "Do not boast" and "Do not lift up your
horn," mean the same thing. Because horns give animals added
strength, they are symbols of strength and, in this context, of
arrogance.

The Judgment of God (75:6-8). Judgment is executed by no
other than God himself. It is symbolized by a cup of intoxicating
wine which the wicked must drain (compare 11:6; 60:3; Jer.
25:15-29).

In Praise of God (75:9-10). The soloist on behalf of his people
praises God for the humiliation of the wicked and the exaltation
of the righteous.

Psalm 76—Human Wrath in Praise of God

This is a song of Zion. Some interpret it as a celebration of
the deliverance of Jerusalem from Sennacherib in the time of
King Hezekiah (701 B.C.; see II Kings 18:13—19:37), or the
victory of some other Judean king over his enemies. Others con-
nect it with the celebration of the kingship of God at the New
Year Festival.

God's Presence in Zion (76:1-3). "Judah" and "Israel" are used as synonyms. God has revealed himself in a special way in Judah. He has made Salem (Jerusalem) his earthly abode. Verse 3 may imply that instruments of war are broken and burned in dramatic ritual to symbolize the destruction of enemy weapons, or it may simply mean that God as the Lord of Zion has defended his city.

God's Rebuke of Zion's Foes (76:4-6). God revealed his glory and majesty in the defeat of his foes, whom he made utterly helpless.

God's Judgment from the Heavens (76:7-9). God's rebuke of his foes is a reminder that he inspires awe and dread, and that no one can successfully resist him. This leads to a prophetic anticipation of his final judgment from heaven upon all the earth for the purpose of saving all the oppressed. However, since God is always Judge, his final judgment is the culmination of an activity already and repeatedly manifested in history.

God's Praise from Men (76:10-12). "The wrath of man shall praise thee," for God rules and overrules in the affairs of men and nations (see Gen. 50:20; Exod. 9:16; Rom. 9:17). God's people are enjoined to pay their vows of thanksgiving which were made in their time of peril, and neighboring nations are also exhorted to bring gifts to Israel's God who is sovereign over all princes and kings.

Psalm 77—Grief in Historical Perspective

This Psalm begins like a lament and ends like a hymn. It may be regarded as a lament of the community on the lips of a devoutly patriotic citizen. He speaks of "my trouble" (vs. 2), but it is the nation's trouble which he has made his own. "The sons of Jacob and Joseph" (vs. 15) may mean that the Psalm originated in Northern Israel (see Amos 5:6, 15), or it may be only a general reference to the entire nation (see Obad. 18).

The Day of Trouble and Grief (77:1-10). In his trouble the psalmist cries out to God day and night without being comforted. He meditates upon God's former mercies to his people and is constrained in the midst of their present distress to ask, "Will the Lord spurn for ever . . . ?" The source of his grief is God's apparent change in the treatment of his people.

God's Wonders of Old (77:11-20). Here the psalmist calls to mind God's wonders in the history of his people. God's way is, like God himself, in a category by itself. "What god is great like our God?" is a rhetorical question (compare Exod. 15:11). There is only one sovereign God. The redemption of his people in the Exodus from Egypt was a signal revelation of his sovereignty (compare 74:2; Exod. 6:6; 15:13, 16).

In verses 16-20 three examples of God's mighty deeds are blended together: creation, thunderstorm, and the Exodus. There are allusions to the ancient Near Eastern account of victory over the forces of Chaos (see comment on 74:12-17). These allusions (vss. 16, 19) are figures of speech used to emphasize God's sovereignty in creation and simultaneously to symbolize the deliverance at the Red Sea. This latter interpretation is confirmed by verse 20 (see Num. 33:1). The thunderstorm (vss. 17-18) symbolizes God's glory and power in his continuing control of creation (compare Ps. 29).

When verses 11-20 are understood in relation to verses 1-10, it is evident that the psalmist and his people are strengthened as they set their grief in the context of God's mighty acts. This perspective assures them that he will save his people again.

Psalm 78—God's Wonders and Israel's Rebellion

In the Outline, this Psalm is classified both as a hymn dealing with the history of salvation and as a mixed poem. The author's purpose is multiple: (1) to warn his people to avoid the sins of their forefathers, (2) to encourage them to commit themselves to God in faith, (3) to emphasize God's choice of Judah and the House of David, and (4) ultimately to praise God for his marvelous deeds in behalf of his people. The Psalm may have been used at Passover when the Exodus redemption was celebrated.

The Teacher's Invitation to His People (78:1-8). The psalmist assumes the role of a teacher and seeks to instruct his people in "the glorious deeds" (literally, "praises") and wonders which the Lord has wrought. The words "testimony" and "a law" refer especially to the command that parents are to teach their children concerning God's mighty acts in Israel's history (see Exod. 10:2; 12:26-27; 13:8, 14; Deut. 6:4-25). It is expected that such instruction will keep the coming generations from being stubborn and rebellious as their fathers were.

The Rebellion of the Fathers (78:9-20). The reference to the Ephraimites in verse 9 is of uncertain meaning. It may mean that the psalmist holds the Northern tribes responsible for the failure of Israel to attack the Canaanites (Num. 14:1-10), or it may mean that in the invasion of the land they did not drive out the inhabitants (Judges 1:22-36). In any case, they forgot God's Covenant (see Exod. 19:5; 24:3-8). Furthermore, the fathers forgot the miracles which God performed on their behalf: (1) the plagues in Egypt (Zoan is also known as Avaris and Tanis), (2) the Exodus itself, (3) the guidance by cloud and fire, and (4) the production of water at Rephidim (Exod. 17:6) and at Kadesh (Num. 20:1-13). In spite of God's goodness to the fathers, they rebelled (literally, "were bitter") against him and "tested" him by demanding food and water. Verse 20 suggests that water was provided before the manna and the quails, but this order is the reverse of that found in Exodus 16:1—17:7 and Numbers 11:4-35 and 20:1-13.

The Manna and the Quails (78:21-31). Because the people had no faith in God, as evidenced by their complaining, God's anger was kindled (compare Num. 11:1-3). Yet he provided the manna and the quails (see the comment on Exod. 16-17 and Num. 11 and 20). The manna is designated by two very interesting expressions: "the grain of heaven" (vs. 24; compare 105: 40; Exod. 16:4, 15; Num. 11:8; Neh. 9:15; John 6:31-32) and "the bread of the angels" (vs. 25; literally, "bread of the mighty ones"; compare 103:20, where a different Hebrew expression is used). Before the people had finished eating the quails, many of the ablest were slain (see Num. 11:33).

Sin in Spite of Grace (78:32-39). In spite of all God's wonders in their behalf, the people did not have faith. Therefore, "he made their days vanish" (compare Num. 14:29, 35; 26:64-65). Temporarily they repented and turned to their Rock and Redeemer, but their hearts were insincere. Nevertheless, on the basis of his compassion God covered their guilt and did not utterly destroy them (compare Num. 14:15-24). "He remembered that they were but flesh."

God's Mighty Acts from Egypt to Canaan (78:40-55). The Israelites rebelled over and over again in the wilderness, and their rebellion is regarded as all the more heinous because they did not keep in mind the events of the Exodus. The psalmist dwells upon some of the plagues sent upon the Egyptians but in an order somewhat different from that of Exodus 7:1—12:51. Not only did God lead his people out of Egypt and overthrow their enemies in the sea, he also brought them to the Holy Land, drove out the nations who were there, and settled them in it (compare Joshua 23:4-5).

Israel's Early History in Canaan (78:56-66). Israel's record in Canaan was no better than it had been in the wilderness. "They twisted like a deceitful bow." They provoked God by their adoption of Canaanite idolatry. He forsook the Tabernacle at Shiloh, where the Ark had dwelt (see Joshua 18:1; I Sam. 1:3), and delivered his "power" and "glory" (that is, the Ark; see I Sam. 4:21-22) to the Philistines (I Sam. 4:1-22). On account of the defeat and fire of war, virgins remained unmarried, priests were slain (see I Sam. 4:11), and widows did not make their customary lamentations. Then God put to rout the Philistines and other enemies of his people under Samuel, Saul, and David.

God's Choice of Judah and David (78:67-72). God rejected the Northern Kingdom and chose Judah, at the center of whose life stands Mount Zion and the Temple in all its grandeur. Earlier he chose the shepherd lad, David, to be the shepherd of his people (I Sam. 16:1-13) and implicitly established the Davidic dynasty. Throughout this entire Psalm, however, no emphasis is placed upon the great achievements of men, for hope does not rest in sinful man but in the mighty God.

Psalm 79—The Temple Defiled and Jerusalem in Ruins

This is a lament of the community upon the occasion of the defilement of the Temple and the destruction of Jerusalem (compare 74). Various dates are suggested, but the fall of Jerusalem to the Babylonians in 587 B.C. is the best suggestion.

The Reasons for Lament (79:1-4). Heathen people have invaded the Holy Land, defiled the Temple, destroyed Jerusalem, and left the dead bodies of God's servants unburied, so as to make the survivors a scorn to their neighbors (see II Kings 25:8-30).

Appeal for Help and Vengeance (79:5-12). These survivors, as well as the prophets, understand the nation's calamity as God's wrath against its sinfulness (see Jer. 25:1-14; Deut. 4:24). At the same time they recognize that Judah's enemies are guilty in the very execution of the divine wrath (compare Hab. 1-2) and pray that God will pour out his anger upon them.

They pray that God will not continue to remember the sins

of their forefathers against them (see Exod. 20:5; Lam. 5:7), resting their appeal on his compassion. Further, they base their plea for help, deliverance, and forgiveness (atonement) on God's concern for his own honor, since the nations say in ridicule, "Where is their God?" (compare 42:3, 10; 115:2). They petition God to hear "the groans of the prisoners" and to "preserve those doomed to die" (literally, "the sons of death"). These expressions may refer to prisoners of war who are to be executed, or to those in the living death of exile (see Isa. 42:7; 49:9; 61:1). Of course it is possible that these two meanings are combined. Finally, they ask God to send the proverbial sevenfold (complete) vengeance upon Judah's taunting neighbors (compare Gen. 4:15; Prov. 6:31; contrast Matt. 18:21-22). These neighbors include such groups as the Edomites, Moabites, and Ammonites.

Vow of Thanksgiving (79:13). In anticipation of the granting of their requests, the people vow to give unceasing praise to their Shepherd.

Psalm 80—Prayer to the Shepherd of Israel

The theme of this lament of the community is carried by the thrice-repeated refrain (vss. 3, 7, 19). God's people need his favor in some kind of restoration, but the historical situation is uncertain.

The Initial Appeal (80:1-3). The congregation appeals to God as the "Shepherd of Israel," a distinctive title but a frequently occurring idea (see 74:1; 78:52, 70-72; 79:13; Gen. 49:24; Micah 7:14; Isa. 40:11). While the title speaks of God's tender care, it also speaks of the people's dependency and folly. "Israel" may, upon occasion, refer to the whole nation, to the Northern tribes, or to Judah. Here it refers either to the Northern tribes or to the whole nation. "Joseph" sometimes refers to the Northern Kingdom; in the parallelism of verse 1 it appears to be a synonym of "Israel." The mention of Ephraim, Benjamin, and Manasseh tends to identify Israel in this Psalm primarily as the Northern Kingdom. Benjamin is sometimes grouped with the Northern tribes and sometimes with Judah.

God is also addressed as the one "enthroned upon the cherubim" (see I Sam. 4:4). A cherub is a composite figure (sometimes a winged lion with a human head) mentioned in the Bible as symbolizing the presence and unapproachability of God. The reference here may be to the cherubim which were thought to support God's heavenly throne (Ezek. 10:1-22; 9:3; compare 1:4-28), or to the cherubim in the Holy of Holies of Solomon's Temple (I Kings 6:23-28; 8:6-7), or to cherubim which may have been used at the sanctuaries of Northern Israel. God as Shepherd and King is called upon to shine favorably upon his people by restoring them (compare 67:1; Num. 6:24-26).

The People's Complaint (80:4-7). God is now appealed to as the "LORD God of hosts" (compare vss. 7, 14, 19). Several interpretations have been placed upon the word "hosts": (1) the armies of Israel, (2) the armies of the stars, (3) the armies of the heavenly beings, and (4) power such as that summed up in all armies in heaven and earth. Whatever its exact origin, the title means that God is the universal King. His people are living on a diet of tears, made all the more unbearable by the ridicule of neighboring enemies.

The Ravaged Vine (80:8-13). Thus far the Covenant relation between God and his people has been expressed under the figures of Shepherd and sheep, and King and subjects. Now the relation is expressed under the figure of the Vinedresser and the vine (compare Isa. 5:1-7; Matt. 21:33-43; John 15:1-11). God brought his vine, Israel, out of Egypt, cleared the Promised Land of its old inhabitants, and transplanted his vine in Canaan. Ideally described it flourished so as to cover the mountains in the south and the cedars of Lebanon to the north. It spread from the Mediterranean to the Euphrates. The psalmist and his people are thinking in terms of the ideal boundaries of the land (see Deut. 11:24), which were more nearly realized in the days of David and Solomon than at any other time. But God has permitted its walls to be broken down, and those passing by "pluck its fruit." The wild boar (Israel's unclean enemies) ravages it.

Appeal for Restoration Renewed (80:14-19). God's vine has suffered greatly. Therefore, his people pray that their enemies may perish and that God's power ("hand") may be upon Israel, who is described as "the man of thy right hand" and as "the son of man." The first of these phrases refers to Israel as the one who has enjoyed God's honor and favor. The second is simply another way of saying "man" or "human being." In gratitude for national restoration the people promise that they will not turn away from God again but will continue to worship him sincerely.

Psalm 81—A Prophet at the Festival

This prophetic liturgy is composed of a brief hymn (vss. 1-5) and a prophetic oracle (vss. 6-16). It probably originated in connection with the celebration of the Feast of Tabernacles.

The Festive Hymn (81:1-5b). The hymn begins with a summons to praise "the God of Jacob," who entered into Covenant both with the patriarch and with the twelve tribes descended from him. The summons is addressed to all the people (vs. 1), to the musicians (vs. 2), and to the priests who blow the trumpets (vs. 3; compare Num. 10:8-10; Joshua 6:4-5). The occasion is designated by verse 3. The "trumpet" mentioned here is the *shofar*, the horn of a ram, wild goat, or cow—not the silver trumpet that was blown at the beginning of each month. On the first day of the month known as Ethanim or Tishri (our September-October), which was the seventh month of the religious calendar and the first of the civil calendar, the festival of blowing the trumpet was celebrated (Num. 29:1; Lev. 23:24). On the fifteenth of the same month the Feast of Tabernacles was begun (Lev. 23:39). The "new moon" of verse 3 refers to the festival of trumpet blowing and the "full moon" to the Feast of Tabernacles. "Statute," "ordinance," and "decree" all refer to the festival. "Joseph" may mean that the Psalm originated in the Northern Kingdom, or it may be a synonym for all Israel. Verse 5 points to the ten plagues.

The Prophetic Oracle (81:5c-16). "Voice" in verse 5c is God's voice to the prophet, through whom he speaks to the Israel of the present as they are identified with the Israel of the past. God set them free from Egyptian slavery (see Exod. 1:8-14; 5:5-11), answered them from the thunder of Sinai (Exod. 19:18), and tested them at Meribah in the wilderness (Exod. 17:1-7). According to the Exodus account it was the people who tested God. This suggests that when men seek to test God, they really put themselves on examination. Verses 8-10, in harmony with the Law and the Prophets, are a warning to Israel to yield absolute allegiance to the Lord who brought them out of the land of Egypt (compare Exod. 20:2). Similarly, the Christian is to yield wholehearted allegiance to the God who, through Jesus Christ, has delivered him from the bondage to sin.

But God's people would not listen to him. Therefore, he left them to their own devices (compare Rom. 1:24-32). Yet in love he calls them to obedience. If they would obey him, he would free them from their enemies and cause them to live on the fat of the land (compare Exod. 3:8; Deut. 32:13-14). Even in the midst of religious festivity his people sometimes need a warning. The Church must hear the prophetic voice.

Psalm 82—Judge of Heaven and Earth

This Psalm has been a battleground for interpreters. The battle has centered around the identification of the "gods" of verses 1 and 6 (compare 58:1). In general the several specific identifications may be divided into two groups: (1) those in which "gods" are heavenly beings, and (2) those in which they are earthly rulers or judges. The position taken here is that both of these identifications are simultaneously true, the first being expressed and the second implied. The Psalm follows the pattern of a prophetic liturgy with freedom.

The Divine Assembly (82:1). This is one of several Old Testament passages in which God is pictured as the heavenly King with a court composed of beings in the general category of what we know as angels (see 29:1; 58:1; 103:20-21; 148:2; I Kings 22:19-22; Job 1:1—2:10).

God's Address to the Assembly (82:2-7). God accuses at least some of these heavenly beings of showing partiality to the wicked and calls upon them to deal fairly with the various kinds of needy people. But injustice on earth is executed through unjust rulers and judges, and it is with the correction of injustice as found among men that the psalmist is immediately concerned. By clear implication God holds judgment in the midst of earthly judges and rulers also.

Verse 5 is a kind of aside rather than a direct address to the assembly, for the "gods" are characterized in the third person, "they." The heavenly beings and their human counterparts lack adequate knowledge, understanding, and light, and consequently the moral order of the world is imperiled.

In verses 6-7 God again addresses the assembly directly. The members are called both "gods" and "sons of the Most High" (compare Job 1:6; 2:1; 38:7). The word "sons" stipulates a subordination rather than a relationship established through procreation. The sentence of death is pronounced on these heavenly beings. By ironical implication human representatives of God are reminded that "six feet of earth make us all one size" (see the reference to verse 6 in John 10:34).

Judgment on Earth (82:8). Here God's people petition him to judge the earth. He is the one final Judge of both heaven and earth.

Psalm 83—The Enemies of Israel

The national emergency which called forth this lament of the community cannot be identified with certainty. A Bible dictionary will give complete data on the places and people named.

Israel's Danger from Conspiracy (83:1-8). After the very brief appeal to God in verse 1, the reasons for the appeal are laid before him in verses 2-8. God's enemies show their hostility toward him by plotting against his "protected" (literally, "treasured") people. Their covenant against God is the conspiracy to obliterate "the name of Israel," his people. The conspirators include Edom, located south of the Dead Sea; bedouin Ishmaelites (see Gen. 37:25-28); Moab, located east of the Dead Sea; Hagrites near Hauran, east of Gilead; Gebal, a mountain district close to Petra; Ammon, located east of the Jordan and north of Moab; Amalek, a bedouin tribe from the southern desert of Palestine; Philistia along the southern Mediterranean coast; Tyre, a Phoenician seaport; and Assyria, tribes living in the territory earlier known as the Assyrian Empire. "The children of Lot" (the Moabites and the Ammonites) as the chief enemies are supported by the other peoples. Since we have no knowledge from the historical books of the Old Testament or from extrabiblical materials of such a widespread conspiracy against God's people, it is possible that the psalmist is showing the quality of the opposition by drawing many of Israel's enemies from different periods of history into a single focus.

Imprecation Upon the Conspirators (83:9-18). God's people pray that he will destroy their present enemies as he destroyed the Canaanites by Deborah and Barak (Judges 4-5) and the Midianites by Gideon (Judges 7-8). Midian is south of Edom and east of the Gulf of Aqabah. Jabin was king of Canaan, and Sisera was his general. Their army was defeated at the River Kishon in the Plain of Esdraelon, and Sisera was killed by Jael, the wife of Heber the Kenite. Jabin was eventually destroyed.

En-dor is south of Mount Tabor. Oreb and Zeeb were Midianite princes (Judges 7:25; 8:3) and Zeba and Zalmunna kings of Midian (Judges 8:4-21). Israel's enemies seek to take possession of the Holy Land.

Various expressions are used to make the curse upon these enemies vivid: whirling dust, chaff driven by the wind, a forest fire, a hurricane, and shame. One purpose of the curse is that the survivors may acknowledge Israel's God (vss. 16, 18; compare Isa. 37:20).

Psalm 84—Love for the House of the Lord

This is the greatest Psalm concerning the house of the Lord. The psalmist is a pilgrim to Zion who loves God's house. The Psalm may have been composed for the pilgrimage to celebrate the Feast of Tabernacles, which took place about the time of the early rain (see vs. 6), but it would not necessarily be confined to one type of occasion. The thought can best be followed by dividing the Psalm into three parts, each part centering around a beatitude (see verses 4, 5, and 12).

The Happiness of Those Who Dwell in God's House (84:1-4). The Psalm begins with a statement of what the Temple with its various parts means to the psalmist. His whole being (soul, heart, and flesh) longs for the experience of worship at the sanctuary (compare 42-43). That which makes the Temple so appealing is not the buildings themselves but "the living God."

The person who has seen a small bird sitting on her nest in a church building can easily appreciate how the sparrow or swallow found a home for herself and her young in the ancient Temple. To be in God's house was for the psalmist to be at home with God. Many a Christian who has been brought up in the Church, feels as much at home in God's house as he does in his own home. To be at home with God is to experience the highest good in life. Happy indeed are the priests and Levites who have the privilege of living at the Temple as the sparrow does, and singing God's praise continually!

The Happiness of Pilgrims to Zion (84:5-9). Not only are those who live in the Temple precincts counted happy, but also those who make the pilgrimage to Zion. Pilgrims often found the journey difficult and needed the encouraging strength of God. Though the Hebrew of verse 5 lacks the words "to Zion," they are clearly implied by the context. The "valley of Baca" has not been located. The word "Baca" literally refers to a species of balsam tree (II Sam. 5:23). It is related in sound to the word "to weep," and some have translated the phrase "valley of weeping." Apparently the valley of Baca was an arid territory through which pilgrims passed on their way to Jerusalem. But the pilgrims' anticipation of the Temple experience transforms the desert for them into a place of springs. Furthermore, the early rain, which comes from the latter part of October to December, will soon bring the long summer drought to an end. Their strength is renewed as they move closer and closer to Jerusalem (compare Isa. 40:31). God will be seen in the sense that his presence will be vitally felt at the sanctuary.

Here the psalmist, apparently as the leader of the pilgrims, interjects his prayer (vss. 8-9)—first for a favorable hearing and then for the reigning king, with whom the life of the nation was intimately bound. For God to look upon the face of his anointed is for him to receive the king favorably.

The Happiness of the Man Who Trusts in God (84:10-12). The psalmist now returns to the theme of his love for God's house. The word rendered "doorkeeper" may refer to some kind of menial servant (see I Chron. 26), or to a beggar who stands at the entrance to the sanctuary to secure his living, or to some other humble suppliant. But whatever the exact meaning may be, the psalmist prefers it to a life among those who cut themselves off from God by wickedness. In other words, the ethical and the ceremonial are woven together. As a sun and shield God gives blessing and protection to those who walk as his Covenant people in integrity (compare 15:2; 101:2, 6). True happiness is not confined to those who live in the Temple or to those who are able to make the pilgrimage to Zion, for every man who trusts in God is blessed. For the Christian this Psalm may be a needed lesson on enjoying the Church.

Psalm 85—The Fortunes of Jacob

Psalm 85 is a prophetic liturgy in three parts: verses 1-3, 4-7, 8-13. Parts one and three were apparently rendered by individuals and part two by the congregation. The setting seems to be the days of Haggai and Zechariah, shortly after the return of a remnant of the Jews from the Babylonian Captivity.

Past Mercies (85:1-3). "Restore the fortunes" does not mean the same thing in every context. Here it seems to refer to the restoration of some of the Jews to their homeland in 538 B.C. under Cyrus the Persian. This restoration was evidence that God had forgiven their guilt and sin.

Present Need (85:4-7). But the expectations aroused by the Prophet of the Exile (Isa. 40-66) have not been realized (see Hag. 1:6-11; 2:15-19; Zech. 1:12-17), and the people feel that God's wrath still rests upon them. Therefore, they plead for a restoration that will be a full salvation in every sense.

Future Expectation (85:8-13). The psalmist, whether he is technically a prophet or not, receives a prophetic message from God and delivers it prophetically. God will grant his well-being ("peace") and salvation to those who revere him, and the Temple will be rebuilt that God's "glory" or revealed presence may dwell in the land (see 63:2; Ezek. 43:4; Zech. 2:1-5; compare Exod. 40:34-35; II Chron. 7:1-3). The Temple of Zerubbabel was completed in 516 B.C. But the ultimate revelation of God's glory in the midst of his people was to be made in the Incarnation of the Son of God (John 1:14; II Cor. 4:6).

Verses 10-13 are similar in thought and language to Isaiah 40-66. God's Covenant love, faithfulness, righteousness, and peace will bless his people, who in turn will reflect the character of their Savior. Material blessings will accompany spiritual growth (compare Matt. 6:33).

Psalm 86—Praying in the Language of Scripture

In this personal lament the psalmist prays in the language of earlier psalmists and writers of other parts of the Old Testament-to-be, just as today a person well versed in the Bible may use an abundance of Scripture quotations in his prayer.

Supplication in Trouble (86:1-7). The psalmist describes himself as "poor," "needy," and "godly." He is godly in the sense that he has been the recipient of God's steadfast love and is in turn devoted to God in the Covenant relation. He describes God as "good," "forgiving," and "abounding in steadfast love." The word "forgiving" suggests that he feels the need of God's forgiveness.

God, the Ground of Hope (86:8-13). Israel's God is incomparable. There is none like him among the so-called gods of the

Gentiles or among the heavenly hosts. He is the Creator of all nations, and one day they will bow before him in worship (compare 22:27-28; 65:2; 66:4, 8; 67:1-7; Isa. 45:22-23; 66:23). For he alone is God (compare Isa. 44:6). Clearly the "gods" of verse 8 are not rivals of the one true God. The psalmist wants this one true God to be his teacher, in order that he may live according to his revealed will; and further prays for single-hearted devotion to him in worship and service. He gives thanks to God as a continuing experience, for in time past God has shown his steadfast love by delivering him from premature death.

Supplication Renewed (86:14-17). Now as God's "servant" and as the son of a mother who also belongs to God, the psalmist prays for deliverance from "insolent" and "ruthless" men.

Psalm 87—Mother Zion

This is a song of Zion about which there has been much debate. Do verses 4-6 refer to Jews living outside Palestine? to converts from non-Jewish faiths? or to the consummation of the Kingdom of God when all nations shall be adopted into the .family of God? The mention of Babylon rather than Assyria and the implicit reference to public religious ceremonies (vs. 7) suggest an early postexilic date, after the rebuilding of the Temple (520-516 B.C.).

Zion, City of God (87:1-3). God founded Jerusalem on a group of hills, and he loves Zion more than all the other cities and villages of the Holy Land (compare 78:68). As the City of God (compare 46:4) it is associated with David, Solomon's Temple, Isaiah's preaching, the Temple of Zerubbabel, and the hopes of God's people. The glorious things already spoken of Zion by God (for example, Isa. 2:2-4) are in harmony with what he now speaks (vs. 4).

Zion, Mother of God's People (87:4-6). Those who know God in Egypt ("Rahab"), Babylon, Philistia, Phoenicia (of which Tyre is the representative city), and Ethiopia include both Jews and converts who live in these countries. The psalmist and some of the prophets understood Israel's missionary role among the nations (Isa. 2:2-4; 43:8-13; 56:3-8; Zech. 8:20-23). "This one was born there" means that Zion is the spiritual mother of all God's children. But winning people to Israel's faith cannot be separated from the consummation of God's Kingdom when the nations turn to Israel's God (see Isa. 19:19-25; 60:1-3; Zech. 2:11). God keeps a record (see 56:8; 69:28; 139:16; Isa. 4:3) of all those whose spiritual birthplace is Zion. This is very close to the New Testament doctrine of regeneration.

Zion, Source of Life (87:7). Religious dancing (see 30:11; 149:3; 150:4; Exod. 15:20; II Sam. 6:16), as well as singing and music, was an expression of Israelite worship. Singers and dancers greet Mother Zion with a song, rejoicing in her as the fountain of salvation and life (compare Isa. 12:3; Joel 3:18; Zech. 14:8).

Psalm 88—Unrelieved Darkness

In most laments there are an assurance of request granted and a vow of thanksgiving, but in this "saddest Psalm in the whole Psalter" the psalmist's darkness is unrelieved. He is suffering from a disfiguring disease, is forsaken by friends, and is about to die.

The Opening Cry (88:1-2). The psalmist cries for God's help day and night, and here appeals for a hearing.

Full of Troubles (88:3-12). His whole being ("soul") "is full of troubles." Already he draws close to the realm of the dead. In fact, he is "reckoned among those who go down to the Pit" (another designation of Sheol). To him, as well as to most of his contemporaries, Sheol was a place from which God's care was absent. He feels that his troubles are the result of God's wrath, though he does not explicitly confess any sin. He is overwhelmed by the waves of trouble (compare 42:7). He is such a horrible sight that his friends shun him (see vs. 18; 31:11; Job 19:13-22). Some have interpreted the words "I am shut in" to mean that he is a leper and therefore cut off from society and the public worship of God (see Lev. 13:1-8, 45-46; II Chron. 26:21). His eye is dimmed through his affliction.

He now returns to the subject of Sheol by asking a series of questions, to which the implicit answer is "No." God does not "work wonders for the dead." "The shades" (a description of the dead in their weak and shadowlike existence) do not praise God (6:5; 94:17). God's Covenant love and faithfulness are not declared in the grave or Abaddon (a proper name for Sheol, meaning "ruin"; compare Job 26:6; 28:22; 31:12). His marvelous deeds are unknown in the "darkness" of the underworld, and his "saving help" (literally, "righteousness") "in the land of forgetfulness." For God does not remember the dead (vs. 5), the dead do not remember God (6:5), and men forget their own dead (31:12). For a different point of view see 49:15; 73:24; 139:8 (compare Introduction).

Faith in the Midst of Darkness (88:13-18). Death offers no hope for the psalmist. In unquenchable faith he continues to cry to God morning after morning. He has been "close to death" since he was a boy. The second half of verse 18 should probably be read, "my companions are darkness." Amidst the darkness of this world our hearts go out in gratitude to God for the resurrected Christ "who abolished death and brought life and immortality to light through the gospel" (II Tim. 1:10).

Psalm 89—The Davidic Covenant

Like Psalm 63 this is a royal lament by or on behalf of a Davidic king. It is thought by some to be composed of two or more originally independent poems. However, as it stands, it is a unity centering in God's Covenant with David. The occasion is the defeat and deposition of a Judean king, and the probable time is the early sixth century B.C. Many think Jehoiachin is the king involved (see II Kings 24:8-17).

God's Steadfast Love and Faithfulness (89:1-4). In this brief hymnic preface the key words of the Psalm are introduced—"steadfast love" and "faithfulness." The fact that both of these words occur in every major division of the Psalm is evidence for its unity. These attributes of God are placed in juxtaposition to a statement of God's Covenant with David, both because they were manifested in the making of that Covenant and because the psalmist is to raise a question about them in his lament proper (vs. 49). Verses 3-4 are to be understood in the light of II Samuel 7 and 23:5.

In Praise of the Incomparable God (89:5-18). The mention of Tabor and Hermon (vs. 12) has caused some to assign the original composition of this section to the Northern Kingdom in the eighth century B.C. However this issue may be decided, in the present Psalm these verses are a source of encouragement to the discouraged king and people and a basis for the later appeal for help.

God is praised for his "wonders" and "faithfulness." No one

in his heavenly court (see comment on 82) can be compared to him. (On the title "LORD God of hosts," verse 8, see comment on 80:4.) In verses 9-12 he is praised specifically for the wonder of his creation. Allusion is made to a Canaanite story in which Yam, the sea-god, is conquered by Baal (vs. 9). Rahab corresponds to the dragon Tiamat who, according to the Babylonian account of creation, is overcome by the god Marduk. Obviously the Lord replaces Baal and Marduk in the psalmist's version of the stories. Unlike the Canaanites and Babylonians who accepted the stories literally, the psalmist uses them metaphorically to celebrate the sovereignty of God in creation. Righteousness and justice are the basis of the Lord's reign. Happy are the people who participate in worshiping the incomparable God with jubilant shouting (see 27:6; 33:3; II Sam. 6:15) and live in the favor of his presence. He is the source of his people's strength ("horn" is a symbol of their strength), and the channel of this strength is his representative, the king. As "shield" the king is the protector of God's people.

God's Promise to David (89:19-37). The Covenant with David has already been briefly mentioned in verses 3-4. Here the same theme is elaborated (see II Sam. 7 again) and for the most part is clear without comment. The "faithful one" to whom God gave the oracle of old is Nathan, who in turn passed it on to David, whose dominion will be from the Mediterranean to the Euphrates and its canals (vs. 25). The promise of sonship to God by adoption, made on behalf of Solomon and his successors (II Sam. 7: 14), is here also applied to David (vs. 26). As God's "first-born," David and his successors are to have pre-eminence among the kings of the earth (vs. 27). God will punish David's descendants for their trangressions, but nothing can ever void the Davidic Covenant.

The Promise Broken or Fulfilled? (89:38-51). Because the present Davidic king ("thy anointed") has been defeated in battle, has lost his throne, has been made prematurely old, and is covered with shame, the psalmist claims that God has renounced his Covenant with David. Further, he appeals for a speedy restoration in view of the shortness of life and the certainty of death. His final appeal is to God's steadfast love and faithfulness with which the Psalm begins. (Verse 52 is the doxology which closes Book III of the Psalter, not a part of Psalm 89.)

Did God break his Covenant promise to David? (vs. 39). Perhaps the psalmist means to say that the facts make it seem so. But, as he himself affirms, God will punish David's heirs for their sins. This is what happened in the sixth century B.C. Furthermore, there was yet to come a fulfillment of the promise to David of which the psalmist was unaware (see Luke 1:32-33; Acts 2:30; 13:22-23).

BOOK IV—PSALMS 90-106

Psalm 90—O God, Our Help in Ages Past

The ascription to Moses was the ancient editor's way of paying this Psalm the highest compliment possible in Israel. It has the style of a lament but the spirit of faith and praise. The congregation is at prayer on a fast day or after some national calamity.

Eternal God and Transitory Man (90:1-12). In view of God's eternity and wrath, and man's mortality and sin, God's people seek to live wisely. God has been their true home in all the generations of their history (compare Deut. 33:27). Before creation, even from the infinite past to the infinite future, he is God. Creation is depicted under the metaphor of birth (compare Job 15:7; 38:8). "The mountains" are specifically named because they are regarded as the oldest parts of the earth (see Deut. 33:15; Prov. 8:25; Hab. 3:6).

In contrast to the infinite God stands finite man in his transitoriness. Man is wholly under the control of God, who turns him back to dust (see Gen. 2:7; 3:19). Even a thousand years are a very small thing to God, no more than yesterday or one of the three watches of the night (compare II Peter 3:8). In order to set forth man's transitoriness the psalmist makes use of the figures of a flood, the sleep of death, and short-lived grass (vss. 5-6).

God's people see the reason for human mortality in his wrath upon sin (see Gen. 3:3, 19; Rom. 6:23), and are especially aware of their own sins. Their deviations from God's will and the secret sins of the heart are all revealed in the searching light of God's presence. Life comes to an end as quickly as a sigh. Even at its best (seventy or eighty years) it has its share of toil and trouble and is of short duration. The implication of verse 11 is that men in general do not take the wrath of God seriously enough. Therefore, his people pray that he will enable them to recognize their limited number of days in such a way as to use them wisely (compare Deut. 32:29).

A Plea for God's Favor (90:13-17). The people pray that God will return to them in favor and satisfy them soon with his Covenant love in order that they may enjoy the short span of life allotted to them. They have been made very conscious of God's wrath upon sin (vss. 7-8) because of the affliction which they have experienced (vs. 15). Therefore, they plead with God to give them joy in proportion to the evil they have undergone. Such a reversal of fortune will indeed be a manifestation of his "work" to his "servants" and of his "glorious power" to their children. This Psalm is a "work" of its author, and as such it has been preserved and used by God's people.

The psalmist has gone as far as a man may go in facing the transitoriness of human life apart from the light of God's grace shining on the other side of death. But since God has set eternity in the human heart, it can never be completely satisfied with threescore years and ten.

Psalm 91—The Shadow of the Almighty

The theme of this Psalm is God's protection of the person who cleaves to him in love. From a literary standpoint the Psalm combines characteristics of the lament, of the affirmation of faith, of wisdom poetry, and of divine oracle (vss. 14-16). Perhaps it is best classified as a wise man's affirmation of faith.

Assurance to Every Man of Faith (91:1-13). God's protecting care is called "the shelter of the Most High" and "the shadow of the Almighty." "Shelter" sometimes designates the Temple (61: 4), but is used here figuratively (compare 32:7). "Shadow" is sometimes found in the expression "the shadow of thy wings" (17:8; 36:7; 57:1; 63:7; compare 91:4). "Most High" and "Almighty" are ancient names of so-called deities that came to be applied to the one true God. The psalmist enumerates the evils from which God protects his faithful one. "The snare of the fowler" is a metaphor for plots against one's life by evil men (124:7; 141:9; compare II Tim. 2:26). "Wings" in verse 4 denotes the protective wings of a mother bird (see comment on 17:8; compare Matt. 23:37; Luke 13:34). "The terror of the

night" may be a designation of a night demon (see Isa. 34:14).
"The arrow that flies by day" may be a designation of a demon
causing sunstroke (compare 121:6), or it may refer to the plans
of evil men (see 11:2; 64:3). It is possible that "the pestilence
that stalks in darkness" (see vss. 3, 10) is a demon that spreads
a plague at night, or just the plague itself. "The destruction that
wastes at noonday" may be a demon thought to roam in the heat
of the day, or simply the devastating oriental sun.

While God protects the believer from the evils listed above,
retribution falls upon the wicked (vss. 7-10). (For the limitations
of this view see comment on 37, 49, 73.) Over against the destructive demons are ministering angels (compare 34:7) sent
by God to protect his loyal one. Verses 11-12 are quoted by the
Devil in his temptation of Jesus (Matt. 4:6; Luke 4:10-11). The
believer will be able to overcome all dangers as symbolized by
the lion, adder, young lion, and serpent (compare Luke 10:19;
Rom. 16:20).

A Divine Confirmation (91:14-16). These verses are an oracle,
presumably delivered by a priest in the Temple, which confirms
the message of assurance in the preceding verses. God promises
deliverance, protection, the divine presence, honor, long life, and
salvation to the person who cleaves to him in love and knows his
name. To know his name is to recognize his revealed character.
"Salvation" covers all the blessings enumerated.

Psalm 92—Gratitude for God's Works

The psalmist expresses his gratitude for God's works in general
and for specific blessings on his own behalf. The form and content of the Psalm place it in the category of a hymnic thanksgiving of an individual.

The Hymnic Introduction (92:1-4). The impersonal beginning
is more in the style of a hymn than of a personal thanksgiving.
It is good to show gratitude to God by singing praises to his
name and declaring his steadfast love and faithfulness to the accompaniment of stringed instruments. "In the morning" and "by
night" probably refer to the burnt offering made every morning
and every evening (Exod. 29:38-42; Num. 28:1-8). The psalmist is moved to express himself in thanksgiving for some specific
"work" on his behalf and for all God's "works" of creation and
redemption.

The Fate of the Wicked (92:5-9). God's great works are the products of profound thoughts. But the fool cannot understand that wicked troublemakers ("evildoers") are doomed because they are the enemies of God.

The Psalmist and His Enemies (92:10-11). But God has delivered the psalmist. He has made him strong like the wild ox ("horn" is a symbol of strength). God has moistened him with "fresh oil." This may refer either to the festive anointing with perfumed oil (23:5; 45:7), or to the priest's anointing of a sick man who has been healed (compare Lev. 14:10-20). The enemies, who probably gloated over the psalmist's calamity, have fallen. Both his deliverance and their downfall are grounds for thanksgiving, because they are evidence of God's moral government of the world (on retribution and reward see comment on 37, 49, 73). On the basis of his personal experience narrated in these verses, the psalmist has already spoken of the destruction of the wicked (vss. 5-9) and will now speak of the prosperity of the righteous.

The Prosperity of the Righteous (92:12-15). Various figures are used to describe this prosperity. The date palm is fruitful, and both it and the cedar of Lebanon are tall, beautiful, and long-lived. Whether trees literally grew in the Temple area or not, the righteous are said to flourish there in the presence of God. Even in old age they are fruitful and very much alive.

Psalm 93—The Lord Reigns

This is the shortest of the so-called enthronement Psalms (47, 93, 96-99; see Introduction), in which the kingship of the Lord is celebrated. The precise nature of the celebration is uncertain.

The Throne of God (93:1-2). "The LORD reigns" is translated "The LORD has become king" by those who associate this Psalm with an enthronement ceremony. They claim that God is re-enthroned as the King of the universe. The former translation is preferable, for the kingship of God which is being praised is past and future as well as present. God is pictured as an earthly monarch, robed in the garments of royalty. His "throne" or sovereignty is of old, and he himself is from eternity. His sovereignty is manifested in his stable control of the world. His reign may be celebrated by men, but all their ritual adds nothing to his stature as King.

King of Creation (93:3-4). Here we find an echo of the ancient Near Eastern story of creation when the forces of Chaos were overcome (see comment on 74:12-17; 89:9-10). This story is used figuratively to assert the Lord's kingship in creation, and, as verse 4 shows, to give assurance that he is always "mightier" than the waves of any chaos.

King in Law and Worship (93:5). Since God is King, his laws and warnings are dependable. His house is set apart for the worship of the only One of his kind.

Psalm 94—The God of Vengeance

This Psalm is composed of two major parts, a lament of the community (vss. 1-15) and a lament of an individual (vss. 16-23). The two parts have a single theme: God's judgment upon the wicked.

The Lament of the Community (94:1-15). The community appeals to God (vss. 1-3) to manifest himself as the "God of vengeance" (compare Deut. 32:35; Rom. 12:19) and the "judge of the earth" (compare 82:8; Gen. 18:25). Vengeance in the hands of God is not a matter of a personal grudge; it is the righting of wrongs and the establishing of justice. The wicked are persons of power and influence within the community. They are troublemakers ("evildoers") who are guilty of arrogance, pride, cruelty, and practical atheism (vss. 4-7). But for them to say, "The LORD does not see," is to mark themselves as dull fools, who are guilty of willful stupidity. It is absurd to think that the Creator of the ear and the eye cannot himself hear and see. It is absurd to think that the One "who chastens the nations" does not chastise the wicked within the Covenant community. The Teacher of men certainly knows the thoughts of men. According to the Hebrew text, "they" in verse 11 is masculine, agreeing with "men" rather than with "thoughts" which is feminine. However, the construction of the sentence seems to mean that human thoughts are fleeting (see I Cor. 3:20). Whatever the precise meaning of the verse, it is true to say that both men and their thoughts are "but a breath" (see 39:5).

That man is happy whom God chastens (compare Prov. 3:11-12; Heb. 12:5-6; Job 5:17) and teaches out of his Law. It is implied that God's chastisement is a part of the education of his people. "Law" probably denotes the Pentateuch but may include the whole of God's teaching of his people as it was known to the psalmist. Through the divine instruction the happy man knows that the "days of trouble" will pass and that the wicked will be destroyed.

The Lament of the Individual (94:16-23). This lament is in the spirit of an affirmation of faith. When the psalmist questions, "Who rises up for me against the wicked?" he is not at all in doubt concerning the answer. Of course the Lord rises up for him. If this had not been true in times past, he would have taken up residence in Sheol, "the land of silence" (see comment on 88:10-12). God has supported him through "steadfast love" and "consolations." Verse 20 seems to mean that "wicked rulers" (literally, "the throne of destruction"), who perpetuate evil under the cloak of legality, cannot be allied with God. They are cruel murderers (see vss. 5-6).

Psalm 95—Worship and Warning

Psalm 95 is a prophetic liturgy in which a hymn (vss. 1-7b) and a prophetic oracle (vss. 7c-11) are blended. The psalmist teaches that the people who worship God must also obey him. The occasion is one of the major festivals, perhaps the Feast of Tabernacles, in the postexilic period.

Invitation to Worship (95:1-7b). This first part is actually a double hymn (vss. 1-5, 6-7b), each subdivision being composed of a call to worship (vss. 1-2, 6) and a recital of the reason for the call (vss. 3-5, 7ab). These verses (1-7b) are sung by the worshipers under the leadership of a choir or a precentor. Verses 1-5 apparently are sung as they approach the Temple area. The worshipers encourage one another to praise the Rock of their salvation with singing, a joyful noise, and thanksgiving (vss. 1-2). The reason given for the call is that the Lord is the sovereign Creator. When the psalmist says he is "a great King above all gods," he does not mean that he believes in the existence of pagan deities. He is emphasizing the kingship of the one true God as being particularly manifest in creation.

Verses 6-7b are sung as the procession enters the gates of the Temple. This time the call to praise (vs. 6) includes an invitation to literal prostration and kneeling, which are tokens of unqualified devotion. "Maker" (vs. 6) refers primarily to God who created Israel to be the Covenant people (compare 100:3; 149:2;

51:18). In other words, creation in this case is election. This is
borne out by the reason given for the call to praise (vs. 7);
namely, that the Covenant relation between God and Israel is
like the relation between a shepherd and his sheep (see comment
on Ps. 23).

Warning Against Hardness of Heart (95:7c-11). The solo voice
of a prophet or priest takes over at this point. The singer first
addresses the people (vs. 7c), calling them to hearken to God's
voice in their time ("today"). Then he quotes the divine oracle
(vss. 8-11). God warns the people that they should not repeat
the obstinacy and unbelief of their fathers at Meribah ("con-
tention") or Massah ("testing") in the wilderness wanderings
(Exod. 17:1-7; Num. 20:1-13). The fathers mistrusted God, although they had seen his mighty work of deliverance at the
Exodus. For forty years God endured these disgusting people
who went astray in their hearts and made no real commitment to
his will (compare 81:13). As a penalty for their sin he refused
to permit them to enter the Promised Land (Num. 14:20-24:
Deut. 12:9). "Rest" in the psalmist's day included the presence
and favor of God as well as living in Canaan. These verses are
quoted, with variations, from the Septuagint translation in Hebrews 3:7-11 and are commented upon further in Hebrews 3:12—
4:13, for the purpose of warning Christians against unbelief
that would prevent them from entering the "rest" which still remains for the People of God.

Psalm 96—King and Judge

Psalms 96-99 along with Psalms 47 and 93 are frequently
classified as Psalms of the enthronement of the Lord (see Introduction). Some claim that the Psalms were used in a festival of
the enthronement of the Lord at the turn of the year in the fall,
a festival comparable to the Babylonian New Year Festival, in
which Marduk was enthroned. However, at times this theory is
so presented that the impression is given that the Lord was re-
enthroned through magic ritual, which means that man controls
God. Any such notion as this is out of harmony with known
biblical data, the theology of the Old Testament, and the thought
of the Psalms themselves.

The style and thought of Psalms 96-99 suggest that they were
written by the same man. They are closely related to Isaiah 40-66.

Three different approaches are made to the interpretation of these Psalms: the historical, the cultic, and the eschatological. In the historical, the Psalms are related to some historical event, such as the return from the Babylonian Captivity and the rebuilding of the Temple. In the cultic, stress is laid upon the significance of ritual drama. And in the eschatological, the kingship of God is seen primarily in relation to the end of the Old Age and the beginning of the New. No one of these approaches alone is adequate; the past, the present, and the future aspects of the Kingdom of God are woven together.

A Call to Praise the Lord (96:1-6). The worshiping community is summoned to "sing to the LORD a new song," and all the earth is invited to join in the singing. The Psalm itself is the "new song." God's people are to announce the glad tidings of his saving power on their behalf and declare his manifest splendor and marvelous works of creation and redemption to all peoples. For he is worthy of praise and reverence. The gods of the nations are "idols" ("things of nought"; compare 97:7; Isa. 40:18-26; 41:23-24; 44:6-8; 46:5-8). But in contrast to these impotent idols is the Lord who made the heavens. "Honor and majesty" are personified as his constant attendants, and "strength and beauty" characterize his earthly Temple.

A Missionary Invitation (96:7-9). Imaginatively and in the spirit of the great Prophet of the Exile (Isa. 40-66), the psalmist invites the families of the nations to worship Israel's God. The presence of Jews and converts at the festival in Jerusalem is prophetic of the eventual turning of the nations to the Lord. As the worshipers "bring an offering," so the peoples of the nations shall one day show their submission to God. Those participating in the festival are to be clothed in garments free from ceremonial uncleanness (see Lev. 11:24-28) and appropriate to the occasion.

The Universal Judgment of the King (96:10-13). The worshiping people are to proclaim the universal reign of God. This proclamation is sometimes associated with God's return to Zion in glory after the return of his people from the Babylonian Captivity and the rebuilding of the Temple (Isa. 52:7). This association is supported by a part of the Psalm's title in the Septuagint, "When the house was built after the Captivity." As God manifested his kingship in the past by making the heavens (vs. 5), he now manifests it in his dependable government of the world. But his Kingdom shall come in its fullness as he executes his

final judgment in righteousness and truth. Since the consummation of God's Kingdom is thought to include a transformation of
nature as well as of human nature (see Isa. 11:6-10; 35:1-10;
55:12-13; Rom. 8:19-25), the heavens, the earth, the sea, the
field, and the trees are all exhorted to join in the praise of the
Lord who is both King and Judge.

Psalm 97—The Lord of All the Earth

For the theories concerning the setting of this Psalm see the
comments on Psalms 47, 93, and 96, and the Introduction.

The Reigning King (97:1-5). The announcement is made:
"The LORD reigns," and in response all the earth and the many
islands and coastlands of the sea are called upon to rejoice
("coastlands" may also mean "islands"). This emphasis upon
world-wide praise looks to the future fulfillment of God's dominion. However, the reign of God is not wholly future. Though
God comes in mystery, righteousness and justice are the foundations of his Kingdom. "Clouds," "thick darkness," "fire," and
"lightnings" are expressions taken from the accounts of God's
former appearances to his people (Exod. 13:21-22; 19:16-18),
to symbolize his presence among them now and his coming in
future glory. His power is so great that mountains melt before
him like wax (compare Micah 1:4; Nahum 1:5).

The Exalted Lord (97:6-9). God's works in creation and in
history have been made manifest to the world. Yet there are
those who worship carved "images," which are nothing but
"worthless idols" (compare Jer. 10:14; Isa. 42:17; 44:9). They
will be put to shame. All the members of the heavenly court
("gods") worship the Lord (compare Heb. 1:6). Jerusalem and
her daughter cities and towns of Judah rejoice concerning God's
judgments in historical events. Some specific recent events may
be in the psalmist's mind. God is exalted "over all the earth" and
"far above" all the members of the heavenly court ("gods").

The Joyous People (97:10-12). The psalmist has moved from
his thought of the universal praise of God and the coming of the
end of the age (vss. 1-5) to a concern for blessings upon the
righteous remnant of the Covenant people in the present time.
These blessings include preservation of life, the gift of light and
joy, and deliverance from the wicked. "Light" is almost a synonym for blessing, since it embraces life (36:9), prosperity (Job

29:3), joy (as the parallelism of this verse shows), and enlightenment of the heart.

Psalm 98—Savior, King, and Judge

This is the only one of the "enthronement Psalms" (see comment on Ps. 96) which does not contain the statement, "The LORD [or God] reigns." However, it does contain the noun "King" (vs. 6). Verses 1-3 reflect a specific historical situation, probably deliverance from the Babylonian Exile.

Praise to the Savior (98:1-3). God's marvelous deeds call forth this new song of praise. The verb "have gotten victory" is the verb "to save" in Hebrew. In verse 2 the noun "victory" or "salvation" is from the same root. "Vindication" is literally "righteousness." God's victory over the enemies of his people was a saving work by which he revealed his redemptive righteousness (compare Isa. 51:6; Rom. 3:21-26). The parallelism of verse 2 shows that salvation ("victory") and righteousness ("vindication") are almost synonyms.

God's victory demonstrates that he has been faithful to his Covenant relation with Israel. People in the extreme parts of the earth have witnessed his victory. The return from Babylon seems to be at least a partial fulfillment of the promise made in Isaiah 52:10. At the same time it is the pledge of complete salvation at the end of the Old Age and the beginning of the New.

Praise to the King (98:4-6). By his victory God has manifested his kingship anew. All the earth is summoned to join Israel in praise to its Sovereign. Both stringed and wind instruments accompany the singing in the Temple. "Trumpets" were slender tubes made of silver, and "the horn" was usually an instrument made from a ram's horn. Verses 4-6 are a salute to the Heavenly King apparently patterned after the acclamation of a newly installed human king (see I Kings 1:39; II Kings 11:12, 14).

Praise to the Judge (98:7-9). Not only has God revealed his kingship in the past by delivering his people (vss. 1-3) and not only is he King at the present moment (vs. 6), but he will bring his Kingdom to its fulfillment when he executes his final judgment—a judgment of condemnation for the wicked, but a judgment of salvation for the righteous. Nature, as represented by the sea, the rivers ("floods"), and hills, is bidden to join with men in praise to the universal Judge (compare 96:11-13).

Psalm 99—The Holy God

This is the last of the "enthronement Psalms" (see introduction to 96). It centers in the holiness of God as that holiness is expressed through God's reigning, executing justice, and exercising forgiveness and vengeance. The refrain which marks the divisions of the Psalm (vss. 3, 5, 9) is progressively lengthened.

The Universal Sovereign (99:1-3). The announcement, "The LORD reigns," is followed by a summons to tremble (see Isa. 64:2; compare Ps. 97:1). Joy and deep reverence are complementary, not contradictory (see vs. 3). (For the possible interpretations of the phrase, "enthroned upon the cherubim," see the comment on 80:1.) The quaking of the earth is nature's counterpart to the trembling of the peoples. Zion is regarded as the religious capital of the world, from which God's sovereignty extends "over all the peoples."

The Executer of Justice (99:4-5). The translation of verse 4a is a free conjecture, but its meaning is not essentially different from a literal translation: "And the King's strength loves justice." In his dealings with Israel, God has executed justice and righteousness. Therefore, the Covenant people are to have a distinctive role in praising God and worshiping at his "footstool." "Footstool" is variously used as a figure for the earth (Isa. 66:1), the Ark of the Covenant (I Chron. 28:2), and, as here, the Temple (132:7; Lam. 2:1; Isa. 60:13).

The Forgiver and the Avenger (99:6-9). Through historical retrospect God's people are encouraged to pray and are warned against wrongdoing. Moses and Aaron are numbered among the Levites (Exod. 2:1-10; 4:14), but this is the only passage in the Old Testament where Moses is specifically called a priest. Nevertheless, he frequently performed priestly acts (for example, Exod. 24:6-8; 40:22-27; Lev. 8). The stress in this passage, however, is upon the priestly ministry of intercession and mediation carried on by Moses (Exod. 14:15-18; 17:11-13; 32:30-34), Aaron (Num. 16:44-48), and Samuel (I Sam. 7:8-11; 12:16-23). According to the Law, God speaks to Moses (Exod. 33:9) and Aaron (Num. 12:5) "in the pillar of cloud," but no such reference is made to Samuel in the Historical Books.

The thought of the Psalm moves almost imperceptibly from God's answer to the prayers of these great religious leaders to his answer to the prayers of his people (vs. 8). The mention of God's forgiveness and vengeance refers primarily to the repeated lesson of Israel's history. Forgiveness brings restoration of fellowship with God but it does not abolish all the consequences of sin (see Num. 14:20-25; II Sam. 12:1-23). God both punishes and pardons. The Covenant people are summoned to worship the Holy God on "his holy mountain," for he will be faithful in every generation to what he has revealed himself to be.

Psalm 100—Old Hundredth

Apparently verses 1-3 were sung by a procession of worshipers as they approached the gates of the Temple to sacrifice the thank offering (Lev. 7:11-18), and verses 4-5 were sung in response by a choral group already within the Temple. The expression "thank offering" in the title of the Psalm may also be translated "thanksgiving" (vs. 4) or "praise." This Psalm is a great hymn of praise whose structure gives the impression of the combination of two shorter hymns—verses 1-3 and verses 4-5. In each case there is a call to praise followed by the reasons for the call. These reasons constitute a confession of faith. In verse 3 they include: (1) "the LORD is God," (2) he is our Creator, and (3) we are his Covenant people. In verse 5 they include (1) "the LORD is good," (2) his steadfast love is eternal, and (3) his faithfulness endures to all generations. The thought of the Psalm is similar to that of Psalm 95. The famous metrical rendering known. as "Old Hundredth" was first published in the sixteenth century.

The First Call to Praise (100:1-3). The call is to a quality of worship that overflows with joyous singing. The biblical faith is a singing faith and is characterized by abundant joy (compare Phil. 4:4-13; John 15:11; 16:22-24, 33). The word translated "lands" is literally "earth" or "land." It is possible that the entire human race is called to join with the postexilic Jews in the worship of the one true God, but the call is primarily to those who acknowledge themselves to be the Lord's people.

Verse 3 contains an affirmation of monotheism. Israel's God is the one true God. He is the Creator of his people in every sense of the word, but the psalmist here stresses God's creative activity in the choice of Israel to be his special possession (see Deut. 7:6-11). The Covenant relation between God and his

people is expressed in terms of the relation of the shepherd and
his sheep (compare 23; 80:1).

The Second Call to Praise (100:4-5). Verse 4 parallels verses
1-2 in thought. "Steadfast love" and "faithfulness" are virtually
synonyms which express God's loving dependability to each succeeding generation of his people.

Psalm 101—A King's Mirror

This is a mirror in which a Davidic king sees not so much
what he actually is as what he ought to be. Its principles are
applicable to all persons in authority in any age, and emphasize
the rooting of political ethics in religious commitment.

The Source of the King's Ethics (101:1-2b). The king sings of
"loyalty" (usually translated "steadfast love") and "justice," for
he knows that the Lord is their source. He commits himself to
the blameless way, because it is patterned on the character of
God. True worship and godly behavior are inseparable. The
king longs for an even closer walk with God (vs. 2b).

The King's Personal Ethics (101:2c-4). The king pledges himself to a godly morality from the inside out. He hates the work of
those who are unfaithful to God. Crookedness of heart he will
spurn, and he will not choose (or borrow) evil.

The King's Administrative Principles (101:5-8). The king does
not attempt to compartmentalize his ethics. He realizes that he
is accountable to the same God in the privacy of his house and
in the administration of his public responsibilities. He will not
tolerate the slanderer, the proud, the deceitful, or the liar, especially as a servant in the royal palace. Rather will he search out
men from among "the faithful in the land" to assist him. Every
morning he will hold court and see that justice is done. By this
process he will seek to purge Jerusalem of wicked men, that it
may increasingly become "the city of the LORD."

Psalm 102—Lament and Hymn Combined

This is one of the seven laments of the individual which have
been regarded by the Church as penitentials (6, 32, 38, 51, 102,
130, 143). In this case the note of penitence is more implicit
than explicit. Verses 12-22 are a fragment of a song of Zion used
by the psalmist as a source of encouragement in his distress.

The Psalmist's Distress (102:1-11). After the openirg appeal
to be heard (vss. 1-2), the psalmist describes his condition. He
likens his days to smoke, because smoke disappears suddenly
(compare 37:20). His very being ("bones") is burning with
fever. Vigor of life and appetite for food are gone, and his body
is emaciated. He makes his sense of loneliness vivid by the references to lonely birds. Enemies taunt him and even use his name
in their formulas for cursing others. He considers his distress as
the result of God's indignation.

The Eternal King of Zion (102:12-22). Here the psalmist finds
strength by lifting his eyes to God as the Lord of Zion and
thereby placing his problem in the setting of God's purpose for
his people. These verses seem to come from the time of the
Babylonian Exile. God as the eternal King will now show favor
to his people by returning them to Zion, thereby inspiring fear
among the nations. This act will be performed "so that a people
yet unborn [literally, "yet to be created"] may praise the LORD"
(compare 22:31; Isa. 43:21). On verse 20 see the comment on
79:11. Verse 22 is a prophetic vision of the gathering of the
peoples "to worship the LORD" (see vs. 15; 22:27; 67:7; 96:7;
Isa. 2:2-4; 60:3).

Return to the Psalmist's Distress (102:23-28). The psalmist
now returns to his distress and pleads that God, whose years
endure, will not let him die prematurely. God created the world,
which is sometimes spoken of as enduring (78:69; 104:5; Eccl.
1:4); and it is enduring in contrast to the life span of a man who
lives in it. But in contrast with the eternal God even the heavens
and the earth will pass away (compare Isa. 34:4; 51:6; Matt.
24:35). In Hebrews 1:10-12, verses 25-27 are quoted from the
Septuagint and applied to Christ as the agent of creation. "Thou
art the same" is literally "Thou art he," meaning that God always is, and is always adequate to the situation. Whether his
request is granted or not, the psalmist finds his peace in the
eternal God who will be the security of future generations.

Psalm 103—Bless the Lord, O My Soul

This Psalm is an individual's grateful praise to God expressed
in the form of a hymn. When it was first used in public worship,
it may well have been rendered as a solo.

Praise for Personal Blessings (103:1-5). The psalmist calls upon

his whole being to its deepest recesses to praise God with gratitude. To "bless his holy name" is essentially to "bless the LORD,"
since his name stands for all that he has revealed himself to be
in his holiness or "godness." The benefits for which the psalmist
is particularly grateful are forgiveness, healing, redemption from
premature death, the royal crown of steadfast love and mercy,
and the renewal of life. God is the Great Physician who ministers
to the whole man. "Pit" is a synonym for Sheol. The eagle is
used as a figure of renewal both because it is long-lived and because it molts annually.

Praise for National Blessings (103:6-18). The goodness of God
to the psalmist is of a piece with his goodness to the nation.
Therefore, the call to "bless the LORD" is made with these national blessings in mind also: "vindication [literally, "righteousness"] and justice for all who are oppressed," the revelation of
his activity and character to Moses and Israel, his gracious forgiveness of sins (see vs. 3), his fatherly compassion for his children, and his enduring Covenant love and righteousness to those
who maintain the Covenant relation with him (see Exod. 20:6;
Deut. 7:9). Verse 7a recalls Moses' prayer in Exodus 33:13,
and verse 8 is based on the answer to that prayer in Exodus 34:6.
God punished the people of Israel for their sins, but not as much
as they deserved. The figure of a father and his children is one
way the Covenant relation is expressed in the Old Testament
(see Exod. 4:22; Isa. 1:2; Hosea 11:1). The statement of human
frailty in verse 14 echoes Genesis 2:7.

Praise from All Creation (103:19-22). Though God is sometimes thought of as dwelling among his people, his throne is "in
the heavens" (compare 11:4; 93:2) and his kingship or "kingdom" is universal. Therefore, "angels" (see 29:1; 148:2) or
"mighty ones," other members of the heavenly assembly, and
all the other parts and powers of creation are summoned to join
in the anthem of universal praise. Then, as the "Hallelujah
Chorus" of heaven and earth fades into the background, the
Psalm ends as it began with the voice of one deeply grateful man
of God, "Bless the LORD, O my soul!"

Psalm 104—The Glory of the Creator

This is one of the four hymns of the Psalter which center in
praise to God as the Lord of creation (8; 19:1-6; 29; 104). For

this reason it is assigned by some to the celebration of the New Year Festival. The author seems to have been acquainted with various accounts of creation current in the Near East of his day: Babylonian, Egyptian, Persian, Canaanite, and Genesis 1 or its prototype. Outside the parallels with Genesis 1, the most distinctive parallels are those found between verses 20-30 and the hymn to the sun composed by the Egyptian Pharaoh Amenhotep IV (Akhnaton), 1370-1353 B.C. These parallels do not prove direct literary dependence, for the differences between the two hymns are even more striking than the similarities. For example, in the hymn of Akhnaton the sun is the creator, but in the Psalm the sun is one part of the Lord's creation. Whatever the Psalm's literary relationships may be, its author used his wide knowledge as a servant of the Lord, the one true God.

The Heavens (104:1-4). The psalmist begins with the summons to himself also found at the beginning and the end of the preceding Psalm. He pictures God as clothed in the royal attributes of honor and majesty. The remaining verses in this section center around his activity in relation to the heavens. Light is the King's mantle; according to Genesis 1:3 it was the first element created. It is the basis of life, the source of joy, and the symbol of deity both revealed and hidden on account of its dazzling brilliance (see Exod. 3:2; Isa. 60:1; John 1:5; I John 1:5; I Tim. 6:16; Rev. 21:23). God stretched out the heavens as easily as a man stretches out a tent curtain, and laid in the waters below the beams which support the heavenly chambers (compare Amos 9:6). For the significance of God's making the clouds his chariot, see the comment on Psalm 68:4 (compare 18:10; Deut. 33:26; Isa. 19:1; Dan. 7:13; Matt. 24:30; Acts 1:9). God makes wind and fire his servants (see the Septuagint reading of verse 4 in Hebrews 1:7).

The Earth (104:5-9). The establishment of the earth and its separation from the waters is the theme of this section (compare Gen. 1:9-10). The psalmist's language reflects a knowledge of the ancient Babylonian and Canaanite stories of creation, in which creation is the result of a struggle (see comment on 74:12-17). But the psalmist has discarded the theology of the stories, for he depicts no struggle at all. The one true God speaks and the waters covering the earth recede to their appointed bounds. The language here is similar to that used in describing the Flood in Genesis 7:19-20: 9:11-15.

The Water (104:10-13). By stream-forming springs and rain God provides the necessary water for animals, birds, and man. There is no exact parallel for these verses in Genesis 1, but in Genesis 2:5-6 the two major water sources are recognized. According to the ancient Semitic world view, rain came from the storerooms of heaven.

Vegetation (104:14-18). These verses parallel Genesis 1:11-12. God provides grass for cattle; food-producing plants, wine, olive oil, and bread (the same word as "food" in verse 14) for man; and trees for birds. Verse 18 is not on the subject of vegetation, but shows how God has provided even for undomesticated animals. Grain, grapes, and olives were the principal products of Palestine.

The Moon and the Sun (104:19-23). The moon and the sun were worshiped as deities by many of Israel's neighbors, but to the psalmist they are creations of the Lord (compare Gen. 1:14-19). The moon is especially important because it marks the times for the religious festivals. Night is mentioned before daylight because the Hebrew day began in the evening (see Gen. 1:5, 8, 13, 19, 23, 31). Darkness is a part of God's providential ordering, that the wild beasts, including the young lions, may seek their food. God ordained daytime for man to work.

The Sea (104:24-26). Verse 24 is a general statement about God's works (compare Prov. 3:19; 8:22-31). Verses 25-26 are in part parallel to Genesis 1:20-21. In addition to the innumerable things with which the sea teems, the psalmist thinks also of the man-made ships which excite his wonder. In the Old Testament the meaning of "Leviathan" varies. Sometimes it refers to a dragon (see Isa. 27:1 and the comment on Ps. 74:12-17), sometimes to the crocodile (Job 41, see margin), and, as here, sometimes to a huge marine animal (Job 3:8).

Life (104:27-30). "These all" is a reference to all the creatures which the psalmist has mentioned, including man. God provides for all their needs (compare 145:15-16; 147:9; Gen. 1:29-30). The hiding of God's face means here the withdrawal of his sustaining grace. When God withdraws the breath he gave them (see Job 27:3), his creatures die (Job 34:14-15; Eccl. 12:7) and "return to their dust" (see 103:14; Gen. 2:7). But God sends forth his creative Spirit to renew the earth with new life.

Praise to the Creator (104:31-35). The psalmist concludes with a doxology. He expresses the desire that the glory of God seen in creation may continue into the indefinite future, and that God may find joyous satisfaction in his work (see Gen. 1:31; Prov. 8:31). Yet, he remembers the awesome fact that the Creator can destroy the world he has made (vs. 32; compare Amos 9:5; Ps. 144:5). As God rejoices in his work, the psalmist rejoices in God (compare Phil. 4:4-7). Verse 35 is the psalmist's way of praying that God will remove all the disharmony from his creation. "Praise the LORD" is the Hebrew "Hallelujah."

Psalm 105—God of the Covenant

Psalm 105 belongs among the hymns in which God is praised as the Lord of history. It is closely related to Psalms 78 and 106 in content, but, unlike these Psalms, it contains no mention of Israel's sins. The purpose of the Psalm is to praise the Lord as God of the Covenant in a ceremony of Covenant renewal. The psalmist makes use of much of the material in Genesis 12 through Exodus 17. Verses 1-15 are quoted by the chronicler in I Chronicles 16 together with Psalm 96 and three verses from Psalm 106, as representative of the thanksgiving sung on the occasion of David's transferring the Ark to Zion.

Summons to Grateful Praise (105:1-6). The People of God are summoned to proclaim God's marvelous deeds to the nations (compare 9:11) and to praise him with joy and gratitude as they remember his marvelous work in their behalf (see Deut. 7:18; 8:2) and his "judgments" (see Exod. 6:6; 7:4; 12:12). The designation of the worshiping community as "offspring of Abraham his servant, sons of Jacob, his chosen ones" (vs. 6) lays stress upon election to privilege (see vs. 43), service, and obedience (see vs. 45).

The Patriarchs (105:7-25). The psalmist now spells out God's deeds in the patriarchal period. Though he stresses the fact that God is ever mindful of the Covenant and promises (compare Lev. 26:42-45) made with Abraham (see Gen. 12:7; 13:14-18; 15: 18; 17:1-14; 22:16-18), Isaac (Gen. 26:3), and Jacob (Gen. 28:13-14; 35:9-12), he does not forget that God is also the Judge of all the earth (vs. 7).

When the patriarchs and their families were few and lived a seminomadic life in Ur, Haran, Canaan, Egypt, and Philistia, God protected them (see Gen. 12:10-20; 20; 26:11). The patriarchs are called "anointed ones" (a word ordinarily used in the

singular of a king or priest) because they were set apart by God
as instruments of his plan of salvation. They are designated
"prophets" because Abraham is so designated in Genesis 20:7,
as one called to be the channel of God's message of world-wide
blessing.

The famine in Canaan in the time of Jacob (Gen. 41:54) is
considered an act of God (compare II Kings 8:1; Haggai 1:11).
The expression "staff of bread" (see Lev. 26:26; Ezek. 4:16)
carries the same meaning as our present-day reference to bread
as "the staff of life." Joseph was sent ahead to Egypt as a slave
and tested by the word of promise, which had come through
dreams in his youth (see Gen. 37:5-11), until the promise was
fulfilled by his exaltation at the hand of Pharaoh (Gen. 41).

Jacob and his family sojourned in Egypt (see Gen. 46:1—
Exod. 1:22), which is also called "the land of Ham" because in
the table of the nations (Gen. 10) Egypt is listed as one of the
sons of Ham (compare 78:51). Through his blessings upon the
Israelites, God caused the Egyptians to hate them and thereby
to prepare the way for the Exodus (see Exod. 1:8-22).

Moses and the Exodus (105:26-42). Moses and Aaron, just as
Abraham and the Israelites as a whole (vss. 6, 43), were elected
by God for special service as leaders. Through them God sent the
plagues upon the Egyptians. Only eight of the plagues are listed,
and their order differs from that found in Exodus 7-12 (compare
Ps. 78).

When the Exodus took place, the Israelites took spoils in com-
pensation for long-enforced slavery (Exod. 12:35-36). On account of the plagues, the Egyptians were glad to see them leave
(Exod. 12:33). In Exodus 13:21-22 the pillar of cloud and the
pillar of fire are the symbols of God's presence and guidance.
Here (vs. 39) the cloud is considered a protection against the
desert sun (compare Isa. 4:5-6). Because the murmurings of the
people do not contribute to the psalmist's purpose, he omits any
direct reference to them, and simply says, "They asked . . ."
(vs. 40); and in answer God gave the quails, the manna, and the
water (see comment on 78:18-31). God did all the wonderful
things mentioned in the preceding verses because "he remembered his holy promise to Abraham his servant" (a better translation of vs. 42; compare vs. 9; Exod. 2:24).

The Purpose of God's Blessings (105:43-45). God delivered his
Chosen People with joyous singing (see Exod. 15) and gave

them the lands of the peoples living in Canaan, to the end that
they should obey his laws (compare 78:7; Deut. 4:1, 40; 26:17-
18). Privilege enjoins a corresponding responsibility (see Amos
3:2; Luke 12:48).

Psalm 106—God's Grace and Israel's Sin

This Psalm combines characteristics of the hymn and the lament of the community. The introduction (vss. 1-5) and the allusions to God's mighty acts in Israel's history tend to identify it
as a hymn in praise of the Lord of history. But for the most part,
the narration of Israel's history from the Exodus to the settle-
ment in Canaan is presented as a lamenting confession of sin.
This use of Israel's history is also found in Psalm 78; Ezra 9:6-
15; Nehemiah 9:5-37; and Daniel 9:4-19. The kind of setting
appropriate for the use of Psalm 106 is depicted in I Kings 8:
44-53. While there was a dispersion as early as the eighth century B.C. after the fall of the Northern Kingdom, it is probable
that the reference in verse 47 is to the scattering in the postexilic
period.

Introduction (106:1-5). The introduction is composed of a brief
call to praise (vss. 1-3; compare 107:1; 118:1; 136:1) and a
personal petition of the psalmist (vss. 4-5). God's Covenant love
is the ground of Israel's hope, and in view of what is to follow
in the Psalm, Israel certainly needs that ground. Verse 2 implies
that no one can adequately praise God for his mighty acts, yet by
indirection the psalmist does praise God for the manifestations
of his grace to his undeserving people. Nevertheless, those are
accounted particularly happy who obey God's will (vs. 3). In
verses 4-5 the psalmist prays that he may be permitted to share
in the future restoration of the fortunes of his people.

A Confession of Israel's Sin (106:6-46). Verse 6 is the theme
of the next forty verses. The translation of the Revised Standard
Version is true as far as it goes: the Israel of the present and the
Israel of the past have both been perverse and have deserved to
be cut off from the Covenant (this is the implication of the verb
"have done wickedly"). But the literal translation of the Hebrew,
"We have sinned with our fathers," seems to mean more. In a
sense, all generations of Israelites came out of Egypt at the Exodus, just as all Christians were present "when they crucified my
Lord." This means that the Israel of the psalmist's day shares in

both the sins of the fathers and God's blessings upon them. The Scripture passages cited are the best commentary on the sins that are listed below:

1. Rebellion at the Red Sea—106:6-12 (compare Exod. 14: 10—15:1).

2. Murmuring for the fleshpots of Egypt—106:13-15 (compare Num. 11:1-35; Exod. 15:22—17:7).

3. Jealousy toward Moses and Aaron—106:16-18 (compare Num. 16; Deut. 11:6). Korah was also involved in this incident with Dathan and Abiram but the psalmist does not mention him, perhaps because he is not mentioned in Deuteronomy 11:6 or because his sons did not die (Num. 26:11).

4. Making and worshiping the golden calf—106:19-23 (compare Exod. 32:1-35; Deut. 9:8-21). "Horeb" (vs. 19) is the name for Sinai in Deuteronomy. "The glory of God" is literally "their glory"; that is, God is his people's glory, but they traded it for the likeness of an animal (see 3:3; Jer. 2:11; Rom. 1:23). The calf was set up to represent God, not to take his place, but God would have no such representation. On "the land of Ham" (vs. 22) see comment on 105:23. To present Moses' intercession for the wayward people, the psalmist pictures him as a soldier standing in the breach of a city wall to repulse the enemy at the peril of losing his life.

5. Unbelief and disobedience after the return of the spies— 106:24-27 (compare Num. 13-14). Verse 27 reflects the warnings of Leviticus 26:33 and Deuteronomy 28:64 and the fulfillment of the warning in the dispersion of the psalmist's own day.

6. Participation in Moabite worship—106:28-31 (compare Num. 25:1-18; Exod. 34:15). "Peor" was a place in Moab where a particular Baal was worshiped. "Sacrifices offered to the dead" may mean that the gods of the Moabites were dead (see 115: 4-8), or that offerings for the use of dead persons were left in their tombs or at their graves (see Deut. 26:14).

7. Murmuring at Meribah—106:32-33 (compare Num. 20:1-13). Not only did the people murmur at Meribah, but even Moses sinned on account of the people and was forbidden entrance to the Promised Land (Num. 20:12; Deut. 3:26-27). For a leader, sin comes at a very high price. Moses' sin seems to have been a combination of unbelief (Num. 20:12), irreverence (Deut. 32: 51), rebellion (Num. 27:14), bitterness (106:33), and rashness (106:33).

8. Pollution through sharing in Canaanite practices—106:34-39. The Israelites failed to exterminate the Canaanites as God had commanded them (Deut. 7:2, 16; 20:16-18; Judges 1:21—2:5). This command is difficult to interpret, but can be at least partially understood if the following facts are remembered: (1) At the outset of Israel's history God was working with rough, semi-nomadic tribes; (2) in order to carry out his purpose both for Israel and for the world, a land was needed; (3) the Canaanites were wicked and their religion degrading (Deut. 9:4-5); (4) God also punished the Israelites themselves severely for their sins throughout their history.

The Israelites became contaminated by Canaanite idolatry (Judges 2:11-12), even to the point of practicing child sacrifice (see II Kings 3:27; 16:3-4; 21:6, 16; compare Deut. 12:31; 18:9-10) to "demons" (some kind of inferior spiritual beings; see Deut. 32:17). Thus Israel was unfaithful to her marriage vow (vs. 39).

9. Repeated disobedience in the period of the Judges—106:40-46 (compare the Book of Judges). The psalmist has the period of the Judges primarily in mind, but he does not confine his thought to that time. He sets forth the repeated sequence which has characterized Israel's history: rebellion, chastisement, cry for help, pardon, and deliverance.

Concluding Prayer for Restoration (106:47). The people have forgotten the Covenant (vss. 7, 13, 21), but the gracious God remembers (vs. 45). Therefore, the psalmist and his people can pray that he will gather the dispersed of Israel, that his people may unitedly offer their praise to him. Verse 48 is the doxology closing Book IV of the Psalter.

BOOK V—PSALMS 107-150

Psalm 107—The Redeemed of the Lord

Psalm 107 is composed of three parts: a call to thanksgiving (vss. 1-3); a litany of thanksgiving by four groups of redeemed pilgrims: desert travelers, prisoners, sick men, and seafarers (vss. 4-32); and a wisdom hymn on the providence of God (vss. 33-43). Each thought division in part two is characterized by a

double refrain (vss. 6 and 8, 13 and 15, 19 and 21, 28 and 31),
which suggests some kind of antiphonal rendering in which each
of the four groups mentioned above participated in turn.

Invitation to Thanksgiving (107:1-3). The invitation begins
with the words also found in the preceding Psalm (compare Jer.
33:11) and is addressed to "the redeemed of the LORD" (see Isa.
62:12). These are the particular groups listed in verses 4-32, who
have been brought together from the four points of the compass
to worship God in the Temple.

The Gratitude of the Redeemed (107:4-32). Each of the four
divisions in this litany is made up of three elements: a description of the group's trouble (vss. 4-5, 10-12, 17-18, 23-27), the
record of their cry to God and his deliverance of them (vss. 6-7,
13-14, 19-20, 28-30), and a summons to thanksgiving (vss. 8-9,
15-16, 21-22, 31-32). The following groups express their gratitude
in turn.

1. Desert travelers who had lost their way (vss. 4-9).

2. Literal prisoners or exiles in the postexilic time (Isa. 42:7)
who had been punished for rebelling against God (vss. 10-16).

3. Sick men whose sickness had been a punishment for rebellion (the literal meaning of "sinful ways") and "iniquities" (vss.
17-22). The word "sick" (vs. 17) in Hebrew is very similar in
appearance to the word "fools." The context here makes it clear
that sickness is involved (vs. 18; compare Job 33:20). However,
"fools" may be correct, since folly is a type of sin. In Old Testament times sickness was ordinarily thought to be the direct consequence of sin. Although this view is not the whole truth (see
Job), many a sick person needs to have his sins forgiven more
than he needs anything else (compare Ps. 32). God's mighty
word of healing is almost personified as an agent (vs. 20; compare 147:15; Isa. 55:11). The "sacrifices of thanksgiving" (vs.
22) were of two kinds: those offered in fulfillment of a vow
made in the time of distress, and those offered altogether volun-
tarily.

4. Seafarers who had been caught in a storm (vss. 23-32).
God is presented as the Master of nature as he both produces and
calms the storm (see Mark 4:35-41).

Meditation on God's Providence (107:33-43). God is Lord of
nature and men. He smites fertile lands with barrenness on account of human sin and transforms desert lands into a fruitful
dwelling place for the hungry (vss. 33-38; compare Isa. 42:15

and 50:2 with verse 33, and Isa. 41:18 with verse 35). When
the needy are oppressed and brought low, he raises them up and
pours contempt upon their wicked oppressors (vss. 39-43; compare Job 12:21, 24 with verse 40, and Job 22:19 with verse 42).

Psalm 108—A New Combination

With only minor variations verses 1-5 are identical with
Psalm 57:7-11, and verses 6-13 are identical with Psalm 60:5-12.
Apparently the compiler formed Psalm 108 by borrowing from
these two Psalms. However, he may have borrowed them from
sources also used by the authors of Psalms 57 and 60.

Psalm 109—Curse and Blessing

Perhaps Psalm 109 is the best known of the imprecations because of the severity of its curses. The crux of interpretation is
the identification of the speaker in verses 6-19. Is it the psalmist
who speaks in verses 1-5 and 20-31? Or is it the psalmist's enemies, whose imprecation against him he quotes as a part of his
own lament to God? The position taken here is that verses 6-19
are a quotation of the curse placed upon the psalmist by his
enemies (compare 2:3; 41:5; 52:7). The reasons for this are
not theological, for the psalmists have already given evidence of
their ability to curse their enemies (for example, 35:4-8; 58:6-9;
59:11-13; 69:22-28; 83:9-17; compare Jer. 11:18-20; 15:15; 17:
18; 18:19-23; on imprecation see Introduction). The reasons are
grammatical, logical, and textual. First, the psalmist's enemies
are referred to in the plural in verses 1-5; suddenly only one
man is being cursed (vss. 6-19); and equally suddenly the psalmist's enemies are referred to in the plural again (vss. 20-31). Second, the imprecations which are admittedly the psalmist's own
(vss. 28-29) are so mild in comparison with those in verses 6-19
that they would be weak and anticlimactic if the psalmist were the
original speaker in 6-19. Third, there is good support for translat-
ing verse 20 as follows: "This is the work of those who hate the
LORD and speak evil against my life." In other words, the word
"work" is a reference to the enemies' imprecation quoted in verses
6-19. Fourth, "Let them curse" (vs. 28) is more easily understood in this interpretation.

Opening Appeal for Help (109:1-5). The psalmist appeals to

God for defense against wicked enemies who accuse him falsely and, in base ingratitude, reward him "evil for good" and hate for love (compare 35:12; 38:20; Jer. 18:20).

Imprecation Upon the Psalmist (109:6-19). This imprecation requires little comment. The psalmist's enemies wish to have him tried and found guilty and even request that "his prayer be counted as sin." They seek his premature death and pray that another may "seize his goods" (vs. 8). The word "goods" may mean "office," and it is so translated in Acts 1:20 where verse 8b is applied to Judas. The concept of social solidarity involved a man's family in his sins and their consequences and involved him in the sins of his forebears (compare 37:28, 38; 51:5; 69:28; Exod. 20:5; 22:24; Matt. 23:32-36). The psalmist is accused of persecuting the needy and cursing them with black magic. Therefore his enemies pray that his curse may cleave to him like a garment and soak in like water and oil. Oil was used as a medicine (Isa. 1:6) and as a luxurious unguent (Amos 6:6).

Appeal for Help Resumed (109:20-29). The psalmist grounds his appeal in God's steadfast love and in his own predicament. He is about to disappear as the evening shadow or as a locust "shaken off" one's clothes. "Shaken off" may be translated "tossed," referring to the locust's disappearance in a stormy wind (see Exod. 10:19; Joel 2:20). The psalmist is gaunt from lack of food and illness, and is "an object of scorn" to his accusers. But no matter how much they curse, God's blessing is all that ultimately matters (vs. 28).

Vow of Thanksgiving (109:30-31). Assurance is granted the psalmist that he will be delivered, and he vows to thank God "in the midst of the throng" of worshipers in the Temple.

Psalm 110—The Priest King

This royal Psalm was probably written by a court poet in the early pre-exilic period to celebrate the enthronement of a new Davidic king. However, the poet of necessity would have had in mind not only the king of the moment but also the succession of kings in the House of David. This fact, together with the poet's exalted language, made it inevitable that the Psalm should eventually be interpreted in relation to the Messiah par excellence of the future, for no Old Testament king measured up to the expectations aroused by the psalmist. God in his overarching providence has a way of tying one historical event into another in such a way that the two events become one elongated event. In fact, the biblical story of salvation is God's way of tying many revelatory events into One Saving Event, Jesus Christ.

Psalm 110 is more frequently quoted or alluded to in the New Testament than any other Psalm, and it is always interpreted messianically (see footnotes in the Revised Standard Version). Its thought centers around the two oracles (vss. 1, 4) printed within quotation marks. The first division of the Psalm presents the king who is also priest (vss. 1-3), and the second the priest who is also king (vss. 4-7). These are two ways of saying the same thing.

The King Who Is Priest (110:1-3). Verse 1a is literally, "The oracle of the LORD to my lord." This means that the court poet delivers a prophetic oracle to his lord the king (see I Kings 1:13). The oracle itself is the remainder of verse 1. The king is instructed to sit at God's right hand because that is the place of honor (see 45:9; I Kings 2:19; Matt. 20:21). "Till I make your enemies your footstool" is a figurative way of promising the subjugation of the king's enemies (see Joshua 10:24; I Kings 5:3; I Cor. 15:25). In the original setting of the Psalm, this promise was of necessity understood in relation to a strong sense of Israelite nationalism, but in its fulfillment in the exaltation of Christ it is entirely stripped of its nationalism. Yet God's sovereignty is the source of all sovereignty (Rom. 13:1).

The poet continues his encouraging address to his king (vss. 2-3). By the power and will of the "LORD," the king rules in the midst of his foes from Zion. "Scepter" is the emblem of power and authority. Verse 3 should be translated as follows:

> Your people are freewill offerings
> on the day of your valor
> in holy array.
> From the womb of the morning
> you have the dew with which
> I have begotten you.

The day of the king's enthronement is depicted as the day when he assumes responsibility for battle with his enemies in the future. His people are present with him in the Temple and offer themselves as freewill offerings to him as their king who is also priest. "In holy array" (compare 29:2; 96:9) may apply to the people and to the king, for both they and he were dressed in garments appropriate to the happy occasion. The morning is personified as mother of the dew. In such a country as Palestine where it rains only at certain times of the year, dew is especially thought of as giving new life (compare Isa. 26:19). Here it is used to express the rebirth of the king as God's son on the occasion of his accession to the throne (compare 2:7); the king of Israel was regarded as God's son, not by procreation, but by adoption at the time of his coronation (see 2:7; II Sam. 7:14). He was not deity but the representative of God. The One who fulfilled this Psalm was the Son of God at the level of deity itself.

The Priest Who Is King (110:4-7). The second oracle is presented by the court poet in the form of a divine oath, identifying the king as a perpetual priest "after the order of Melchizedek." David (II Sam. 6:12-19), his sons (II Sam. 8:18), Solomon (I Kings 8:14, 55-56, 62-63; 9:25), and Ahaz (II Kings 16:12-15) performed priestly rites upon occasion. As representative of God before the people and of the people before God, the king was of necessity a priestly mediator. "For ever" corresponds to the promise of perpetual kingship to David and his descendants recorded in II Samuel 7:13-29. But Israel's king was not an Aaronic priest; he was "after the order of Melchizedek." According to Genesis 14:18-20, Melchizedek was "king of Salem [Jerusalem]" and "priest of God Most High." The psalmist is saying that each Davidic king stands in a long succession of priest-kings who have reigned in Jerusalem and whose most illustrious representative is Melchizedek. Perhaps he also means to say that the Davidic king is to have a priestly or "in-behalf-of" concern for his people.

The poet resumes his assuring words to the newly enthroned king (vss. 5-7). In verse 1 the king is seated at God's right hand, but in verse 5 the Lord is at the king's right hand as his protector (16:8; 109: 31; 121:5). "The day of his wrath" (compare Zeph. 2:3) and the portrayal of God's universal judgment suggest that the psalmist may be looking ahead to the future Day of the Lord, of which God's victories in behalf of the present Davidic king are an earnest. The king will refresh himself at the brook along the way and continue his victorious campaign (vs. 7).

Psalm 111—In Remembrance of His Wonderful Works

In this hymn God's wonderful works in behalf of his ancient people are gratefully remembered by a devout descendant. He has expressed his praise in twenty-two short lines, each succeeding line beginning with the next letter of the Hebrew alphabet. "Praise the LORD" is not a part of this structure. Psalms 111 and 112 are closely related in language and thought. While the activity and attributes of God are extolled in Psalm 111, the corresponding deeds and character of the godly man are declared in Psalm 112. Inasmuch as the Exodus from Egypt, the giving of the Law at Sinai, and the provision of food in the wilderness are all alluded to in Psalm 111, it could have been appropriately used at the celebration of any one of the great festivals—Passover, Weeks, or Tabernacles.

Thanks to the Lord (111:1). This verse suggests that the Psalm was sung as a solo in the presence of and on behalf of the congregation in the Temple.

The Works of the Lord (111:2-9). The great works of the Lord in which his people delight include: the Exodus (vs. 4; compare Exod. 12:14; 13:8-9); the provision of food, especially the quails and the manna in the wilderness (vs. 5; compare 34:9-10; Exod. 16:11-36; Matt. 6:25-34); the Covenant at Sinai (vss. 5, 9; compare Exod. 19:5); the gift of Canaan (vs. 6; compare 78:55; 105: 11, 44); the gift of the Law (vs. 7; compare Exod. 19-20); and the redemption of his people (vs. 9). The reference in ve ses 4 and 9 certainly includes the Exodus (compare Deut. 7:8), but is not necessarily confined to it. Verse 9 seems to refer to the deliverance from the Babylonian Exile as well (compare Jer. 31: 11). Through his mighty works God revealed aspects of his character.

The Fear of the Lord (111:10). The word "terrible" in verse 9 is from the same Hebrew root as "fear" in verse 10. Since God has revealed himself as one to be feared (revered), "the fear of the LORD is the beginning of wisdom" (compare Prov. 9:10; 1:7; Job 28:28). "The fear of the LORD" is almost synonymous with the religion of Israel; it includes worship, law, and life (compare 19:9; 34:11). Wisdom, or meaningful life, begins at the point of reverence for God.

Psalm 112—The Man Who Fears the Lord

Identical acrostic structure, similarity of vocabulary, and a common emphasis on the fear of the Lord (111:10—112:1 indicate that Psalms 111 and 112 were written by the same poet.

"Praise the LORD" stands outside the acrostic structure in both Psalms. However, Psalm 111 is a hymn and Psalm 112 is wisdom poetry, in which the psalmist seeks to instruct others in the desirability of living a God-fearing life.

The Happiness of the God-fearer (112:1). The Psalm begins with the wise man's pronouncement of a beatitude upon the man who so reveres the Lord that he keeps his commandments with joy (compare 1:1-2; 40:8; 119:35, 97). The psalmist seems to have carried over the thought of the fear of the Lord from the last verse of the preceding Psalm.

A Description of the God-fearer (112:2-9). In these verses the beatitude of verse 1 is developed. The God-fearer will have a powerful and influential posterity. He himself is prosperous and so uses his prosperity in benevolent deeds that he continually enjoys the rewards of such righteousness (see Ezek. 18:20), since it is patterned on the righteousness of God (111:3). The light of prosperity and joy (see 97:11; Isa. 58:10) follows the darkness of trouble and sorrow in the lives of the upright. The subject in the clause of verse 4b is uncertain. As the clause stands, it means that God is the source of such light because he is gracious, merciful, and righteous. But if the God-fearer is the subject, his character reflects the character of God as set forth in Psalm 111:4b.

The God-fearer is generous and lends (compare 37:21, 26), and conducts his affairs so as to injure no one. Borrowing took place usually in the case of critical need, and a lender was forbidden to profit out of his brother's misfortune by charging interest (see 15:5; Deut. 23:19-20). Generous living issues in stability (compare 15:5) and in the gratitude of those who will not let the name of their benefactor be forgotten (vs. 6; compare 111:4a). On account of the security of faith the righteous man is undisturbed by evil reports. He is confident that God will administer justice to his adversaries. Verse 9ab is parallel to verse 3 and is quoted by Paul in II Corinthians 9:9 to encourage Christian liberality.

The Antagonist of the God-fearer (112:10). The wicked man is infuriated at the happiness of the righteous man, but his purpose will not be fulfilled (compare Prov. 10:24). Obviously the psalmist has presented only the general principle of reward and punishment, for some God-fearers are not prosperous. Nevertheless, there is need for an optimism that does not overlook any of God's blessings, material or spiritual.

Psalm 113—The Exalted and Humble Lord

In Judaism, Psalms 113-118 are known as the Hallel, Hymn of Praise, or the Egyptian Hallel (see 114:1); and are sung at the Feasts of Passover, Weeks, Tabernacles, and Dedication (Hanukkah). At Passover, Psalms 113-114 are sung before the meal, and Psalms 115-118 after it. The hymn sung by Jesus and his Apostles after the Last Supper (Matt. 26:30; Mark 14:26) was probably Psalms 115-118; it is also possible that Psalms 113-114 were sung before the Supper. Psalm 113 is a hymn of praise to the name of the Lord, who is supreme over all the universe yet stoops to meet the needs of his people.

Call to Praise the Lord (113:1). A soloist calls the congregation as the "servants of the LORD" (see 34:22) to "praise the name of the LORD." "The name of the LORD" is mentioned three times in the first three verses; it stands for the revealed character of God. This strong emphasis upon the name of God is not far removed from the emphasis in the Lord's Prayer, "Hallowed be thy name."

The Exalted Lord (113:2-4). A Temple choir here responds to the call to praise. Temporally speaking, God's name is to be blessed "from this time forth and for evermore" (for the use of this expression see 115:18; 121:8; 125:2; 131:3). Geographically speaking, it is to be praised universally from east to west (see 50:1; Mal. 1:11).

The Humble Lord (113:5-9). Although God is the transcendent Lord of glory, he stoops to meet the needs of his people. Verse 6 should probably be read, "who humbles himself to look upon the heaven and the earth" (compare 102:19; 138:6; Isa. 57:15; Phil. 2:5-11). Verses 7-8 are taken almost verbally from the Song of Hannah in I Samuel 2:8 (compare Luke 1:52). "The needy from the ash heap" is the most extreme example of debasement and wretchedness. The ash heap was the village dump, from which those who were stricken with abject poverty or a loathsome disease sought their livelihood. "To make them sit with princes" is a figure for elevation to honor and dignity. The giving of a home and children to the barren woman is probably a further reference to Hannah (I Sam. 1:1—2:11). Throughout these verses (7-9) the psalmist is illustrating God's concern for lowly and needy persons and also for lowly and needy Israel (compare Isa. 54:1; 66:8).

Psalm 114—Exodus Set to Music

Psalm 114 is a hymnic confession of Israel's faith in the God of the Exodus, the wilderness wanderings, the Covenant at Sinai, and the entrance into Canaan—all of which events are mighty acts of God. This poetic gem is part of the Egyptian Hallel (see comment on Ps. 113) and may have been written for the celebration of Passover, the festival commemorating the Exodus events. It is particularly appropriate for us as Christians to use it at the Easter season, for at that time we celebrate God's mighty deliverance in our Exodus from bondage to sin through the death and resurrection of Jesus Christ.

The Birth of a Nation (114:1-2). The patriarchs were forerunners of the nation of Israel but they were not a nation. It was the Exodus from Egypt that made the nation possible. The Egyptian language was foreign to the Israelites and was an additional barrier between the two peoples. It was through the Exodus that the nation whose chief divisions were to be Judah and Israel was set apart unto God.

Miracles Along the Way (114:3-6). At the very outset of the journey from Egypt the waters of the sea were parted (Exod. 14:21-22), and at the end the Jordan "turned back" (Joshua 3:9-17). The giving of the Law at Sinai was accompanied by an earthquake (Exod. 19:18; Judges 5:5). In verses 5-6 the psalmist challenges the sea, Jordan, the mountains, and the hills—as if they were persons—to explain their unusual behavior.

The Author of Israel's Redemption (114:7-8). By indirection it is clear that the answer to the question of verses 5-6 is that Israel's God is the Author of the unusual events of Israel's beginnings. All the earth is called upon to tremble at his presence, for he is Lord of all history and creation. It was he who provided water for his people in the wilderness (Exod. 17:6-7; Num. 20:8-13; Deut. 8:15; Pss. 78:15-16, 20; 107:35; compare Isa. 41:18). As Lord of nature and men, God causes nature to serve his historical purposes.

Psalm 115—Glory to God's Name

This Psalm is a part of the Egyptian Hallel (see introduction to Psalm 113). It is a liturgical hymn of praise with an intricate antiphonal arrangement (compare Ezra 3:10-11; Neh. 12:40).

Praise Through Lament (115:1-2). It is unusual for a hymn to begin with words of lament. But in this case the lament actually contributes to praise. Israel (probably Judah after the Exile) is being mocked by surrounding peoples as they say, "Where is their God?" (compare 79:10). Therefore, the Covenant people pray that God will raise them from their low estate, not for their own sake but for his glory (compare Dan. 9:18-19), because such a blessing will demonstrate anew that he is true to his Covenant love and faithfulness revealed to his people of old (see Exod. 34:6; Deut. 7:7-8).

Praise Through Ridicule (115:3-8). In spite of outward circumstances, God's people know that he is sovereign and is able to do all his holy will. Their predicament is not a lack of power on his part. The gods of those who taunt them are but man-made idols without any capacities corresponding to the human senses (compare 135:15-18, where verses 4-8 recur; Isa. 44:9-20; Jer. 10:1-16; Hab. 2:18-19). Those who make idols and trust in them are false and powerless also. Thus, through the ridicule of idols and idolaters, God is praised in a reverse procedure.

Praise Through Affirmation of Faith (115:9-13). Praise is next offered through a call to trust and a declaration of trust and blessing. Three groups are addressed: all Israel, the priests, and those "who fear the LORD." The identification of the third group is uncertain. It may be composed of Gentile converts to Judaism (see I Kings 8:41-43; Isa. 56:6-7; Acts 10:1-2; 13:16; 16:14), or an inner circle of the truly devout (see 111:10; 112:1), or both the laity and the priests already mentioned separately. The same three groups are addressed in Psalms 118:2-4 and 135:19-20, a fourth, the "house of Levi," being added in the latter case. God is the help and shield (protector) of each of the three groups mentioned in 115:9-11. He will bless them all without regard for their rank or station in life (vss. 12-13).

Praise Through Priestly Blessing (115:14-15). At this point a priest pronounces a blessing, which is by its very nature an expression of praise, for God is acknowledged as the Giver of all good things (compare James 1:17). His blessing includes the increase of family (compare 127:3-5; Deut. 1:11; 28:4). As the Maker of heaven and earth (see 121:2; 124:8; 134:3; 146:6), God controls all blessings in heaven and on earth.

Praise Through Commitment (115:16-18). The Psalm is brought to its conclusion by the vow of the people to praise God for evermore. The heavens and the earth are God's by creation (see Gen. 1:1), but he has made men the stewards of earth (see Gen. 1:28-29). The psalmist moves from heaven and earth to the underworld of the dead, where in his thinking men do not praise God (on Sheol see Introduction and Pss. 6:5; 30:9; 88:4-5, 10-12; Isa. 38:18). But God's people or "we, the living," as the Septuagint puts it, "will bless the LORD."

Psalm 116—I Will Lift Up the Cup of Salvation

This personal thanksgiving is a part of the Egyptian Hallel (see comment on 113), in which the psalmist narrates the circumstances of his thanksgiving (vss. 1-11) and pays his vows in the Temple (vss. 12-19).

The Reason for the Psalmist's Thanksgiving (116:1-11). The reason for the psalmist's thanksgiving is that God saved him from the realm of the dead (vss. 1-4). Apparently he had been sick. Through this deliverance God made known to "the simple" or inexperienced psalmist his grace, righteousness, and compassion (compare 111:4; Exod. 34:6), and brought to him a renewed inner calm (vss. 5-7). Yet, even in the midst of his complaining the psalmist never lost his faith in God, though his faith in man was undermined (vss. 10-11; Paul, in II Cor. 4:13, quotes vs. 10a from the Septuagint and seems to allude to vs. 11b in Rom. 3:4). Verse 11b is literally, "All men are liars."

The Psalmist's Payment of His Vows (116:12-19). In expressing his gratitude for deliverance from death, the psalmist lifts up "the cup of salvation," offers a sacrifice of thanksgiving, calls on the name of the Lord, and pays his vows in the Temple court (vss. 14 and 18 are identical). "The cup of salvation" or "deliverance" is a designation of the drink offering poured out at the altar as an accompaniment of the animal sacrifice (Deut. 32:38; Lev. 7:11-18). To call "on the name of the LORD" is to acknowledge him as Deliverer. Payment of vows includes all the items listed and anything else the psalmist may have promised during his distress. Gratitude expressed publicly is a witness to God's grace. Verse 15 means that the life of each person devoted to God is considered valuable by him, and therefore his death is costly. The most significant aspect of the psalmist's gratitude is stated in these words: "O LORD, I am thy servant . . . the son of thy handmaid" (see 86:16)—for thereby he rededicates himself to the will of his divine Master.

Psalm 117—A Precious Gem in a Small Package

This shortest of the Psalms is a hymn, composed of a call to praise, a statement of the grounds of the praise, and a conclusion. The call to praise is a missionary invitation addressed to all the nations (vs. 1). It is quoted by Paul in Romans 15:11 in support of God's missionary purpose among the Gentiles (compare 67; 22:27; 86:9). The basis of this invitation is God's Covenant love and faithfulness shown to Israel (compare 47:1-2). According to the Septuagint the concluding "Praise the LORD" belongs at the beginning of Psalm 118. If the Septuagint tradition is correct, Psalm 117 is left without a conclusion. If the Hebrew tradition is correct, the conclusion is an invitation to praise God, addressed to the congregation.

Psalm 118—A Processional Litany of Thanksgiving

This Psalm, known as the favorite of Martin Luther, is the last unit in the Egyptian Hallel (see comment on 113). It is a litany of the community based on an earlier thanksgiving of an individual (perhaps a king), who was delivered from enemies (vss. 5-14) and from severe chastisement (vss. 17-18).

Call to Thanksgiving (118:1-4). The Psalm both begins and ends with the liturgical formula found in 106:1; 107:1; and Ezra 3:11. On the threefold division of worshipers in verses 2-4 see comment on Psalm 115:9-13.

Thanksgiving in the First Person (118:5-21). Verses 5-19, 21, and 28 are sometimes identified as the original song of individual thanksgiving (see above). In the present Psalm they are rendered by a soloist (or a choir) on behalf of the congregation. God's people had called on him at various times in their distress and he had granted them freedom (vs. 5). Verse 6 is quoted in Hebrews 13:6 (compare Ps. 56:9, 11).

If verses 10-14 are a part of an earlier thanksgiving of an individual, they can be more easily understood on the assumption that the individual was a king. As they now stand, they refer to God's deliverance of the nation from surrounding enemies (on verse 14 see Exod. 15:2; Isa. 12:2). "Victory" or "salvation" (vs.

15) is another way of referring to God's deliverance of his people. Though he has chastened them severely, he has not exterminated them (vss. 17-18).

The procession of worshipers has been advancing and is now standing before the Temple gates. The soloist or choir addresses the gatekeeper in the words of verse 19 (compare 24:7-10). The gates are called "the gates of righteousness" because they give access to the earthly dwelling of the righteous God (compare Jer. 31:23). Verse 20 is the gatekeeper's reply. Verse 21 is a repetition of the theme (see vss. 5, 14, 15-16, 18).

Praise in the Inner Court (118:22-29). Israel is likened to a stone which was at one time rejected by the builders; that is, Israel seemed unimportant. "The chief cornerstone" probably means the most important cornerstone used in the foundation of a building to bond the walls together (see Isa. 28:16), or it may be a reference to the keystone of the arch, which bonds the walls and c mpletes the structure. The point is the same in either case. God has made his disciplined remnant "the chief cornerstone" in his Kingdom.

Jesus applied these verses to himself (Mark 12:10-11; Luke 20:17; compare Matt. 21:42). Verse 22 is also quoted in relation to Jesus in Acts 4:11 and I Peter 2:7 (compare Eph. 2:20). These applications to Christ rest upon the fact that in him the mission of Israel finds its fulfillment.

The day of festivity at the sanctuary was made possible by God (vs. 24). On it the people both rejoice (vs. 24) and pray God's blessing upon them in the days ahead (vs. 25). In response, the priests pronounce their blessing upon the procession of worshipers (vs. 26). Verse 26a is quoted by the crowd on the occasion of the Triumphal Entry of Jesus into Jerusalem (Matt. 21:9; Mark 11:9; Luke 19:38; John 12:13). The word "Hosanna," which occurs in all these references except Luke 19:38, is derived from the Hebrew expression, "Save us, we beseech thee," found in verse 25. In Luke 13:35 verse 26a is quoted as a prediction that the people of Jerusalem will not see Jesus until they acknowledge him as Messiah (that is, on the occasion of the Triumphal Entry). In Matthew 23:39 the same quotation is used in relation to Jesus' return as the glorified Son of Man.

God has given his people "light" (vs. 27), which means he has shown them favor (see 67:1; 80:3, 7, 19; 119:135; Num. 6:25). The reference to binding the festal procession seems to apply to a part of the ceremony of the Feast of Tabernacles. The worshipers carried branches of palm, myrtle, and willow trees as they processed around the altar. The branches may have touched the projections ("horns") at the corners of the altar. Verses 28 and 29 are a concluding expression of thanksgiving and praise.

Psalm 119—The ABC's of the Law

This Psalm is a combination of four literary types. First, it is the most elaborate acrostic in the Bible. It is composed of twenty-two strophes corresponding to the twenty-two letters of the Hebrew alphabet in order. Each strophe contains eight pairs of lines, and each pair within a given strophe begins with the same letter of the alphabet. This structure makes for length and repetition. Second, the Psalm is a hymn in praise of the Law, or, ultimately, the God who gave the Law. Third, it is a wisdom poem, in which the psalmist teaches others concerning the Law. Fourth, it bears some of the marks of a lament as the psalmist prays for deliverance from his enemies.

The Law in this case seems to be what we know as the Pentateuch. The psalmist probably wrote after the work of Ezra, about 400 B.C. His approach to the Law is one of deep spiritual understanding. The Law does not take the place of God but guides the believer in doing God's will. The psalmist seeks God's personal instruction in understanding what the written word means. This is what the Christian calls the guidance of the Holy Spirit. The Law is no burden to the psalmist; it is a means of joy, refreshment, and life in communion with God. In other words, it is his Bible.

Many different words are employed to describe the Law: law, testimonies, precepts, commandments, ordinances, statutes, word, ways, and promise. Though the words are essentially synonyms in this Psalm, they do suggest slightly different approaches to the Law. For the meaning of the first five terms, see the comment on Psalm 19:7-9. As "statutes" the Law is that which is written down and prescribed. As "word" it is the communication of God's will to man. Sometimes one of the two terms meaning "word" is translated "promise." As "ways" the Law is a pattern of behavior in accord with the will of God (compare Deut. 5:33).

Comment (119:1-176). Only brief comment is required since the thought of the Psalm is for the most part very clear. Obedi-

ence to God's Law is a basis of happiness (compare 1:1-2; Deut.
28:1-14); therefore, the psalmist seeks God's help in understanding and keeping it (vss. 1-8). God's word laid up in the heart is a
means of sin prevention and joy (vss. 9-16; compare Prov. 7:1-5;
Jer. 31:33; Matt. 4:1-11). In view of the brevity of his life as "a
sojourner on earth," the psalmist longs to make the most of it by
studying the Law as a source of strength in the midst of persecution at the hands of irreligious leaders (vss. 17-24). In humiliat-
ing distress he seeks the new life promised to those who obey
God's word (vss. 25-32; compare Deut. 30:1-20). He asks that
God teach him his Law and keep him from covetous gain and
other worthless pursuits (vss. 33-40; compare I John 2:15-17).
He prays further that God will grant him the deliverance promised to obedient servants, in order that he may answer those who
ridicule his faith; he then promises that he will bear witness to the
faith in him even before kings (vss. 41-48; compare Matt. 10:18;
Acts 26:1-2). Though godless or insolent men have derided him,
he has remained true to God's laws which have been his songs
throughout his earthly sojourn (vss. 49-56; compare vs. 54 with
vs. 19). In gratitude for the Law he rises in the middle of the
night to praise God (vss. 57-64). He went astray, was benefi-
cently afflicted, and now keeps God's word (vss. 65-72). He
recognizes his affliction as the judgment of God and prays for
God's mercy upon himself and God's punishment upon those
who led him astray (vss. 73-80). He is deteriorating as "a wine-
skin in the smoke" while he hopes for God's judgment upon his
persecutors and his own deliverance from peril (vss. 81-88).
There is a limit to the perfection of all man-made creations, but
God's word or Law has no such limitation (vss. 89-96). Through
the study of God's Law the psalmist is wiser than his enemies or
his teachers and older persons who have not given themselves to
the Law with such diligence (vss. 97-104; with vs. 103 compare
19:10; John 4: 32-34). Amid the darkness of affliction and persecution he is able to value God's word as a guide (vss. 105-112;
compare Prov. 6:23). His devotion and hope stand in contrast
to the faithlessness and certain doom of the wicked (vss. 113-
120). Since his oppressors have broken the Law, "it is time for
the LORD to act" in his behalf (vss. 121-128). He continues his
prayer for God's favor and expresses sorrow because men do not
keep God's Law (vss. 129-136). The Law reflects the eternal
righteousness and faithfulness of God (vss. 137-144). The psalm-

ist draws near to God in prayer before the dawn and in meditation upon his promises before the three watches of the night, and God is near him in the midst of persecution (vss. 145-152). As the psalmist repeats his petition for redemption from the wicked, he commits himself with unswerving loyalty to God's testimonies, of which he can say: "The sum of thy word is truth" (vss. 153-160; compare John 14:6). Frequently during the day he praises God for his Law, because all who love it are secure (vss. 161-168). He ends his Psalm with a petition for understanding and deliverance, a recommitment to the Law, and a confession that in spite of all his striving he is a lost sheep in need of the Shepherd's gracious care (vss. 169-176).

Psalm 120—Living Among Enemies

Psalms 120-134 are known from the title found at the beginning of each of them as the Songs of Ascents. Although they vary in origin and character, they appear to have been taken from a collection of songs which were sung by pilgrims as they went up to the great festivals at Jerusalem (see Deut. 12:5-7). Psalm 120 is the lament of a man who is living in a hostile environment.

A Cry in Distress (120:1-2). The psalmist prays for deliverance from those who are guilty of such things as treachery, false accusation, and hypocrisy (compare 52:1-4; Micah 6:12).

Retribution Upon Enemies (120:3-4). The "deceitful tongue" is personified in verse 3 as in verse 2 to represent the psalmist's deceitful enemies. Under this designation they are questioned (vs. 3) and answered (vs. 4) in rhetorical fashion. Verse 3 reflects the formula for an oath or curse: "May God do so to you and more also" (see I Sam. 3:17; I Kings 2:23; Ruth 1:17). In other words, the retribution which the psalmist's enemies are to experience will be that indicated by their offense. Since they have shot arrows of falsehood at the psalmist to destroy him (compare Prov. 25:18; Jer. 9:8), so shall they be destroyed. As the psalmist's enemies have kindled the fire of enmity by deceit, the fire of divine judgment will consume them (compare 140:10). The "broom tree" is noted for holding fire a long time.

The Psalmist's Predicament (120:5-7). The psalmist's neighbors are like the wild nomadic tribes of Meshech and Kedar. Meshech was a people descended from Japheth (Gen. 10:2);

they lived between the Black Sea and the Caspian and traded in slaves and vessels of bronze (see Ezek. 27:13; 32:26-27; 38:3; 39:1). Kedar was a people descended from Ishmael (Gen. 25: 13); they lived in the Syrian Desert south of Damascus (see Song of Sol. 1:5; Isa. 21:13, 16-17; 42:11; 60:7; Jer. 2:10; 49:28-29).

Psalm 121—The Lord Is Your Keeper

Pilgrims and their leader sang this affirmation of faith antiphonally as they journeyed to Jerusalem for the celebration of the festivals at the Temple. The theme of faith revolves around the word "keep," which is used six times.

The Source of Help (121:1-2). The leader lifts his eyes to the hills surrounding Jerusalem (87:1; 125:1-2; 133:3), the place of God's earthly dwelling, from which he sends help to his people (20:2). But his help does not come from the hills; rather does it come from the One who is suggested by the sight of the hills, the One who made not only the hills but heaven and earth as well (compare 115:15; 124:8; 134:3; 146:6).

The Keeper Who Does Not Slumber (121:3-4). Verse 3 is better rendered: "May he not let your foot slip, may he who keeps you not slumber" (compare 35:23). Some of the terrain over which the caravan of pilgrims traveled was treacherous, and pilgrims were in danger of serious falls. But assurance is given in the response in verse 4. The sentries keeping watch over the pilgrim camp at night may drop off to sleep, but the Lord guards all his people without interruption.

The Keeper Who Protects by Day and Night (121:5-6). The Lord as Keeper of the pilgrims is called a shade (compare 91:1), stationed at the right hand of each pilgrim (compare 16:8; 109: 31), to protect him from sunstroke by day (91:6; II Kings 4:18-19; Isa. 49:10) and moonstroke by night. There were some who thought the stroke in either case was produced by a demon. The fear of moonstroke seems to have arisen from the assumption that there was a relationship between the moon and certain diseases. For example, the New Testament Greek word for "to be epileptic" means literally "to be moonstruck" (Matt. 4:24; 17:15).

The Keeper Who Preserves Life (121:7-8). God preserves his people by guarding them from all sorts of evil in all their undertakings ("going out" and "coming in"; compare Deut. 28:6).

Psalm 122—The Significance of Jerusalem

This is a song of Zion written by a grateful pilgrim. Certain grammatical constructions and the backward look to the time of the Davidic kings (vs. 5) indicate a postexilic date.

Jerusalem, the Joy of the Pilgrim (122:1-2). The psalmist begins by reflecting upon the joy he experienced when his friends invited him to accompany them on their pilgrimage to the Temple in Jerusalem (see Deut. 12:5-7). Pilgrims journeying from distant places banded together for protection and fellowship. To what specific moment does verse 2 refer? Are the pilgrims approaching the city, or have they already entered? Are they about to leave, or have they already returned home? It seems most appropriate to think that they have enjoyed the festival and that, as they are about to leave, one of their number voices this song of gratitude and petition for Jerusalem.

Jerusalem, the Symbol of Unity (122:3-5). Verse 3 is not primarily a reference to the brick and mortar of Jerusalem's walls and buildings, but is a way of saying that Jerusalem is the means of the religious and political unity of God's people. The three major festivals "to which the tribes go up" each year are Passover, Weeks, and Tabernacles (Deut. 16:16-17). The psalmist has probably just attended the Feast of Tabernacles because, in a special way, it was the time "to give thanks to the name of the LORD" for the blessings of the past year (Deut. 16:13-15). He also recalls that David made Jerusalem the capital of his kingdom and that from his day justice was administered from that city.

Jerusalem, the Object of Prayer (122:6-9). The psalmist now calls upon others to join him in praying for the peace of their beloved city. "Peace" includes soundness, wholeness, and well-being in every possible sense. Specifically it includes security within the "walls" (ramparts or outer walls) and "towers" of the city. There are several examples of alliteration in the Hebrew of this passage, the most notable occurring in the phrase "the peace of Jerusalem." The psalmist probably regards "salem" (see 76:2) as meaning "peace" also. He prays for God's blessing upon all who love Jerusalem and that for which she stands. What makes Jerusalem so significant in his day is the presence of God's house there (vs. 9; compare vs. 1).

It is possible that Jesus had this Psalm in mind as he wept over

Jerusalem, saying, "Would that even today you knew the things that make for peace!" (Luke 19:42).

Psalm 123—Looking to the Lord

This Psalm is a free composition of mixed type, though it is primarily a lament of the community. The first verse is in the first person singular and may have been sung by a priest. The remainder of the Psalm is in the first person plural and was probably sung by the congregation. This combination of persons also gives the Psalm the form of a liturgy.

Eyes of Hope (123:1-2). The priest or other representative of the people looks to God as the King of the universe, enthroned in heaven, and therefore able to grant his people's request. As slaves turn to their masters and mistresses for everything good, so God's people look to him for grace in time of need (compare Isa. 30:18).

A Plea for Grace (123:3-4). "Have mercy upon us" is better translated, "Be gracious unto us." The enemies of God's people are "at ease" in their privileged position and therefore scornful and proud (compare Job 12:5; Amos 6:1; Zech. 1:15). Some identify these enemies as the Samaritans and the other neighbors of the Jews in the time of Nehemiah. Others identify them as the people among whom the Jews of the Dispersion were living. It is significant that the psalmist heaps no imprecation upon them.

Psalm 124—Gratitude for Escape

The nation has experienced a recent deliverance and the people express their gratitude. Language and syntax point to a postexilic date.

The Danger (124:1-5). These verses are a figurative description of what would have happened to God's people if the Lord had not been on their side. A priest or precentor sang the first verse to sound the keynote, and then the congregation, probably assisted by the choir, sang the remaining lines. The enemies of God's people are compared to a monster who would have swallowed them up alive (compare Jonah 1:17), and to a raging torrent that would have overwhelmed them (compare 69:1-2, 15).

The Escape (124:6-8). The people thank God for their deliverance from their enemies, who are now depicted as ravenous beasts of prey and as fowlers (compare 91:3). The people face the future in the assurance that the God who delivered them is the Maker of heaven and earth (see 121:2).

Psalm 125—The Defense of the People

Most affirmations of faith center in the individual's relation to God. This one is sometimes classified as a lament, but trust in God is far more prominent than lament. Some see the occasion of the Psalm in the opposition to the rebuilding of the walls of Jerusalem in the time of Nehemiah (see Neh. 4:7-9; 6:1-14), but this is only one of several conjectures.

The Lord Round About His People (125:1-3). Those who have faith in the Lord are like Mount Zion, unmovable. Zion here is the hill on which the Temple stands. Today the geographical spot remains, but the Temple was destroyed in A.D. 70 by Titus the Roman. Yet the real Zion, the people of faith, remains unshaken. As a girdle of mountains protects Jerusalem, so the wall of God's embracing presence "is round about his people." Jerusalem and the surrounding territory are under oppressive foreign rule. But God will not allow "the scepter of wickedness" to remain permanently over the land allotted to his people, lest they succumb to the temptation to join forces with the wicked.

A Prayer and a Warning (125:4-5). In verse 4 the worshiping congregation prays for God's blessing upon the righteous, who are designated "good" and "upright." They are the true Israel—those who trust in the Lord (vs. 1). In verse 5a, warning is issued to those who are tempted to become disloyal to God and country (see Neh. 6:12-13, 17-19). Renegades will be classified with "evildoers" (that is, troublemakers) in the time of God's judgment. "Peace be in Israel" is a prayer that God will deliver his people from all evil and bless them with all material and spiritual good (compare 29:11; 122:6-9; 128:6; Num. 6:26). Paul must have had this Psalm in mind as he wrote concerning the Church: "Peace and mercy be upon all who walk by this rule, upon the Israel of God" (Gal. 6:16).

Psalm 126—The Restoration of Zion's Fortunes

In form this Psalm is a prophetic liturgy, though the proverb-like oracle in verse 6 may have been announced by a priest.

Verses 1-3 reflect the great expectations of the Remnant that returned from the Babylonian Exile, while verses 4-6 reflect the disappointments of a later period. In thought and form the Psalm should be compared with Psalm 85.

Gratitude for Past Restoration (126:1-3). The expression "to restore the fortunes" means to bring back prosperity and well-being. Here it is applied to the restoration from the Babylonian Captivity. The psalmist identifies himself with the people of the return (vss. 1-3) as well as with those of his own generation (vss. 4-6). He seems to draw his picture of the return from such glorious prophecies as those found in Isaiah 40-55. The return was like a dream—too good to be true (compare Luke 24:41). It was an occasion of laughter and joy (compare Isa. 44:23; 48: 20; 51:11). Even people in other nations recognized the greatness of God's mighty acts on Israel's behalf (compare Isa. 52: 10).

Prayer for a New Restoration (126:4-6). Because the expectations of the postexilic Jewish community are still unfulfilled, the worshiping people pray for a new restoration of fortunes; and this restoration is likened to "the water-courses in the Negeb." The Negeb is the dry territory to the south of Judah which is quickly changed by the autumn rains into a place of life-giving streams. God's people pray that their tears of disappointment may issue in a harvest of joy (compare Isa. 9:3; Matt. 5:4). Through the oracle of verse 6 they are assured that God will grant their request. This verse seems to reflect the ancient Near Eastern custom of weeping at the time of sowing with a view to ensuring the fertility of the seed. The custom originated in the non-Israelite religions whose devotees believed that their god of fertility died and was then brought back to life through a ritual of weeping, thereby producing fertility for another season. This origin was probably unknown to the psalmist; certainly he gives an ancient form a new theological interpretation in keeping with the faith of Israel.

Psalm 127—Man's Dependence Upon God's Blessing

The psalmist is a sage who teaches that man is utterly dependent upon God. The Psalm came to be associated with Solomon chiefly because the word "house" in verse 1 was early taken to mean the Temple.

Wisdom for the Laborer (127:1-2). The efforts of the builder, the watchman, or any other diligent laborer fail to achieve their purpose apart from the blessing of God (compare 33:16-17; 91: 9-10; Deut. 28:30; Zeph. 1:13; Prov. 21:31). This implies that man should undertake only that which is in harmony with the will of God. Missiles and bombs in and of themselves are inadequate protection (compare 121:4-5). Even hard work from early morning to late evening does not achieve its good apart from the trust of the laborer in God. God's blessing rests upon the person who labors in the Lord and so trusts him that he also rests in him. The psalmist gives no invitation to sloth or idleness, but warns against fretting anxiety (compare Matt. 6:25-34; Luke 12: 22-31; Mark 4:26-29; I Peter 5:7).

Wisdom for the Homemaker (127:3-5). Sons are regarded as a special blessing from God (compare Deut. 7:13). Sons born while the father is a young man are likened to "arrows in the hand of a warrior" because they will be strong enough to protect their father in his declining years. That man is considered particularly happy who has many sons. They will ensure his just treatment in the city gate where court is held. In the light of the theme of the Psalm, it is obvious that the builder of a home stands in need of God's help as truly as does the builder of a house.

Psalm 128—Reverence the Basis of a Happy Home

The affinities between this and the preceding Psalm are evident. Both are wisdom Psalms, and in both the home is a major theme. The combination of wisdom teaching and a strong love for Zion places the date in the postexilic period.

The Happiness of the Reverent Man (128:1-2). That man is happy with internal and external blessings whose reverence for God issues in right conduct. This psalmist would agree with the author of Psalm 111 that "The fear of the LORD is the beginning of wisdom" (vs. 10; compare Prov. 9:10). One of the external aspects of happiness is to be able to eat the fruit of one's labor (see Isa. 65:21-22), for in the history of the ancient People of God war, oppression, drought, blight, and insects have often caused the farmer to go hungry. It is not the psalmist's purpose to deal with exceptions to his general pronouncement of happiness.

The Fruitfulness of His Wife (128:3-4). Another aspect of happiness is a fruitful wife within one's house. "Within your house" means "in the inner parts of your house," which are reserved for the women. As the reverent man's sons gather about the table, they appear to him as young olive shoots which have grown up around the parent tree. The olive tree is an evergreen and therefore a symbol of continuing vitality (compare 52:8; Jer. 11:16). Again the psalmist does not deal with the exceptions to his general principle. All of us know godly couples who are childless.

The Prosperity of His People (128:5-6). These verses are cast in the form of a priestly benediction. God is thought of as sending forth his blessing from Zion because it is his earthly dwelling (compare 14:7; 20:2; 134:3). But the blessing is not confined to a long life and numerous descendants; it includes also "the prosperity of Jerusalem." As the center of Jewish life, Jerusalem is the mother of all God's people (Ps. 87) and therefore their representative and symbol. In other words, the godly man is a member of the Church, and his happiness is incomplete apart from the well-being of God's larger family (compare Heb. 11: 40). Appropriately, then, the Psalm is concluded with the words, "Peace be upon Israel" (compare 125:5).

Psalm 129—The Survival of Zion

Vocabulary, grammar, literary type, and thought content date this Psalm in the postexilic period. It is a free mixing of thanksgiving (vss. 1-4) and imprecatory lament (vss. 5-8). Psalm 129 should be compared with Psalm 124 in style and general meaning.

Thanksgiving for Preservation (129:1-4). Israel is here personified as an individual. From his youth in Egypt (Hosea 11:1) he has been sorely oppressed by his enemies: Egyptians, Canaanites, Philistines, Arameans, Assyrians, Babylonians, Persians, and others. Yet, these enemies have not been able to obliterate him (compare II Cor. 4:8-10). They are described as plowmen who plow long furrows upon the back of prostrate Israel (compare Micah 3:12; Isa. 51:23). Two things account for this metaphor: the identification of Israel with his land and the furrows made on the back of the beast by the lash of the plowman. Because God is righteous he has always delivered Israel (compare Isa. 45:21-25) by cutting the cords of his wicked enemies. If the figure of verse 3 continues in verse 4, "the cords" are the straps by which the yoke is held on the neck of the beast. Therefore, the cutting of the cords brings plowing to an end. However, if the figure is changed, Israel is the beast which is set free when the cords are cut. The historical meaning is the same in either case. God's people are grateful for their preservation.

Imprecation Upon Enemies (129:5-8). The Jewish community is confronted by enemies and prays for their destruction, for they are regarded as God's enemies also. Their destruction means the deliverance of the struggling Jewish community. "Zion" not only refers to Jerusalem but also to all who are faithful to the Covenant. This kind of usage of the word helps to prepare the way for its Christian interpretation as the Church. The congregation prays that Zion's enemies may be like the grass which sprouts in the dirt that collects on Palestinian housetops and soon withers because it has "no depth of soil" (compare II Kings 19:26; Isa. 37:27; Matt. 13:5-6). With this kind of grass no reaper fills his hand to hold the grass as he cuts it with the sickle, nor does a binder fill the loose fold of his clothes with it until he has gathered enough to bind into a sheaf. Furthermore, "those who pass by" do not call down God's blessing upon reapers and binders, for there is no harvest.

The main thrust of the Psalm suggests that Zion as the People of God is indestructible (compare Matt. 16:18).

Psalm 130—Out of the Depths

This lament of an individual is known in Christendom as one of the seven penitentials (6, 32, 38, 51, 102, 130, 143). The psalmist is in deep distress, primarily because of sin. Therefore, he cries out to God who alone can meet his need.

Supplication to the Lord (130:1-2). The psalmist figuratively describes his distress in terms of the overwhelming waters of the underworld (see 69:1-2, 14). But there is no indication that he is about to die. It is his guilt and alienation from God which give the dimension of depth to his cry for help.

The Forgiveness of the Lord (130:3-4). These verses are in effect a confession of sin and a plea for pardon. The psalmist sees his own sinfulness as a part of man's universal predicament (compare 143:2). By implication man's need can be met only by the undeserved grace of God (compare Gal. 2:16; Rom. 3:20). But there is forgiveness with God (compare 86:5) in order that he may be feared (compare I Kings 8:39-40; Rom. 2:4). Of course perfect love casts out unwholesome fear (I John 4:18). But fear as reverent devotion and obedience is engendered by the forgiving love of God.

Waiting for the Lord (130:5-6). The psalmist waits expectantly for God's "word" of pardon and deliverance but does not indicate how it will be communicated. In fact, he waits with greater eagerness for God's word than the weary sentinels wait for the dawn, when they will be released from their responsibility.

Israel's Hope in the Lord (130:7-8). But the psalmist is not selfishly concerned with his own problem; he is a member of the Church and calls his people to "hope in the LORD." For God is the Redeemer of the Covenant people as well as of the individual (compare 25:22; Isa. 43:25; Neh. 9; Eph. 5:25). The salvation of the individual is bound up with the salvation of the Church, since salvation is a family (Covenant) affair as well as an individual affair. The words "redemption" and "redeem" mean "ransom." Only God can ransom his people from their iniquities (see Mark 10:45). "Iniquities" include sin, guilt, and punishments for sin.

Psalm 131—From Pride to Faith

This is an affirmation of faith in the form of a personal testimony by a man who was once proud, haughty, and pretentious (see Luke 18:9; John 7:49) but is now humble, calm, and contented. Now he is satisfied with an honest self-appraisal because his security is in God.

Verse 2 is hard to translate meaningfully. The literal translation is preferable: "But I have calmed and quieted my soul, like a weaned child upon its mother; like a weaned child is my soul upon me" (compare Matt. 18:4). The psalmist pictures himself calming his soul upon his bosom as a mother calms her child. In this case the child has been weaned and therefore no longer frets for its mother's milk but is content with her presence. Thus the psalmist has been weaned from worldliness and self-centeredness and is content with God's presence. Verse 3 demonstrates a concern for all the People of God (compare 128:6; 130:7-8). It may have been added to adapt the Psalm to congregational use.

Psalm 132—David and Zion

This royal Psalm was rendered liturgically by several different voices. The stress upon the Davidic Covenant and the Ark of the Covenant dates it in the pre-exilic period. Several interpreters associate it with the festival in the autumn, but they differ as to the exact nature of the occasion. In any case, God's election of Zion as his earthly habitation and his covenant with David are interrelated. Second Chronicles 6:40-42 seems to be a free reproduction of verses 8-9, 16, 10b, 1.

Prayer for the Davidic King (132:1-5). The Psalm begins with a prayer for the Davidic king and, by implication, for the whole House of David by the king himself or some other solo voice. David's hardships, perhaps especially his concern for establishing a sanctuary in Jerusalem and his preparation for building the Temple (see I Chron. 22:14), are pleaded as a ground for God's favor upon his successors. Verses 3-5 recall David's strong intention to find a dwelling place for the Ark. They seem to blend his transfer of the Ark to Jerusalem (II Sam. 6) with his desire to build the Temple (II Sam. 7:1-3; I Kings 8:17). "The Mighty One of Jacob" means that God is the Champion of his Covenant people (see Gen. 49:24; Isa. 1:24; 49:26; 60:16).

The Transfer of the Ark Re-enacted (132:6-10). The procession of worshipers is outside the city, and at this point a choir representing David and his followers picks up the hymn (vss. 6-7). David heard of the Ark while he was in Ephrathah (Bethlehem), his home (I Sam. 17:12), and later "found it in the fields of Jaar" (a poetic abbreviation of Kiriath-jearim—see II Sam. 6:2-12; I Chron. 13:1-14). The choir summons the other worshipers to go up to the Temple to worship at God's "footstool" (the Ark; see I Chron. 28:2). God as represented by the Ark is addressed with words reminiscent of Numbers 10:35-36: "Arise, O LORD"; and with a shout by the people the procession is on its way to the Temple, led by the Ark which is borne by the priests. When the procession arrives in the inner court of the Temple, presumably the king offers sacrifices (see II Sam. 6:13-15; I Kings 8:1-11) and prays for the divine favor upon himself as God's anointed one (vs. 10). The Ark is placed again in the Holy of Holies.

God's Promise to David and Choice of Zion (132:11-18).

These verses are composed of two oracles (11-12, 13-18), which may have been sung by one or two soloists. Verses 11-12 are a summary of God's promise to David as recorded in II Samuel 7:2-17 (compare Ps. 89:3-4; Acts 2:30). Verses 13-18 record God's choice of Zion as his dwelling place and his promise to bless her, the poor within her, her priests, those who worship there, and the House of David established there. God "will make a horn to sprout for David"—that is, he will cause the Davidic line to flourish and be strong. The Davidic king will always have "a lamp" in the form of an heir (see I Kings 11:36; 15:4; II Sam. 21:17). The king's enemies will be defeated but his own crown will shine brightly.

The Christian sees the fulfillment of the promise to David in Jesus Christ (see Luke 1:69) and the fulfillment of the promise concerning Zion in his Body the Church.

Psalm 133—The Beauty of Family Unity

The family is a favorite subject of the wise man (see 127; 128; Prov. 1:8-9). In this brief Psalm he extols the beauty and loveliness of harmony among brothers. In pre-exilic times great stress had been placed upon family unity, but the home was not as secure in the postexilic community. The figures which the psalmist employs to depict the pleasantness of brotherly concord were very meaningful in his day but are more difficult to appreciate in ours.

The precious oil used for consecrating the Aaronic high priests in pre-exilic times was sweet-scented and compounded with aromatic spices (Exod. 30:22-33). The beard was highly valued in Israel, and a priest was forbidden to cut his (Lev. 21:5). The figure of the oil flowing down upon the beard suggests the figure of the copious and refreshing dew on Mount Hermon in the north flowing down to "the mountains of Zion" farther south. Of course the psalmist did not think that this literally took place. It is a pleasant picture for the mind's eye.

The psalmist is not only thinking about the unity of brothers in the literal family but also and primarily about the unity of his people in the Covenant family, as is made clear by the last sentence of the Psalm (see 132:17). As brothers in Israel go up to the festivals in Jerusalem, their Covenant with God and with one another is renewed and they receive God's blessing.

Psalm 134—Blessing God and Blessing Men

This last of the Songs of Ascents (120-134) is a liturgy composed of a hymn (vss. 1-2) and a priestly blessing (vs. 3). It seems probable that verses 1-2 were sung by the congregation of pilgrims at the sanctuary and that verse 3 was sung by the priests in response.

Invitation to Bless the Lord (134:1-2). A hymn ordinarily begins with a general invitation to praise God. Here the invitation is addressed to those who serve God as special ministrants in the Temple. The word "stand" means "minister" in this context (see 135:2; Deut. 10:8). The word "night" is plural in Hebrew and seems to indicate that services are held for several nights in succession (compare I Chron. 9:33). It appears that such a series of night services was held during the Feast of Tabernacles in the autumn. The priests are called upon to lift up their hands (compare 28:2; I Tim. 2:8) toward the holy place (perhaps the Holy of Holies) and bless God. To bless God is to express to him praise, adoration, and thanksgiving.

The Priestly Benediction (134:3). The priests respond with a priestly benediction (see Lev. 9:22; Num. 6:22-26), which is a prayer that God may bless his people from Zion (see 128:5), his earthly dwelling (see 9:11; 76:2). There are no limits to the potentialities of his blessing because he is the Creator of all that is (see 115:15).

Psalm 135—A Mosaic of Praise

This hymn of praise to God as the Lord of creation and history is a postexilic mosaic of other Psalms and other parts of the Old Testament beautifully woven together.

Introductory Call to Praise (135:1-4). It is not possible to determine how many different groups are called to praise. In any case, the call is most clearly directed to those who minister in the Temple. A very brief summary of reasons for praise is given: God is good, "it [his name] is lovely" ("he is gracious" is not an exact translation), and he has elected Israel as his special possession.

The Reasons for Praise (135:5-18). Here the reasons for praising God are enumerated in fuller detail. The first reason is his greatness, especially in his Lordship over creation (vss. 5-7). He is altogether superior to the so-called gods of the nations. The second reason is his Lordship over history (vss. 8-14) as seen in the defeat of Sihon and Og in Transjordan (Num. 21:21-35; Deut. 2:30—3:11) and the nations in Canaan (Joshua 12:7-24), and in the gift of their land to Israel as a heritage. But God's compassion is not confined to the past; his name and renown will continue through the ages as he vindicates his people. The third reason, by way of contrast, is that the gods of the nations are mere man-made idols without the equivalent of the human senses (vss. 15-18). Those who make them and trust in them shall be like them—that is, a man becomes like the god he worships.

Concluding Call to Praise (135:19-21). This concluding call to praise is clearly addressed to specific groups: laymen, priests, Levites, and "you that fear the LORD." This last group cannot be identified with certainty. It may be composed of Temple servants below the rank of Levites (see I Chron. 9:2), or of converts to Judaism, or of all the other groups already mentioned.

Psalm 136—His Steadfast Love Endures Forever

This is a liturgical hymn of thanksgiving to God as the Lord of creation and history. It is known as the Great Hallel (Praise) both alone and joined with 135, to which it is very similar, and is to be distinguished from the Egyptian Hallel (113-118). It could be used appropriately at the celebration of all the great festivals. Its dependence upon material of late date and the use of certain grammatical constructions place its composition in the postexilic period. The theme is carried by the familiar refrain, "for his steadfast love endures for ever" (see 106:1; 107:1; 118: 1-4; I Chron. 16:34: II Chron. 20:21; Ezra 3:11).

Introductory Call to Thanksgiving (136:1-3). The call to thanksgiving is issued to the whole congregation. God is designated as "the LORD," "the God of gods," and "the Lord of lords." "The LORD" is the name revealed to Moses at the burning bush (Exod. 3), the Covenant name of God. The two other titles characterize God as the supreme ruler of the universe, who exercises sovereignty over all heavenly beings, evil spirits, and human rulers. The over-all reason for giving thanks is that God is good and his Covenant love never ends.

More Specific Reasons for Thanksgiving (136:4-25). Each

series of God's mighty acts rehearsed in these verses is a revelation of his goodness and Covenant love. First, is the series of mighty acts of creation (vss. 4-9; compare Gen. 1:1, 14-18). The relation here set forth between creation and God's Covenant love suggests that God created the world for the Covenant. Second, is the series of mighty acts in the salvation of Israel: the Exodus from Egypt (vss. 10-15; compare Exod. 12-14), the wilderness wandering (vs. 16; compare Deut. 8:15), the conquest of Canaan (vss. 17-22; compare 135:10-12; Num. 21:21-26, 33-35), and deliverance from foes (vss. 23-24; compare Judges 3-8; Neh. 9:26-28). Attached to this long list of mighty acts on Israel's behalf is the fact that God "gives food to all flesh" (vs. 25; compare 104:27-28). Verses 23-24 may have special reference to the deliverance from the Babylonian Exile.

Concluding Call to Thanksgiving (136:26). In this concluding call to thanksgiving God is designated "the God of heaven." This is the only occurrence of this title in the Psalter, though God is often thought of as enthroned in heaven. However, it is found in some of the other later parts of the Old Testament (for example, Ezra 1:2; Neh. 1:4; 2:4; II Chron. 36:23; Jonah 1:9; Dan. 2:18).

Such a Psalm serves the purposes of thanksgiving, instruction, and hope. The psalmist's generation is grateful for God's mercies to the fathers, for apart from these mercies the blessings of the present and the future would be impossible.

Psalm 137—By the Waters of Babylon

This is a deeply moving Psalm of love and hate—love for Jerusalem and hate for her enemies. It is a lament of an individual with a community concern. It was written either during the Babylonian Exile or immediately thereafter by one who knew the Exile from personal experience. This would date it sometime between 587 B.C. and 537 B.C.

The Experience in Exile (137:1-3). The psalmist was among those exiles who lived with a longing for Zion in their hearts. "The waters of Babylon" were the Tigris and Euphrates Rivers and the irrigation canals that flowed from them. The exiles hung up their lyres because they were too sad to play. However, their Babylonian captors called upon them to sing for their amusement "one of the songs" formerly sung in the Temple.

The Imprecation of the Psalmist Upon Himself (137:4-6). But to "sing the LORD's song in a foreign land," regarded as unclean (see Amos 7:17), would be unthinkable and traitorous. Therefore, the psalmist places a curse upon his own hand and tongue, both of which are used in praising God, if he should prove unfaithful to Jerusalem.

The Imprecation Upon Zion's Enemies (137:7-9). Though the psalmist is unwilling to sing "one of the songs of Zion" in a strange land, his Psalm, written either in Babylon or in Jerusalem, extols Zion in part by cursing her enemies. God is asked to remember the Edomites in retributive judgment because they gloated over the destruction of Jerusalem in 587 B.C. (compare Obad. 10-14; Joel 3:19; Jer. 49:7-22; Lam. 4:21-22; Ezek. 25: 12-14; 35:5; Isa. 34; 63:1). The curse upon Babylon takes the form of a blessing upon that nation which requites her according to the law of retaliation (see Exod. 21:24; Lev. 24:20; Deut. 19:21; compare Jer. 25:12; 51; Isa. 47). This retaliation includes that which is unthinkable to the Christian's mind, the dashing of babies against a rock with a view to obliterating a people. However, such cruelty was often practiced in the ancient world (see II Kings 8:12; Hosea 10:14; 13:16; Isa. 13:16; Nahum 3:10). While we as Christians ought to realize that if we had lived in the psalmist's age and circumstances we should probably have felt as he did, we are called to yield ourselves to the Christ who said, "Love your enemies" (Matt. 5:44; see also Matt. 5:38-42). We are also reminded of Paul's admonition to the Romans, "Bless those who persecute you; bless and do not curse them" (12:14).

Psalm 138—An Expression of Personal Gratitude

The psalmist thanks God for answering his prayer. The structure of the Psalm is dependent on that of the royal Psalms, and its thought is similar to that of Isaiah 40-66. These facts may mean that the Psalm is exilic or postexilic.

I Give Thee Thanks (138:1-3). The author gives thanks for deliverance from some kind of trouble. "Before the gods" may mean "in the presence of subordinate heavenly beings," or the psalmist may be using his imagination to ridicule the so-called gods of surrounding peoples (compare 96:4-5). If he is worshiping in the Temple, the phrase "toward thy holy temple" means "toward the Holy of Holies." On the other hand, if he is at some distance from Jerusalem, he bows down in the general direction of the Temple. The meaning of verses 2-3 seems to be that God's deliverance of him is a superlative revelation of his steadfast love and faithfulness, and a source of renewed vigor for the psalmist.

Kings Shall Praise Thee (138:4-6). Here the psalmist has a missionary vision of all the kings of the earth praising the Lord (compare 102:15; Isa. 49:7), for he regards what God has done for him as a token of the salvation of the world. Through his experience he has learned that God cares for the humble in a way the haughty cannot know (compare Luke 18:14).

Thou Dost Preserve My Life (138:7-8). In words that sound much like the Twenty-third Psalm, the psalmist, as he faces the future, affirms his faith in God. Though trouble may come again and again, God will preserve his life until he has fulfilled his purpose for him (compare 57:2; Phil. 1:6). He prays that God will not forsake him since he is a work of his hands.

Psalm 139—A Wise Man's Prayer

This is one of the most profound statements of personal religion in the Psalter. It is best classified as a wise man's prayer. Although his thoughts come from personal experience as a member of the Covenant family, they are of universal application.

Omniscience—"Thou Knowest" (139:1-6). The psalmist recognizes himself as one whom God has examined and knows thoroughly. God knows him when he is at rest and when he is at work. He even knows what he is going to say before he says it. His presence surrounds the psalmist at all times. Such infinite knowledge is beyond human comprehension.

Omnipresence—"Thou Art There" (139:7-12). At some earlier time the psalmist may have tried to flee from God on account of a deep sense of sin. But in these verses he is by no means seeking such flight. Rather is he glorying in God's omnipresence. There is no place or condition where one can hide from God: heaven, Sheol, the sea, or darkness (compare Jer. 23:23-24). Though the psalmist does not develop his statement concerning God's presence in Sheol, he opens the door to a richer understanding of the afterlife than is found in the usual doctrine of Sheol (see 88: 3-7, 10-12). "The wings of the morning," a phrase occurring only here in the Old Testament, is a poetic way of describing the rapid spread of light at dawn.

Omnipotence—"Thou Didst Form" (139:13-18). The psalmist
praises God for his omnipotence, not by enumerating all his
mighty acts in creation and history but by dwelling upon the
marvel of God's creation of him (compare Job 10:8-11). The
meaning of the latter part of verse 15 is uncertain. Some think
it reflects the ancient belief that the embryo was formed "in the
depths of the earth" before being placed in the womb of the
mother. Others emend the text to read, "in the remotest recesses
of the womb." The psalmist clearly asserts God's foreknowledge
and foreordination (compare Jer. 1:5; Rom. 8:28-30; Eph. 2:
10) on the basis of faith that God carries out his purpose in a
human life. While he contemplates the precious value and tre-
mendous vastness of God's thoughts, he drops off to sleep, but
when he awakens he finds that he is still with God.

Omnijudgment—"Thou Wouldst Slay" (139:19-24). Finally,
the psalmist prays to God as the Judge of all: the wicked, himself, and, by implication, all men. He lives so close to God that
the thought of those who defy God and shed blood is unbearable.
He sees such persons as God's enemies and makes them his own.
However, he is aware of his own imperfection and asks God to
examine him further (compare vss. 1-3 and 23-24) to see "if
there be any pain-producing way" (the literal translation) in him
and to lead him in the way that is eternally right.

Psalm 140—Prayer for Deliverance and Vengeance

This imprecation is a prayer for deliverance from enemies
and vengeance upon them.

Prayer for Deliverance (140:1-8). The psalmist's enemies are
called "evil," "violent," "wicked," and "arrogant." They plot
evil against him and are always seeking a quarrel with him ("stir
up wars"). Their hurtful speech is presented by a combination of
metaphors: the sharpened tongue like a sword or razor (compare 52:2; 55:21; 57:4; 64:3) and the bite of a poisonous snake
(compare 58:4). Romans 3:13 is a quotation from Psalms 5:9
and 140:3. The tongues and lips of the wicked may be used in
cursing (see vs. 9; compare 10:7) as well as in slander (see vs.
11). Furthermore, the psalmist likens his enemies to hunters who
seek to trap him (vs. 5). He prays both directly (vss. 1,4) and
indirectly (vs. 8) for deliverance from their plots.

Prayer for Vengeance (140:9-11). These verses appear to be a countercurse pronounced by the psalmist upon his enemies (on imprecation, see Introduction). In other words, he prays that God will let the curse they placed upon him recoil upon them. "Burning coals" and "pits" are figures for destruction.

Assurance in God (140:12-13). The psalmist has an inner confidence that God will maintain not only his cause but that of all the needy, who are here identified with the righteous. Repeatedly they will go up to the Temple to offer thanksgiving for deliverance, and may therefore be said to dwell in God's presence there.

Psalm 141—Facing Temptation

The psalmist is tempted to sin through the influence of the godless in his community, and in this lament he seeks God's help in overcoming the temptation.

The Initial Plea to God (141:1-2). In his initial appeal for help he asks that his "prayer be counted as incense" and the lifting up of his hands in the posture of prayer as "an evening sacrifice." The sacrifice referred to is the cereal offering, which was made in the morning and in the evening (Exod. 29:39-41; Num. 28: 4-8) and was accompanied by incense. The psalmist does not repudiate material sacrifice but does suggest that prayer may take its place (compare 40:6; 51:16-17; 69:30-31; I Peter 2:5).

Prayer for Spiritual Protection (141:3-4). The psalmist is tempted to lose faith in God and to express his unbelief in words, thoughts, and deeds. Perhaps his faith has not paid off in the material dividends he anticipated. The godless wicked seem to prosper. The psalmist finds their social banquets, where enticing dainties are served, to be especially tempting. He knows what it is for the flesh to war against the spirit. Therefore, he prays that God will give him the inner stability needed to win the victory.

The Psalmist's Tempters (141:5-7). Presumably the psalmist is a young man and therefore amenable to discipline at the hands of godly elders (see Prov. 3:11-12), but he does not want the perfumed oil, customarily used for anointing guests at a banquet (see 23:5), to be poured on his head by the wicked. The end of the wicked is condemnation and destruction.

Prayer for Literal Protection (141:8-10). Here the psalmist's enemies are compared to hunters. Like other psalmists, he prays that the evil plans of the wicked may boomerang (7:15-16; 9:16; 140:9).

Psalm 142—No Man Cares for Me

An Audible Cry (142:1-3b). Though this is a private lament, the lonely psalmist does not pray in silence (compare 55:17). He pours forth his pent-up emotion in a gushing stream as he tells God his story. Yet, God already knows it before he tells him (compare Matt. 6:32).

The Psalmist's Trouble (142:3c-4). The psalmist's enemies tricked him into his present predicament. He looks "to the right" where a protector would stand if he had one (see 16:8; 109:31; 110:5; 121:5), but he feels utterly forsaken: "No man cares for me" (compare 22:11; 38:11). This sensation is one of the most horrible kinds of suffering. It is the root of much juvenile delinquency, domestic unhappiness, and crime.

The Psalmist's Refuge and Deliverer (142:5-7). But the psalmist does not turn to crime in his loneliness, he turns to God, his only portion in life, and prays for deliverance from his persecutors whose "trap" (vs. 3) resulted in his imprisonment. He asks that he may be brought out of prison to give thanks to God. Moreover, he realizes that there are those who do care for him; they will surround him as he offers his thanksgiving for deliverance in the Temple. When a man turns to God in his distress, he usually finds that his troubles are not as great as he had previously thought, for he gains a new perspective (see I Kings 19: 1-18).

Psalm 143—No Man Is Righteous

This is the last of the seven penitentials (6, 32, 38, 51, 102, 130, 143; see Introduction). The psalmist acknowledges that his suffering at the hands of enemies is the consequence of his own sin, and he seeks God's forgiveness and deliverance. His dependence on many other Psalms indicates a postexilic date.

Invocation (143:1-2). First, the psalmist invokes God's attention to his prayer. The second sentence in verse 1 should be translated, "In thy faithfulness answer me with thy salvation." The word "faithfulness" shows that the psalmist appeals to God in relation to the Covenant. The word "righteousness" often has the meaning of "salvation," "deliverance," or "vindication" (see 51:14; 98:2; 103:6; Isa. 40-55). Here the psalmist is seeking deliverance from sin and enemies. Implicitly he confesses that he cannot stand guiltless before God; in that sense "no man living is righteous" before God (compare Job 4:17; 9:2; 15:14; 25:4). Paul seems to quote these words freely in Romans 3:20 and Galatians 2:16.

Complaint (143:3-4). The leader of the psalmist's enemies has "pursued" him, "crushed" his life, and made him "sit in darkness like those long dead." The exact nature of their persecution is uncertain. The psalmist may be in the darkness of a prison or at the point of death through the wicked plots of his enemies. He is desolate and appalled at such cruelty, for it goes beyond anything he has deserved as a recompense for his sin.

Backward Look (143:5-6). He recalls God's mighty acts in behalf of his people in times past as a basis of hope that he will deliver him now. As the parched soil thirsts for the refreshing rain, so he longs for a fresh manifestation of God's blessing.

Petition (143:7-12). Here the psalmist makes more specific the appeal begun in the invocation. He does not want to die prematurely ("go down to the Pit"). Therefore he prays, "Let me hear in the morning of thy steadfast love." Although it is possible to take "in the morning" as a figure for "soon," it should probably be understood literally. The psalmist has been falsely accused and anticipates some kind of revelation from God that will vindicate him "in the morning." He seeks God's instruction as well as his deliverance, and requests that his Spirit lead him in a way free from his present obstacles (that is, "on a level path"). As God's servant he bases his final appeal for help on God's name (that is, his revealed character), righteousness, and steadfast love. From the psalmist's point of view the destruction of his enemies is a necessary manifestation of God's character and an essential aspect of his own deliverance.

Psalm 144—Salvation of King and People

From a literary point of view this is a Psalm of mixed type, in which earlier materials have been adapted. Verses 1-11 are a royal Psalm, and verses 12-15 are wisdom poetry in the form of a blessing. These may have been independent compositions, but not necessarily so. The Psalm as we have it is unified by the theme of the salvation of king and people.

The King's Prayer (144:1-11). First, the king expresses his gratitude to God as his rock, teacher in military science, fortress, stronghold, deliverer, shield, and refuge—"who subdues the peoples under him" (vss. 1-2). Then in words which call to mind Psalm 8 he marvels at God's concern for mere man, who, even though he be a king, "is like a breath" (vss. 3-4). In light of God's care for man, the king entreats him to come to his aid in the power manifested in volcanic eruption and storm (compare 18:7-15) and to deliver him from the power of foreigners and malicious liars (vss. 5-8; perhaps this means foreigners who break treaties). Finally, he vows to sing a new song of praise to the accompaniment of a ten-stringed harp upon the occasion of his deliverance. God is the one who has given "victory" (literally, "salvation") to David and his successors in times past and is the present king's Deliverer also (vss. 9-11).

The People's Prayer (144:12-15). In the king's prayer, salvation is predominantly deliverance from enemies and victory in war. In the people's prayer it is synonymous with happiness or all divine blessings. These blessings include vigorous sons and stately daughters, abundant harvests, fertile flocks, and the absence of the "cry of distress" (caused by war, violence, famine, or plague). But above all else the worshiping congregation shouts, "Happy the people whose God is the LORD!"

Psalm 145—A Hymn of an Individual

This profound hymn of an individual was rendered as a solo (vs. 1) in the presence of the congregation (vs. 10). It is the only Psalm which has in its title the Hebrew word which is translated "A Song of Praise," in spite of the fact that the title of the Psalter as a whole in Hebrew is "Praises." Thought, language, grammar, acrostic structure, and dependence on other Scripture passages combine to date the Psalm in the postexilic period.

God's Greatness (145:1-3). The introduction to the Psalm is a statement of the psalmist's intent to praise God as King continually. The basis of his praise is the greatness of God, which is defined in the remainder of the Psalm.

God's Mighty Acts (145:4-7). God's mighty acts include his works as Creator and Redeemer, some of which inspire fear (vs. 6). Each generation will proclaim to the next generation the gospel which it has received.

God's Compassionate Nature (145:8-9). The breadth of the

psalmist's outlook begins to shine forth clearly at this point. Not only is God "gracious and merciful" in his dealing with the Covenant people, he is "good to all" mankind and exercises compassion over every part of his creation (compare Mark 8:2).

God's Kingdom (145:10-13b). The word "kingdom" as used here is essentially "kingship," "reign," or "sovereignty." God's "works" are thought of as giving thanks to him through their obedient response to his will. God's "saints" (Israel) along with his works proclaim his mighty deeds and "the glorious splendor of his kingdom" to "the sons of men." In other words, they proclaim "the gospel of the kingdom" (see Matt. 4:23). The Kingdom continues generation after generation. The first part of verse 13 is quoted almost verbatim in Daniel 4:3, 34.

God's Faithfulness and Grace (145:13c-20). As the universal King, God is faithful to his promises and gracious in everything he does. For example, he supports those falling, provides for all living creatures, is near those who call upon him sincerely, and grants the requests of those who revere and love him. But because he is faithful and gracious, he will destroy those who repudiate him ("the wicked").

God's Praise (145:21). The psalmist ends as he began with a promise to praise God, and adds what is so characteristic of his breadth of soul—an invitation to all men to join him in praise.

Psalm 146—A Hymn of Social Concern

Psalms 146-150 are known as Hallelujah Psalms because in Hebrew they begin and end with "Hallelujah," which means "Praise the LORD!" Psalm 146 is the hymn of an individual who praises God as Creator and Savior in the presence of the congregation. The author places such emphasis upon social righteousness (compare 10, 14, 15, 24, 37, 72, 94, 102, 103, 113) that the reader repeatedly thinks of the prophets and Jesus.

A Pledge to Praise God (146:1-2). After summoning himself to praise, the psalmist pledges himself to the praise of God as long as he lives.

Man an Inadequate Savior (146:2-4). Now he sets the background against which he sings his praise. Man, even though he be a prince, is not an adequate source of "help" (literally, "salvation"). For he will return to the dust as decreed (see Gen. 3:19), and his plans to help will die with him. The author does not deny the necessity of mutual trust in the give and take of life; rather does he say that man cannot save himself.

God the Hope of the Needy (146:5-9). Here we find the reasons for the psalmist's praise. God is the Maker of heaven and earth and therefore has all power at his disposal. He is also the saving Lord of history. He meets the needs of the oppressed, the hungry, the prisoners, the blind, those bowed down by adversity, the resident aliens, the widow, and the fatherless. The Gospels, notably Luke, pulsate with the kind of spirit found here (see Luke 1:53; 4:16-21). According to both Testaments, personal gospel and social gospel are one gospel, and God's punishment of the wicked (vs. 9c) is a reality. Five times in verses 7c-9 the psalmist begins a sentence with "The LORD," thereby stressing the fact that God is the Hope of the needy. "The righteous" whom God is said to love (vs. 8) are those who accept his love.

The Reign of God (146:10). Unlike the reigns of human kings, God's reign continues. Though he is the God of all creation (vs. 6), he has made himself known in and through Zion. This, put in Christian terms, means that the one true God of the whole universe has chosen to make himself known to the world through his Covenant community, the Church. As King he is also the Savior and Judge who has a special concern for those in need.

Psalm 147—Lord of History and Nature

Psalm 147 has the appearance of being three hymns in one because each of its divisions begins with its own call to worship (see vss. 1, 7, and 12). Verse 2 indicates a postexilic date, and verse 18 suggests a date after Ezra had promulgated the Law. Vocabulary, grammar, and the use of other Psalms and Isaiah 40-66 support a postexilic date.

The Builder of Jerusalem (147:1-6). First, God is praised as the Builder of Jerusalem after the Babylonian Exile (see Ezra 1-2; Neh. 6-7). The exiles are called "outcasts," "the brokenhearted," and "the downtrodden." God gathers them, heals them, and lifts them up—but he casts down their oppressors. In addition to his work of rebuilding Jerusalem, "he determines the number of the stars" and "gives to all of them their names." That is, he has created them and has absolute control over them. The context shows that such power and limitless understanding are working in behalf of God's people in every generation.

The Sustainer of Creation (147:7-11). Second, God is thanked for his sustaining providence. As illustrations of his providence the psalmist praises God for rain, vegetation, and food for beast and bird. Yet God does not delight in the physical strength of animal or man; he takes pleasure in those who respond to him in reverence and hope.

The God of Zion (147:12-20). Third, the Lord is praised as the God of Zion. By his word (vs. 13; compare 33:9; Gen. 1:3) God strengthens Jerusalem's defenses, blesses her sons, grants her peace and prosperity; sends the winter with its snow, frost, hail, and cold; and then sends the spring with its melting of the ice, the blowing of warm wind, and the flowing of the life-giving waters again. But God's special word to his Chosen People is the Law, which by the privilege it confers places upon these people a corresponding responsibility.

Psalm 148—Universal Praise

Most of this hymn is a series of calls to praise God, addressed to both animate and inanimate creatures. The hymn is divided into two parts: a summons to the celestial world (vss. 1-6), and a summons to the terrestrial world (vss. 7-14). Each part is concluded by a partial refrain (vss. 5-6, 13-14) within which the reasons for praise are stated. Compare the Psalm with Genesis 1 and Revelation 5:13.

Celestial Praise (148:1-6). First of all, angels and other heavenly beings are summoned to praise God (compare 29:1; 103: 20-21). The heavenly bodies, the "highest heavens," and the "waters above the heavens" are personified and associated in praise with the heavenly beings (compare 19:1-4). In the ancient Gentile world the luminaries were worshiped as deities, but to the psalmist they are but creatures of the one true God. However, the psalmist shares the view that there are several heavens (compare II Cor. 12:2, 4). Along with others of his day (see 104:3; Gen. 1:6-7), he thinks in terms of waters stored above the firmament as the source of rain. While he holds much of the same "scientific" world view as his Gentile neighbors, his theology is distinctive. All celestial creatures are invited to praise the Lord because he created them, established them, and determined the conditions of their operation (compare Jer. 31:35-36).

Terrestrial Praise (148:7-14). Now the psalmist summons all earthly creatures to praise God. He begins with the "sea monsters and all deeps" (see 74:12-14; Isa. 27:1; 51:9-10; Gen. 1:2), words associated with the ancient Near Eastern story of the dragon (see comment on 74). It is debatable whether he is calling upon the forces of evil to praise God. He appears only to be summoning all God's creatures to praise him from the highest heights (vss. 1, 4) to the lowest depths (vs. 7). Associated with the sea monsters and the deeps are lightning, hail, snow, frost, and strong wind. The next group of creatures on the list is composed of mountains and hills, fruit trees and cedars, wild beasts and domesticated animals, creeping things and flying birds (see Gen. 1:21-25). Finally, the summons is addressed to men of all ranks, all ages, and both sexes. Perhaps human beings are mentioned last because man is the crown of creation (Gen. 1:26).

The reasons given for praise by all terrestrial creatures are that "his name alone is exalted," "his glory is above earth and heaven," and he has restored his Covenant people to dignity and power (compare 89:17, 24; 92:10). Indeed, the primary motivation of the psalmist is the restoration of his people. The Psalm suggests to Christians that God's purposes for the Church and the world are closely interrelated (compare Rom. 8:18-25; Rev. 21:1—22:5). What God has recently done for his people is a theme of praise for them, that is, for "the people of Israel who are near to him" in the Covenant relation (compare Deut. 4:7). Of course all of God's acts on behalf of his people are both a call to praise and a summons to service.

Psalm 149—Adorned with Victory

This hymn centers in some specific victory of the Jews over their enemies in the postexilic period and implies that this victory is a token of the future consummation of the Kingdom of God.

Victory (149:1-4). The worshiping people are exhorted to sing "a new song" (compare 33:3; 96:1) in gratitude for their recent "victory." They are designated "the faithful" (a word often translated "saints" as in 145:10; 148:14), "Israel," "the sons of Zion," and "the humble." God is Israel's Maker because he brought the nation into existence as his people (compare Isa. 44:2; 51:13). He is also the King of "the sons of Zion" and therefore their defender. The celebration not only includes singing but also dancing to the accompaniment of timbrel and lyre (compare Exod. 15:20; Judges 11:34; II Sam. 6:14; Jer. 31:4). The sacred dance was an important element in worship among the Israelites and their neighbors. The reason for the call to praise is that God "adorns" ("glorifies") his "humble" people "with victory." The word "victory" is literally "salvation" and includes both literal victory and its accompanying benefits. The people are called "humble" because they have recently gone through a humbling experience.

Judgment (149:5-9). In this sacred dance the warriors have their swords and probably strike them together in time with the rhythm of the music. This celebration of a recent victory has overtones of future judgment upon the nations. Israel is to execute upon the nations "the judgment written." This written judgment may be the sentence recorded in the Lord's book in heaven (Isa. 65:6; Job 13:26; Dan. 7:10) or in the Law and the Prophets on earth (Deut. 32:41-43; Isa. 45:14; 49:7, 23; Joel 3: 12-16). In the psalmist's day it was inevitable that the Kingdom of God was envisioned by many in a nationalistic and militaristic framework. But this framework is set aside in the New Testament: "Jesus answered, 'My kingship is not of this world' " (John 18:36); "for though we live in the world we are not carrying on a worldly war, for the weapons of our warfare are not worldly but have divine power to destroy strongholds" (II Cor. 10:3-4).

Psalm 150—A Crescendo of Praise

Psalm 150 is a festal hymn which serves appropriately as the doxology of Book V in the Psalter (see 41:13; 72:18-19; 89:52; 106:48). As the Psalm is sung, the volume of praise is increased with the addition of the sound of each musical instrument and reaches a thrilling crescendo of instruments and voices (vs. 6). Several interpreters have noted that the psalmist answers four implicit questions: where, why, how, and by whom is the Lord to be praised?

Where Is the Lord to Be Praised? (150:1). The Lord is to be praised both in his earthly sanctuary in Jerusalem and in heaven (see 29:1; 148:1-2; Gen. 1:8).

Why Is the Lord to Be Praised? (150:2). The Lord is to be praised "for his mighty deeds" in creation and history and for the greatness of his character revealed thereby.

How Is the Lord to Be Praised? (150:3-5). The Lord is to be praised with wind, stringed, and percussion instruments; with the sacred dance; and of course with the human voice. The psalmist has given the most complete list of musical instruments found in any one place in the Old Testament, but even here the list is not exhaustive. The "trumpet" is the ram's or goat's horn, ordinarily used for giving signals (47:5; 81:3; 98:6; Judges 3:27; I Kings 1:34, 39; Isa. 18:3). It is not to be confused with the trumpet made of metal (Num. 10:2). The Hebrew word for "lute" also means "wine-skin bottle"; the lute is a stringed instrument resembling the shape of such a bottle. The Hebrew word here translated "harp" is better translated "lyre." "Harp" is more accurately applied to the lute. The "timbrel" is a small portable hand drum (see 81:2; 149:3), sometimes translated "tambourine" (Gen. 31:27· I Sam. 10:5). "Strings" is a designation of stringed instruments in general. The "pipe" is probably a reed flute. The "sounding cymbals" are noisy and heavy and are struck vertically; the "loud clashing cymbals" are clearer and lighter and are struck horizontally.

By Whom Is the Lord to Be Praised? (150:6). The Lord is to be praised by all human beings and perhaps by animals as well. By implication the whole universe is one great temple in which all the creatures of God are summoned to worship him.